PRAISE FOR *MARKETING REVOLUTION*

"Businesses need to rapidly adopt new methods and tools if they are to achieve the transformational change in marketing effectiveness they so desperately need. This book provides an excellent introduction to the subject."

Nigel Howlett, Executive Vice President, OgilvyOne Worldwide

"Marketing isn't working. This book sets out the compelling case for better, faster, more distinctive and more integrated marketing processes. Emerging concepts, such as managing each customer's lifetime journey, and developing a smart and agile dialogue with selected customers, are succinctly presented here. The approach may indeed be revolutionary; so too are the rewards."

Matthew Banks, Senior Director, Marketing Solutions, Siebel Systems

"Marketing Revolution provides a comprehensive exploration of the major issues affecting the marketing profession, and points the way to more effective and rewarding marketing through greater integration and 'sense and respond' marketing. Those serious about marketing would do well to read it."

Christine Cryne, Chief Executive,
The Chartered Institute of Marketing

"Direct and powerful, Marketing Revolution explores how industry leaders are facilitating change in their business through new enterprise marketing approaches."

Karen Richardson, CEO, Epiphany

"This book is a unique opportunity for all marketers to rethink their thinking and join the new marketing game: engaging the customer!"

Bernard Cova, Professor ESCP-EAP Paris, and Visiting Professor, Bocconi University Milan

"Marketing is a discipline not a function. This book is a clarion call for those of us determined to make it part of everyday business practice."

Jennifer Kirkby, Editor, Customer Management Community

D1291123

DEDICATIONS

Paul R Gamble: To Jean, with love

Alan Tapp: For Mum who, like all mums, constantly reminds us to 'count our blessings'

Anthony Marsella: To my wife Camille and children Clara, Laura and William

Merlin Stone: To Kathryn, who has revolutionized my life

MARKET!NG
REVOLUT!ON

The Radical New Approach
to Transforming the Business,
the Brand & the Bottom Line

**Paul R Gamble, Alan Tapp,
Anthony Marsella & Merlin Stone**

KOGAN
PAGE

London and Philadelphia

Publisher's note

Every possible effort has been made to ensure that the information contained in this book is accurate at the time of going to press, and the publishers and authors cannot accept responsibility for any errors or omissions, however caused. No responsibility for loss or damage occasioned to any person acting, or refraining from action, as a result of the material in this publication can be accepted by the editor, the publisher or any of the authors.

First published in Great Britain and the United States in 2005 by Kogan Page Limited
Paperback edition 2007

120 Pentonville Road
London N1 9JN
United Kingdom
www.kogan-page.co.uk

525 South 4th Street, #241
Philadelphia PA 19147
USA

© Paul R Gamble, Alan Tapp, Anthony Marsella, Merlin Stone, 2005

The right of Paul R Gamble, Alan Tapp, Anthony Marsella, Merlin Stone to be identified as the authors of this work has been asserted by them in accordance with the Copyright, Designs and Patents Act 1988.

British Library Cataloguing-in-Publication Data

A CIP record for this book is available from the British Library.

ISBN-10   0 7494 4980 2
ISBN-13   978 0 7494 4980 3

Library of Congress Cataloging-in-Publication Data

Marketing revolution : the radical new approach to transforming the business, the brand & the bottom line / Paul R Gamble ... [et al.].
     p. cm.
  ISBN-13: 978-0-7494-4980-3 (pbk.)
  ISBN-10: 0-7494-4980-2 (pbk.)
  1. Marketing–Management. 2. Product management. I. Gamble, Paul R.
  HF5415.13.M3584 2007
  658.8--dc22

                                                                      2007008627

Typeset by Saxon Graphics Ltd, Derby
Printed and bound in Great Britain by Creative Print and Design (Wales), Ebbw Vale

Contents

Acknowledgements

Thanks go first of all to our many colleagues at IBM who have contributed ideas to this book, especially Ralph Schuler, Rod Street, Gavin Potter, Kevin Bishop, Paul Crick, Jennifer Love and Bryan Foss, and to colleagues in many universities who have helped us by exchanging ideas on the evolution of marketing, especially Clive Nancarrow of Bristol Business School, Martin Evans of Cardiff Business School, Malcolm McDonald and Hugh Wilson of Cranfield Business School, Bob Shaw of City University Business School, Tim Ambler and Paddy Barwise of London Business School, and Michael Starkey and Len-Tiu Wright of Leicester Business School. Thanks to IBM's many software partners for contributing ideas directly and indirectly too, especially Matthew Banks at Siebel, Kevin O'Regan at e.piphany and Mark Cerasale at SAP, and to the teams at QCi – particularly Neil Woodcock, David Williams and Paul Weston – and OgilvyOne – particularly Nigel Howlett and Nick Orsman – with whom IBM has worked closely to explore new developments in managing customers. Most importantly of all, thanks to the many IBM clients who have given us the opportunity to learn with and from them about what revolutionizing marketing really means. Many thanks to Malcolm Bennett of IBM for a detailed review of the manuscript.

Finally, and hopefully not too introvertedly, thanks also to Pauline Goodwin at Kogan Page for putting up with our constantly shifting deadlines with good humour and to each of the other co-authors, for cooperating in a difficult project, teaching each other, sharing knowledge and not getting upset with each other.

Paul R Gamble
Alan Tapp
Anthony Marsella
Merlin Stone

Foreword

That marketing is changing fast is obvious. Marketing as a function is being asked to generate more value, more profit. It can no longer be considered just as a function with a defined set of defined tasks. The focus of marketing has broadened from the classic 'product, price, place, promotion' to include the customer's experience and the customer's journey, both of which require marketers to focus on issues such as processes, people and customer insight. These new areas offer great opportunities for differentiation, but once again threaten those whose competence in these areas is weak. Marketing is now a capability – one which helps companies manage customers, channels, markets and profit, which helps companies avoid commoditization and low margins.

Marketing is changing under the influence of greater global competition in increasingly open markets. Radical improvements in information technology have made it much easier for suppliers and customers to talk to each other and do business with each other, but also expose suppliers' failures more quickly. Marketing effectiveness is a central concern for boards of directors, as they increasingly question the role and cost of marketing.

To meet the new demands placed upon them, marketers are increasingly required to develop new skills, such as re-engineering the company around customers' experience, multichannel optimization, and moving their company from selling products and services to providing solutions.

That's why we at IBM have invested heavily in developing a marketing consulting practice experienced in areas such as process management and integrating marketing with other corporate functions. That's why we have supported the production of this book, which outlines the new marketing agenda to which leading companies are working.

Martin Jetter
General Manager & IBM Business Consulting Leader
North East Europe

Ralph Schuler
IBM Business Consulting CRM Leader
South West Europe

Introduction

> A victorious strategy is not repeated... Water configures its flow in accord with the terrain; the army controls its victory in accord with the enemy. Thus the army does not maintain any constant strategic configuration of power; water has no constant shape... One who is able to change and transform in accord with the enemy and wrest victory is termed genius.

That, according to Sun Tzu in his treatise on *The Art of War*, is the way to win. Transform and change. It's not as easy as it sounds. After all, not every enterprise can be a winner in a competitive marketing environment. In many markets, companies are playing a zero sum game. If the customer buys my product or service, they won't buy yours. Or at least, they might buy less of it or buy from you less often.

This book does not promise to make everyone a winner. What it does is encourage managers to think about their marketing environment in a totally new way, a revolutionary way. We chose that word, 'revolution', carefully. Its original meaning derives from the Latin. As used in everyday speech it simply referred to something which went round and around. That is, until a Polish astronomer called Nicolas Copernicus used the term for the title of a book he braced himself to publish as he approached his 70th year in 1543, *De Revolutionibus Orbium Coelestium* – The Revolution of the Heavenly Orbs. He only saw one copy of that book, as it was put into his hands on his deathbed, but about 60 years later an Italian called Galileo Galilei decided to use a new invention, the telescope, to prove to everyone that Copernicus had been right. The sun does not revolve around the earth; it is the other way about. Since this ran against the central dogma of the Church at the time, it rather upset Pope Urban VIII who then forced Galileo to retract. The consequences of this action were to be devastating. It is hard to kill new ideas. The centre of scientific advance so long based around Southern Europe moved from the Mediterranean to Northern Europe where it was to remain for the next 500 years. The centre and basis of economic and techno-logical advance shifted.

The word 'revolution' now has two levels of meaning. The first refers to something continuous and fundamental. It goes round and around. Like a sound business model. Rather more recent than astronomy, the art and science of marketing requires some funda-mental practices. A sound business model has to be in place for a business to succeed. Which leads us on to the second level. Following the work of Copernicus and Galileo, the word 'revolution' acquired a new, more powerful meaning. Today, revolution refers to a radical change. To be a revolutionary is to be someone who threatens to overturn the world as we know it. This can be threatening, but to ignore the change does not mean it will go away.

Radical changes have been and are taking place in the business world, and companies need to transform themselves radically if they are to survive these changes. Ignoring them or turning away from them forcefully can have devastating consequences.

An enterprise that does not change, that does not reinvent itself from time to time, will be rigid. It will, in the end, be defeated by its competitors. This book draws on the huge amount of established research and good practice in marketing to develop some revolu-tionary ideas. It challenges many of the conventional approaches to marketing as a discipline and encourages managers to think about their customers, their business, their strategies and their marketing tools in a revolutionary way. Like all good revolutions therefore it builds on what has gone before to show how new futures can be invented. It addresses the realities of the current marketplace to consider how different cultures, different demographics and different relationships can be embedded into a modern business to help it compete and survive more effectively.

To work well, new ideas have to be accessible and easy to use. Like pod casting. Take an established idea based on a current technology such as MP3 players and iPods[1]. Think about it in a radical new way like the broadcaster and technologist Adam Curry and ask some simple questions. If you can broadcast music to millions of people over the internet, why not broadcast speech? Anyone with a recording device and a computer can do it. Add a little bit of new software and you have an entirely new medium. Now everyone can own their personal radio station. The only tricky bit remaining is to develop some content that people want to listen to.

CRM (customer relationship management), operational analytics and multichannel marketing are of this form. They use existing and developing enablers to allow marketers to gain insights into their customers in a way never before possible. The trick is, having established that capability, how to develop relationships with a more mature, more marketing savvy, changed customer base in a way that will respond to their changing needs at just the right time.

Marketing Revolution explores how these changes have come about and what companies might do to embed this new approach to marketing within their organization.

NOTE

1. iPod is a registered brand name of Apple Computer, Inc.

1

Why revolutionize marketing?

THE RISE OF THE NEW CUSTOMER

Marketing is facing a mid-life crisis. Emerging as an academic discipline 80 years ago and as a corporate discipline around 50 years ago, marketing has become the sophisticated customer and market discipline we know today, with proven results in many industries. Sadly in its maturity, marketing is struggling to cope with a customer whose teenager-like independence is undermining every conventional effort to communicate effectively with them! Thirty or more affluent years in a highly commercial and largely free market economy has given birth to a new type of customer whose needs, wants and approach is totally different from those of consumers of 50 years ago. Customers have become more demanding of how we interact with them and how we treat them across segments, products and channels. In a world where today's best practice becomes the basic standard of tomorrow, it is becoming harder for companies to retain and attract customers cost-effectively. This has raised questions about marketing effectiveness in the boardroom and about the role and definition of marketing generally. Marketing must recognize and engage with this new customer to succeed in this new customer-driven age.

WHAT'S SO DIFFERENT ABOUT CUSTOMERS NOW?

Customers live a world that is far removed from the one marketing grew up in. It is a world where experiences are at the heart of life and of life's objectives. The mass-produced manufactured products that customers were once happy to buy are being overshadowed by the desire for tailored services, a reflection of our prosperity. Partly as a result, services have grown much faster than products. In most OECD countries for the last 25 years the fastest-growing area of spending has been 'leisure services', up by 340 per cent in the UK since 1980 – not surprising when you consider the growth of health clubs, holidays, nail bars, meals out or night clubs in towns and cities worldwide.

With affluence comes more choice. People are now used to making their own decisions about how they live, what they buy and what they do. This independence has been fuelled by the phenomenal choice that global competition has provided. In market after market the number of products on offer has multiplied as super-segmentation sets in. Just think about how we have gone from a generic 'orange juice' for instance to the many types (fresh, concentrated etc) and variations even within a single brand such as Tropicana.[1] People can indulge their merest whim to get the product that most closely matches their desires. From a historical perspective, the result is stupendous. The average European hypermarket presents a choice of 40,000 different product lines, with 5 to 10 per cent of these changing every year! It is hard to see how someone back in marketing's youth could have foreseen such a choice.

As hypermarkets emerged on the outskirts of towns, the shopping experience they offered was unlike anything some senior retailers had ever encountered. Many of the latter were taken by surprise, and as a result the companies that they ran often suffered, when they failed to offer an effective marketing response. Changes in the retail scene for groceries, financial services, travel, utilities and so on, through both traditional channels and more recent e-channels, have forged a modern customer (of all ages!) who is excellent at making purchase choices. They expect to be able to make their own choices from a wide range of options in most aspects of their lives. It is this sort of attitude that has broken up the kind of marketing cycles that used to sweep across nations merely a quarter of a century ago and created the smorgasbord that can now be seen. In a world where MTV reckon to be able to affect global youth culture within 48 hours or where pensioners in their eighties are doing investment comparison shopping on the internet, things move very fast.

THE GROWTH OF CHOICE

In industry after industry the growth of competition and choice can be seen, even in mature categories. Take for example four industries that have revolutionized themselves since the 1940s:

- *In automobiles*, from 1975 to 1995 it is calculated that the number of models in the US market increased tenfold from 60 to over 600. Even the number of drive trains increased from 5 to over 30.
- *In clothing*, from 1980 to 1990 as average batch sizes fell tenfold, the number of styles being produced in a plant increased fivefold.
- *In detergents*, the growth of choice has seen the rise of far more focused products and a proliferation of SKUs (stock keeping units – referring to one specific product) to address the laundry needs of white, black and coloured fabrics, silk, wools, biological, non-biological, with or without conditioner, and in a dazzling array of packages from ordinary to concentrates, tablets, sachets and liquids.
- *In beverages*, point of sale customization has produced a variety where even a single beverage such as Coca Cola is available in over 50 different pack sizes and versions. You can now choose exactly the Cola that you want, if you have the time!

In the battle to reach this customer, marketers have pioneered new ways to communicate with them, well beyond the conventional television, radio or magazine advertisements of the 1960s. Companies can sponsor almost anything: taxis, supermarket trolleys, bus tickets, programmes, sporting events and facilities, even planes and trains in some countries. New media have appeared and been adopted through the internet, e-mail and text messages.

The new customer fights back against the rising daily flood of commercial messages by ignoring them. Most people can easily blank out the sound, pictures or points, leaving all messages in the background until they are interested in the category or area. That is tough to live with if you are a marketer wanting to help your company grow!

Even worse, technology is now passing yet more control to customers, so they can manage their intake of communications and filter out unwanted messages. As personal hard-drive DVD recorders become more common and people increasingly time-shift their viewing, many customers will eliminate TV advertisements from every recording at the push of a button, furthering the decline in broadcast advertising effectiveness. Unfortunately many of these people will be the most valuable customers.

Such gadgets now form an integral part of most people's lives, regardless of age. Increased mobility, distance and new tools for communication and entertainment have meant that the new customer spends long periods of time interacting with their gadgets, many of which have become an indispensable part of their life. Lose the use of your mobile phone for a week and you will quickly appreciate how much you have made its presence a necessity.

It is possible that we spend 20 times as much time interacting with machines than we did 25 years ago at the birth of the PC. Phones, personal digital assistants (PDAs), games machines, computers, televisions, music players and many other items seem to fill our time. As a result the new customer is much more at home with technology than many marketers assume. They are less patient with glitches, long-winded communications or complex propositions and are used to using shortcuts to increase productivity. Abbreviations, acronyms, sound bites, colours and logos are increasingly the language of commercial messages to exploit this short attention span.

As if this were not enough, tried and tested formulae are starting to fail as consumer values change. Professor Bernard Cova describes how the postmodern consumer is rejecting progressive values linked to the individual, freedom, reason and globalization in favour of regressive values such as the community, authenticity and proximity. This has created a new trend where aspirations and values are based on the past. It has given rise to postmodern marketing such as Tribal Marketing, retro marketing and experience-based marketing. Successful examples include Mini,[2] 'Paul', PT Cruiser[3] and Nomad.[4]

IS THE CHANGED CUSTOMER ENVIRONMENT IMPORTANT?

Some might question the significance of these trends. After all, trends like these last a long time. There may be time to adjust to them as they influence marketing activities. Sadly some marketers are rather slow to react. Many marketing departments fail to see that something is broken and needs fixing. Having mastered the skills of the hammer, they want to nail everything together, when a more subtle approach with screws or glue might work better. Sometimes it is hard to start again and break the mould, but this is essential if marketers are to regain the effectiveness and productivity of the discipline's youth. However, warning lights are flashing. In an IBM survey of CMOs in the top 100 UK companies, 70 per cent admitted that marketing effectiveness was one of their most important challenges. Failure to address these issues can be seen in the heightened turnover of executive marketing staff.

A marketing model that is based on broadcast messaging, product differences, conventional channels and a 'one size fits all' mentality is becoming uneconomic and ineffective. The need to revolutionize marketing is immense. The customer is not listening when many marketing departments want to talk to them through advertising or promotions. The impact of such advertising is declining in many advanced economies – perhaps a reflection of the surge in the number of messages people experience every day where every new media and channel increases complexity and erodes effectiveness.

This is happening at the same time as the cost of presenting messages (regardless of the customers' listening skills) explodes. A TV advertisement in the last episode of *MASH* in the United States reached two-and-a-half times as many people, at half the real cost, of the last episode of *Friends* 20 years later! This is a fivefold increase in unit cost.

To make things even more challenging, when customers do engage with a business they are far more easily disappointed. They come with radically different expectations that many businesses fail to meet. This new generation of customer expects:

- Your company to be able to interact with them at any time and in any way, 'Martini' style, even if that means at midnight on a mobile phone.
- An easy process to follow to meet their needs. Through buying, service and support they expect to be able to choose how and where they conduct their business. They expect to be able to configure the process to suit their needs rather than being told how it will be.
- To be able to unbundle processes and propositions so that they can compare suppliers before committing. Already on average

50 per cent of European customers will search for major purchases and compare suppliers on the internet before then going to buy in the shops.
- To get excellent service, every time. Their benchmark for excellence might well be from an entirely different industry; it will be their best experience in any category.

The cost of not meeting these expectations is high. Customers will buy from someone else and may even encourage others to do so as well. Of course companies cannot afford to treat everyone the same. But knowing and recognizing at the point of interaction the most valuable customers, especially over the lifetime of interactions and across channels, escapes many organizations. This customer-driven agenda is challenging all organizations and institutions, even well-established ones. Companies must be customer-centric. If they are not, then the consequences can be fatal. A quick look at what has been happening in the airline industry illustrates the point. Low-cost carriers offering inexpensive point-to-point fares have maintained their profitability in a market where full-service flag carriers have struggled.

Long-term value can only be created when the customer is the focus. Yet the challenge in doing this is significant: meeting the enhanced service expectations of an increasingly diverse customer set when competitive pressure is eating away at differentiation and margins. It requires a new model of marketing from that which we are used to.

ENGAGING THE NEW CONSUMER

There are many aspects of change that marketing must embrace. Some companies are starting to explore these. Business journals and professional institutes are also starting to comment. By the beginning of 2005 two companies, major global businesses in consumer goods and petrochemicals, launched similar initiatives to explore ways to enhance their marketing posture.

What kinds of changes are needed? Let us consider some of the main themes examined in this book.

The need to enhance the customer experience

Marketing focus needs to move to the customer's experience with the brand and service. Organizations need to build emotional loyalty with their key customers. They need to become brands that customers feel they own, in that category of goods or services. If this is to be achieved, every contact and communication must reinforce that idea. Too many businesses limit their communication perspectives to advertising or point of sale. They miss the reality that many more communications take place, normally with their heavy users through the contact centre, in after-sales care, with support staff in the field or through the billing cycle. Marketing needs to engage through the whole of the customer life cycle because the customer is most receptive to engaging with the brand when they want something. When they are sitting in front of a television watching their favourite programme or browsing the internet to read their latest health tip, they are less receptive to promotional messages.

Processes must be designed to reinforce brand values. This can mean radical change. When Continental Airlines began to turn around its contact centres in the mid-1990s, the emphasis was strikingly moved from scripted responses and a battery of 65 performance indicators to a focus on customer results and far fewer measures. This produced a dramatic turnaround in customer satisfaction and loyalty. Marketing needs to set its sights on these areas to exploit them for communication and competitive advantage, rather than ignore them as merely operations.

The need to develop better channel strategies

Organizations need to pay more attention to their channel strategy. As interactions between companies and customers increase, people buy the service, use the product, but seek enjoyment from the experience. Of course a quick trip to a store to buy milk is hardly an experience – but Tesco installed bakeries in its stores to ensure that the perfume of freshly baked bread made customers more relaxed and comfortable. Companies also struggle with a paradox – they want to talk to customers but this costs money (and may not immediately earn money!). Few contact centres or sales teams do not understand that time is money when they speak to customers. This puts a real premium on planning and on executing a well-planned, 'industrial-strength' approach to channel management. This area is still too much of an orphan in marketing strategy. Little real consideration is given to the design and disciplined execution of channel strategies. Yet it is essential for the new customer.

The difference between an easyJet channel strategy and a standard flag carrier channel strategy can be 10 per cent or more of operating costs. The ability to knock 30 per cent to 40 per cent off customer service costs whilst moving to the top of the customer satisfaction ratings is worth a lot to a business. This is something that the US mobile operator Nextel has done successfully.

Customers need to be encouraged to migrate to the most suitable channel each time they need to contact the company. Channel costs, service levels and efficiency are the factors which determine the best channel to do the job, for each of many different purposes. The right technology must be deployed to deliver a reliable, consistent and customer-oriented experience.

In addition, new channels need to be considered:

- The use of the internet has grown one hundredfold in ten years. Penetration levels are very high across the developed world. We are seeing the gradual institutionalization of the internet as it moves steadily from the province of computer 'techies' to normal acceptance as a part of everyday life for most people. In the most valuable European customer households, as in other regions, people routinely turn to the internet for their daily needs. A low-cost broadband connection puts them in touch with companies on the other side of the world, at no cost. It even allows them to use 'free' VOiP, Voice over internet protocol telephony, to make long-distance calls.

- Mobile phone penetration has reached saturation across most countries in the EU and many parts of Asia. In North America it is at very high levels and multifunction 3G mobile phones provide shopping and investment services along with powerful search and locate facilities. It is possible to establish a fast interconnection between your mobile phone and your e-mail service, to respond to messages or find out if your eBay bid is currently winning. With IMS technology it will soon be possible to speak, and send images and e-mails at the same time.

- Speech recognition technologies are starting to enable reliable, easy to use, automated interactions that customers appreciate.

Channel management must move to the centre stage of strategy. Well-established channels must be given industrial quality and performance standards, to ensure effective and efficient service. New channels must be exploited. All this must be executed to tighter standards and cost controls if it is to help customer and business alike.

Move to sense and respond marketing

Sense and respond needs to replace the push model of selling for generating business. This capability is essential if marketing is to present the right proposition to the most appropriate customer at a time when that customer is willing to listen. Organizations must sense when customers are interested and sell to them at that point, rather than simply broadcast promotional messages at a time that suits the iron imperative of the company's marketing plan. Selling when the customer touches the company means that all contact points with the customer – the web, phone, store, field agent or whatever – are driven by customer insights mined from customer databases and prised out by sophisticated analytical procedures, about potential value and needs. Timing, the proposition and the customer selection will determine effectiveness and this needs marketing input and orchestration. Marketing will need to provide customer understanding, ensure connection to the right touch points, help to educate and train staff to sell, find out what customers' information needs are and shape how best to follow up. Marketing managers will also need to join up their marketing messages seamlessly with service and support functions to make this credible.

Fully integrate segmentation with the core business

Segmentation has to be *fully* integrated with the operations and propositions of the business. To make all this credible and ensure that value is created rather than destroyed, the business will need to carry segmentation and dialogue right through to all operations. This means that marketers will need to integrate the development of propositions and segment-specific offers with all the touch points between organization and customer at a much more granular level than today. They will also need to offer much more strategic insight than tactical offers. Failure to do this effectively will burn money in long, unproductive telephone selling conversations, wasted e-mails and pamphlets with a resulting demoralization of staff. Operationalizing the new model will need marketing's active engagement and at ever-increasing levels. Campaign timing and volumes will become critical. Already in those businesses that are using this approach effectively, managers are seeing the need to take the model further. Even smaller and more personalized customer segments, with even shorter windows of time in which to respond when an appropriate customer event triggers a need, will become the new standard. This problem will quickly escalate as competitors adopt more sophisticated approaches. The customer response rates for the slower or more broadly based companies will fall.

Operationalizing segmentation like this means that customers must be identified personally each time they contact the business. The nature of the customer interaction and proposition to be offered at each touch point must be thought through. An enabling infrastructure must be established so that the right capabilities can be put in place. A relentless campaign management mentality must exist throughout the organization.

POINTING THE WAY FOR MARKETING

All this is placing marketing under unprecedented pressures. These challenges to marketing effectiveness combined with the pressure on profitable growth are raising the marketing function to the top of the corporate agenda and putting the marketing department and chief marketing officer under close scrutiny by CEOs and shareholders. The response must be to create a new model for marketing, less first violin and more orchestra conductor. Marketers must plan customer engagements segment by segment, they must help engineer channel strategy, and establish quality levels based on what is valuable to the customer (not what is easiest to quality manage). They must also think about all the possible touch points in the customer life cycle. They must establish micro-marketing at the heart of a branded delivery. In short, middle-aged marketing must start to reinvent itself for a successful new age.

REINVENTING MARKETING

The marketing function is not operating at a high or strategic level in most companies. According to one report, only 13 out of 100 CEOs of the FTSE top 100 firms in the UK have any marketing background and only 61 per cent of the top 1,000 European firms have a board-level marketing officer. Yet UK government census statistics show that the marketing profession's membership has surged. Marketers now outnumber teachers! So are marketers themselves to blame for their lack of respect from others?

A recent study of the problems from the Chartered Institute of Management (2001), produced some interesting quotes from marketing managers:

> Marketers are desperately short of company wide-vision. We are hopelessly outflanked by management consultancies.

> Before you address e-skills we need to address more basic problems: do marketing people understand money? Cash flow? ROI? These are rhetorical questions to which the answer is no.

When respondents were asked what was needed to change things, what skills marketers needed, they offered some interesting replies:

> Marketers need to develop mini entrepreneur skills – strategising, devising a business plan, making resource allocation decisions, understanding risk. In short, commercial acumen. What marketers lack are MBA graduate skills. At the moment these are in very short supply.

> Stop wasting time hiring and firing agencies. Marketing departments are fiddling with deckchairs on the Titanic. We are playing marbles at the wrong end of the playground, while the grown ups are doing business at the other end.

One interesting by-product of this debate has been the creation of the Marketing and Sales Standards Setting Body (MSSSB) in the UK. This body, accredited by the government, is seeking to define marketing's new functional scope with the help of industry and agencies and to set out professional standards. The trouble is, everyone has confused the things that functional marketing does – branding, market research, advertising, sales support and so on – with marketing itself. These things are important cogs in the wheel, but they must be deployed within an understanding that marketing is about the whole firm going to market with something valuable that customers want to buy.

Consider another problem, marketing double speak. All too often marketers adopt the trappings, but not the substance, of being on the side of customers. If managers are asked what their priorities are, customer satisfaction is always high or highest on their agenda. Customer loyalty is also placed at or near the top. Encouraging? Not when you find that:

- most managers measure success by short-term financial measures like quarterly profit;
- only 13 per cent of managers including marketers spend time personally with customers; and

- according to Ogilvy, less than 30 per cent of firms have any concrete actions in place to actively encourage customer loyalty and 75 per cent do not know why they lose customers.

This is not an impressive record. It must change. However, in a few leading companies, chief executive officers have got the message. They have taken a more holistic, rounded view of the world and recognized that breaking up a job into too many fragments doesn't work if customers, employees, managers, shareholders and suppliers are all to get the same message, experience the same corporate culture. Companies such as Tesco, Orange and HSBC in the UK, Wal-Mart, Sony and MBNA in the United States, know they are not perfect in managing this balance as yet. They know they have to manage it and be better at it not just in their own sphere of activity but across the range of all companies active in the marketplace.

THE CUSTOMER IMPERATIVE

We have referred to some of the changes in society already. Let us look a little closer. The collective mutually agreed template for living, 'this is how we do things round here', has increasingly given way, at least partly, to greater acceptance of individualism. With this shift in favour of individualism has come an abundance of life choices. Abundance of choice facilitates individualism but also creates feelings that life is complex and raises anxiety levels about choosing what is right for oneself. At the same time, trust in traditional advisers has collapsed. So people look for information and help. The general trend is to trust those real people around us more, and institutions less. Our social capital has become important, relating more to whom you know than what you have or spend.

Traditional segmentations based on gender, occupation and income no longer apply as powerfully. Society is more complex now. The last decade has seen the rise of many new groups, all with their own acronyms. 'BoBos' are the bohemian bourgeois. This highly educated, new middle class rejects conspicuous consumption in favour of understated but expensive products that emphasize their cultural capital. BoBos will sneer at a Porsche but will spend £300 on a kettle. SKIers (spending the kids' inheritance) are the over-fifties deciding to enjoy life as they enter the third age. KIPPers are 'kids in parents' pockets', mid-twenties and early thirties, living at home because they cannot find the deposit for their own house or simply because it is more convenient.

OK, that's all very interesting you may say, but so what? Why should businesses care about these touchy-feely changes in our collective psyche? The answer is because businesses urgently need to change the way they currently interface with customers. The model that used to work with brands can no longer be based on an imperative 'Here is what you need to do'. Instead, it has to be the facilitative 'Once you've made up your mind, here is how we can help'. Brands can no longer help with people's objectives in life but they can help with people's strategies to get there. Nimbler companies have already moved their advertising away from persuasion towards involvement. The persuasion model is working less and less well, so firms must move towards other ways of engaging sceptical, marketing-savvy customers.

The days when customers believed TV adverts have gone. Customers are increasingly sceptical about advertising and tend to describe it as brainwashing and lies. Indeed older people are increasingly difficult to reach at all with symbolic brand advertising. Clever, agency creative approaches that take an ironic approach to advertising may slow down the negativity, but the long-term trend against effective brand building using traditional methods continues.

Indeed we can go further and suggest that marketing as a profession is seen in a less than glorious light by the public. In an age when ethical considerations are clearly on the rise and ethical companies and investments are increasingly popular, the marketing profession is lagging rather than leading the trend. Marketers are seen by consumers as trying to manipulate people into buying goods or services that they neither want or need. Irrelevant junk mail is a good example. These perceptions need to be changed because that is often how marketers are perceived *inside* the company as well as outside.

AN EXAMPLE OF RESPONDING TO THE NEW CUSTOMER: THE MUSIC INDUSTRY

If ever there was an example of a leading-edge sector that has created a new model of doing business, it is music. Why was music's traditional structure so vulnerable to the internet? First, the product can be delivered electronically and customers can 'do it for themselves'. This allows customer-to-customer distribution to take place. Second, it is an entertainment sector, so there is plenty of chance for chat rooms to flourish. The fragmentation of the music sector into segments plays to the web's strengths of multiple linkages. With this fragmentation comes a need to gather data so that companies understand the degree of fragmentation. This suggests a shift towards a customer focus and genuine data-driven marketing.

The nature of marketing changes. Music fashions rise and fall in months, even weeks and possibly days. Money can be made today but the same customers may be looking for different kinds of music tomorrow. The product therefore needs to change quickly and communication to potential customers changes day by day. This acceleration, enabled by the internet, demands marketing to be connected with customers in ways never envisaged a few years ago. This revolution is not over yet as customers download music to their iPods[5] and MP3 players. The music industry had to take stern action against companies like Napster to avoid losing huge royalty incomes, but what started as an erosion became a new source of growth. Downloading the music you like onto your personal player, for a small charge, has become the norm. The music industry needed to redefine its end product boldly as a service, and to change its pricing model.

Such social and technological developments affect marketing in other industries more and more. Being able to use these technologies effectively will be key to the marketer of tomorrow. Leading companies have picked up the challenge here. They have realized that when customers contact them and give them more information, they are likely to buy products and services if relevant ones are offered. Properly organized, a marketing network based on sense and respond identifies relevant, timely sales opportunities.

MARKETING AS A WHOLE-COMPANY ENTITY

What does this imply inside the company? Revolution is not about functional marketing issues. It is about recognizing how external events affect the entire business process. As long ago as 1954 management guru Peter Drucker wrote, 'Marketing is not only broader than selling, it is not a specialised activity at all. It is the whole business seen from the point of view of the final result, that is, the customer's point of view.' Today we still grapple with the problem of how a company can manage itself around the customer. If this is done at the expense of staff, management, suppliers or other stakeholders it can turn into a stick to beat up the rest of the company, whilst marketing remains proudly virtuous. It is important to balance the expectations of both the company and the customer for this to work.

First and foremost marketing is an attitude of mind, company-wide, that says that while the customer is the ultimate short-term arbiter of our actions, in the long run it is getting customers, staff, managers, suppliers and owners going where they want to go together, that works. Whether the customer is 'always right' is irrelevant. The truth is more subtle. Customers don't always know best, especially in technical or complex markets. Sometimes marketing's role is to lead the market, not follow it. The key is to focus on balancing the different stakeholders' interests. Successful companies get their internal act together by creating value for all their stakeholders. Unsuccessful companies tend to have lost this focus. They become top-heavy bureaucracies and split themselves into functional specialisms that each fight their own corner with no regard for the bigger picture. The marketer's role is to be expert in understanding the customer as stakeholder, to become the customer advocate, and to work closely with the other groups that are experts in understanding and possibly representing the other stakeholders.

Once marketers understand that creating value for customers and other stakeholders is not done just inside marketing departments, they must engage with the firm's critical processes. These include:

- a strategy process, aligning customers' wants and needs to the businesses' strengths and objectives;
- an innovation process, creating a steady stream of new products and services that people want;
- an efficient operations process;
- a process for going to market, promoting, selling, channels, service, relationships.

Marketers quite clearly have a role to play in the first three but they also have a strong leadership role in the last one. Abdicating this role to IT, operations or a 'customer service' channel risks losing the customer focus that we've agreed is so vital. Running across these processes are very important functional processes: people and organization, technology, information and finance.

SPREADING THE MARKETING STATE OF MIND

Spreading the marketing 'attitude of mind' company-wide is easier said than done. On the office walls of most enterprise HQs, you will find a mission statement. A research company examined 55 statements from some of the world's biggest companies and found overwhelming similarities. Amongst them was always something about delighting their customers. However, sticking this on a wall doesn't mean it happens. At its heart, marketing revolution is about reclaiming marketing. Before you can revolutionize your company around customer, staff, manager, supplier or shareholder value you must drag marketing out of its functional specialisms and replace it in its rightful home, a philosophy at the centre of the company. This is why the buck must stop with the CEO. Only the CEO and main board enjoy the whole picture. Even then, they may not see it as the customer sees it. How many companies have customers on their main board? Great CEOs such as Richard Branson of Virgin, Anita Roddick of The Body Shop, J W Marriott of Marriott Hotels, or Terry Leahy of Tesco run their entire corporation around customers and the staff that manage them.

Case study: the revolution of IBM – the CEO as the head of marketing

One of history's best examples of marketing revolution in action is IBM. In 1992, IBM posted what was at the time the largest commercial loss in history. Not only did it need a new vision but also new, cheaper and faster channels of distribution and a real marketing arm to fill in the gap left by direct selling. When Lou Gerstner took over at the start of the decade, IBM showed all the classic signs of a firm obsessed with internal issues, ignoring the marketplace and getting trounced by the competition. One of IBM's mantras at the time was 'superior customer service'. By 1992 that had come to mean 'servicing our machines on the customers' premises', instead of working out how computer technology can help the customer in their business. Gerstner (2003) observed that customer service had become largely administrative, 'like going through the motions in a marriage that had long since lost its passion'.

Many great companies have run into serious trouble by reaching a comfortable market dominance, then slowly but surely taking their eyes off customers and competitors. They then divert themselves with internal processes, administration or internal politics. Great marketing built the firm but this is lost on maturity. In IBM's case, decision making slowed to a crawl. As firms become more successful, they tend to grow bigger and this makes internal processes, procedures and management more complex and time-consuming. Also, dominance builds complacency. Sales and revenues roll in without anybody having to do very much. This leads to less and less focus on what is going on outside. Large companies are often riddled with internal turf wars: divisions or functions scrapping over power bases and product lines, competing with each other to serve the same customer (even competitively bidding against each other). Departments may even refuse to share market information with other units. Teamwork is not valued or rewarded. Teams should address a common cause, which in business should mean a passion for meeting customer needs better than anyone else. If this is not there, teams disintegrate.

In 1992 Gerstner had to do two things, both of which depended on his natural abilities as a great marketer. First, he had to understand and articulate a strategic direction for the company that would take it back to a position of market leadership. Second, he had to change the culture from an individual, internal focus which was risk averse, to an external focus, team-based, which put the customer first.

First, revolutionize the strategy

Especially in his early tenure, Gerstner spent vast amounts of time talking to and listening to IBM's key customers, usually chief information officers of major companies. He learnt some critical things. He learnt that the notion that the mainframe was dead, to be replaced by PCs, was incorrect. He found that IBM's prices were far too high. He also found that IBM was hard to deal with and had slow, unclear delivery channels. So he cut mainframe prices and promised to sort out the delivery. He cut costs. He fired many people who did not share the new vision or who could not or would not contribute to its achievement. The real achievement was integration. With much complex, new technology coming on board, customers wanted help in using all the different layers of IBM to create solutions. This insight led to a number of important decisions during Gerstner's time at IBM. First, under great pressure to split the company up, he kept it together. He could see that IBM's breadth was a competitive advantage that customers would value, if IBM could deploy it properly. Second, he positioned IBM as a services company, with great people delivering solutions for customers. Third, he realized that in many cases teaming with IBM's suppliers would enable staff to do a better job for customers. Fourth, IBM needed a really excellent team to meet customers' needs. Eventually this was developed even further by buying PriceWaterhouse Coopers' consulting business. The revolution of IBM from a hardware company that dominated the world's supply of computers into a consultancy company that focused on providing customer solutions is shown in Figure 1.1.

Later on, Gerstner's vision for IBM, delivering e-business, was also a market-driven vision. E-business is about using technology to revolutionize your business, making it able to respond more quickly. He saw that IBM could help define business practice, to lead the market once more.

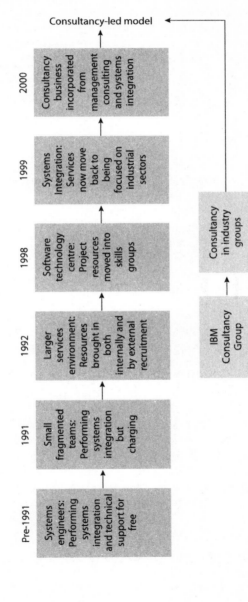

Figure 1.1 *The transformation of IBM*

Second, revolutionize the culture

Culturally, Gerstner started by holding up a mirror to the organization, so people could face up to the internal problems they were inflicting on themselves. In an emotional address to senior executives, he highlighted in depth the behavioural changes needed. Clogging processes were abandoned in place of a number of key principles, the first of which was, 'The market place is the driving force behind everything we do'. He created IBM Leadership Competencies which described some essential qualities such as:

- customer insight;
- breakthrough thinking;
- drive to achieve;
- team leadership;
- straight talk.

These changes were successful but not sufficient. To drive home the changes needed, Gerstner simplified the principles further and inculcated them into every-thing IBMers did through a new performance management system linked to merit awards and variable pay. In the end 'making it happen' came down to personal leadership by the hundreds of senior executives who took up these challenges and inspired their teams.

Third, the marketing revolution

Probably less well known was the revolution in marketing and sales. Traditionally focused on a successful but increasingly costly face-to-face sales approach, IBM found it had to build a more efficient channel mix that would recognize the balance of customer value in an increasingly commoditized market. In the early 1990s, according to measures by the Interbrand Corporation, the IBM brand was at an all-time low. As a reflection of the company's problems, it had fallen to 248th worldwide. In addition to rallying the company around the e-business revolution, IBM rebuilt its marketing function. It consolidated resources and investments, web-enabled the company and created new channel coverage capabilities such as database marketing, direct marketing and call centre sales coverage for customers. It also put in place a well-oiled machine to generate and qualify leads for both its direct sales force and IBM's new business partner and reseller networks. As a result, by 2001 the IBM brand value had risen from 248th to 3rd worldwide.

Creating the customer journey: the SPIN approach

In this book we are going to examine what it takes to revolutionize your marketing. It is a painful process, but it is one that is essential if companies are to respond to the challenge of the new millennium. A truly customer-centric company does more than post slogans on the lobby walls. It makes real changes in its marketing approach. Table 1.1 gives an example of using the framework of the SPIN (Situation, Problem, Implication and Need to do) for revolutionizing your marketing – in this case, revolutionizing the customer experience.

Table 1.1 _Revolutionizing customer experience_

SPIN	Point of value
Situation	Managing the emotional and tangible outcomes that occur each time a customer touches an organization is regarded by 84% of CEOs as the fundamental driver of value creation. The Ogilvy BrandZ research into the top 16,000 worldwide brands shows that customer experience directly impacts upon brand equity and perceptions and that better bonding of top customers leads to market leadership. Customers who experience a consistent set of positive outcomes both emotional (feelings of well-being) and behavioural (repeat purchase) over time, will exhibit behaviours and attitudes that underpin continued consumption and value growth.
Problem	Current approaches to creating and managing customer experiences are ineffective, because: 1. Few organizations prioritize this area to address. 2. Those that do often think in terms of a point experience only and fail to build the environment needed for success to create valued customer journeys. They tend to think in terms of a series of point experiences that are neither consistent nor effective because they fail to address all drivers of the interaction such as people, processes and technology. This is reinforced by (a) approaches to measurement and reward which are primarily functional and (b) career paths which are specialized not generalized. 3. The fragmentation of customer ownership across organizations and channels means that organizations unwittingly destroy and build value and in equal measure. 4. Customers are increasingly demanding and expect positive outcomes on each interaction. The strong link between brand promise and the tangible outcomes customers actually experience, through delivery, is often overlooked, broken or considered too difficult to implement.
Implication	Marketers must engage on the full range of journeys that the customer experiences to devise models built on the value proposition of the brand. This must be designed from the perspective of the customer and be both coherent and consistent in execution through all channels and touch points. A structured approach to developing and implementing customer experiences

establishes and cements the connection between the brand promise and actual brand experience delivered to customers. This generates value, growth and competitive advantage.

Need to do

Step into the customer's shoes

1. Appoint a senior customer champion accountable for aligning process, people and technology to create a seamless marketing and delivery capability. This will then match brand promises and execution consistently across all customer journeys.

2. Establish a baseline for today's customer experience for the buyer/adoption model for a priority segment across all touch points. Identify where and how value is created and destroyed at each touch point. Benchmark performance against best in class competitors, regardless of industry group.

Align marketing and delivery capability

3. Develop the customer experience model for the priority segment defining generic customer expectations and critical success factors at each touch point through a journey. Align these to the brand proposition and join up marketing and delivery capability across touch points.

4. Develop, pilot and evaluate the customer experience model for the market segment. Measure variance in actual outcomes against the desired brand characteristics for each touch point.

Revolutionize

5. Implement the preferred customer experience model with a ruthless focus on embedding effective human linkages, usability and consistent delivery of the brand promise throughout the model. Incentivize and reward cross-functional collaboration.

NOTES

1. Tropicana is a registered brand name of Pepsico.
2. Mini is a registered brand name of BMW.
3. PT Cruiser is a registered brand name of Chrysler.
4. Nomad is a registered brand name of Tiscali.
5. iPod is a registered brand name of Apple Computer, Inc.

2

What is marketing revolution?

EXTREME COMPETITION

To say that the external environment is becoming more turbulent is probably one of the most trite expressions that can be written – it has been said so many times. Unfortunately, it is true. The external environment *is* becoming more turbulent and a recent report from McKinsey (Huyett and Viguerie, 2005) supports this. The 'topple rate' at which companies lost their leadership positions doubled in the 20 years to the mid-1990s as new technologies overthrew long-standing industry leaders and changes in the world's geopolitical systems opened up new countries to the forces of globalization in a way never seen before. This trend will continue.

New technology, the integration of low-cost economies into the world's supply and demand base, liberalization and privatization and the exploitation of the networking and communications infrastructure will all combine to affect rates of innovation and the reshaping of major industries. Mature companies in seemingly dominant positions are probably the most vulnerable, especially so since they face a relative decline in their industry performance. The slow, steady decline of the US automobile industry over 30 years against European and Japanese competition will seem very welcome to industries facing something rather more forceful.

Why is this so? Take for example labour costs. Twenty-five years ago the one-third of the world's population that live in India and China were more or less out of reach of the economic forces of the developed world. In 2005, education, communications and computing power, coupled with massive infrastructure developments achieved by the countries themselves, has made a huge number of people available for a vast range of physical and knowledge work. A day-to-day example of such a change has been the reaction in the West against companies who have increasingly outsourced their service and support centres to India. On both sides of the Atlantic it would be hard to find an ordinary home without finding examples of white goods and consumer electronics that owed their origin in whole or in part to China.

The way these sorts of changes shape an industry can be seen in the world market for PCs. In the early 1990s, the PC industry had three clear leaders: IBM, Compaq and Apple. Over the last 15 years, demand for PCs has become global, 'everybody' has one or has access to one, there has been a massive trend to digital convergence in terms of PDAs, iPods,[1] MP3 players, DVDs and digital TVs. Buyers have become increasingly sophisticated, and low-cost sources of supply and plentiful internet-based information for comparison shopping along with the relatively open architecture of the devices has resulted in the manufacture of digital devices becoming one of the world's most competitive industries. So, what happened? Apple Computer nearly went out of business before reinventing itself in a niche market; Hewlett Packard bought out Compaq but nearly choked on the acquisition; and IBM decided to get out of the business and sold its PC offshoot to... a Chinese manufacturer. At the moment, China accounts for less than 5 per cent of total world production, which does not seem much until you realize that more than half this share was won since 2000. Consider the implications of that in terms of a growth trend!

McKinsey identify four zones of extreme competition:

- *Trench warfare* – this is common in mature, undifferentiated industries such as paper where either demand is shrinking or supply is growing too rapidly.
- *Judo competition* – this is just the opposite. The overall industry is growing but the risk of being toppled and replaced by a more

agile competitor is ever present. The software industry would be a good example.

- _White-knuckle competition_ – the term first coined by Jack Welch, former CEO of GE, refers to industries which are shrinking and where there is high churn amongst industry leaders such as telecoms where Voice over Internet Protocol (VoIP), the growth of mobiles and the rise of broadband have totally revolutionized the basis of the industry.
- _Relative stability_ – this might be found in industries where the risk of dramatic changes in the demand or the supply side are less threatening, such as for example in pharmaceuticals.

To survive in these new conditions of extreme competition requires companies that are more agile and responsive than their forebears. Chief executive officers (CEOs) need to challenge business units to respond more imaginatively and need to intervene more directly within business units to encourage creative responses to new conditions. They must adopt the unpopular role that goes with the territory of a CEO when they seek to lead change. They need to make people uncomfortable with the way things are now. They need to shake business units out of any sense of complacency and encourage them to realize there is a need for an urgency in finding new ways of getting close to their customers as never before.

THE END OF THE COMFORT ZONE

The marketing comfort zone has gone. Gone are the days when mass products were designed for mass audiences, and manufacturers and producers could combine good old mass-distribution methods, face-to-face selling and mass advertising. Marketing used to be straightforward. If you were a product marketer and had a decent product, you could promote it heavily and it would sell. You could fine-tune things on the run. It was not hard to succeed. Unfortunately, markets have changed. The trusted marketing management textbooks that formed the cornerstones of marketing of 5, 10 or 15 years ago are gathering dust. The product is now undoubtedly a very small proportion of the profit in a value chain. Product differences are rarely a sustainable competitive advantage: there has to be something more – it's in the service/solution part of the equation. So everyone is trying to differentiate through services and solution, which is fine, but again this makes it hard for everyone to win.

So what happened? What caused this paradigm shift? Over the last 10 years, the model has changed totally. The IT industry for instance relied from its beginning largely on a face-to-face or direct sales model. When margin permits, this form of one-to-one marketing is the most personalized type of relationship marketing. It is built on knowing the needs of individual customers and building solutions to meet them. The role of marketing in this phase is sales and promotional support rather than mass-awareness advertising and branding. As the market matured, competition increased, product cycles were reduced and costs fell. IT products are becoming commodities in a world of reduced margins. Whilst the face-to-face sales force remains the right solution for complex and/or high-value transactions, commoditized products and services are more suited to lower-cost distribution channels such as the web. The face-to-face sales model is no longer affordable. So marketing needed to take on a new expanded role.

The IT industry, like others such as retail, automotive, insurance or travel, relies on and suffers from the growing role of intermediaries. The supplier may be one or more steps from the end customer. So better customer data and market intelligence is now critical to building and nurturing relationships with end customers.

In many markets, the old approach to marketing is not working. There are more things to play with – whether that is more channels, more media or more technology. In many ways that is a switch from the analogue age of marketing to the digital age of marketing. Markets are more fragmented. The media available to reach consumers have proliferated. The differentiation of roles traditionally attributed to different media has also broken down. For instance, take the mailshots with CDs by internet service providers such as AOL. They are providing product access as well as building the brand in a non-traditional manner. The fragmentation of media and changing of media roles together have an effect which requires even more thought than before about how to integrate communications. As if this were not enough, customers are becoming more discerning, screening media, throwing away or deleting non-relevant mail and zapping adverts. This has made marketing planning more complex.

Even more alarming has been the accelerating rate of change. Activities that once required hours or days, such as inventory assessment, can now be done automatically with the click of a mouse using e-commerce techniques. Marketers need to react faster to the market and are using new technologies to do this. The pressure for speed and efficiency is forcing marketers to consider more innovative

and effective means to building relationships. New forms of partnering are emerging.

Reflecting on the sum of all these changes, one could say that it is
a quite challenging environment, one that could genuinely be
called revolutionary. Evidence from several sources shows that
marketing revolution is high on the chief marketing officer's agenda.
Marketing revolution is critical to coping with change. Marketing
revolution involves combining the best in marketing, sales and
service from anywhere in the world to change marketing and to meet
the challenges described above. At a time when the wingspan of what
we call marketing is much greater, so it is _all_ customer-facing activity
– not just the marketing department controlled stuff; nothing is ruled
out. It includes merging marketing with other functions, outsourcing
or even abolishing marketing. Marketing is also taking partial
accountability for new areas, making the boundaries between
marketing, sales, service, HR, operations, logistics and other functions less impervious. Marketers need to answer questions such as:
How can my marketing be twice as effective at half the cost? How can
I accelerate my marketing activities so I can do everything at four
times the speed and half the cost without sacrificing quality? They
also need to answer tactical questions relating to the cost-effectiveness
of specific marketing activities. All this involves big changes to how
information is created, interpreted, shared and used to manage
customers and business partners.

Companies are starting to realize that their marketing needs to
change radically to succeed. The new emerging and empowered
consumer, an increased product choice and global oversupply are
creating an ever-growing pressure on the marketing function.

The symptoms of a crisis that has slowly been gaining momentum
over the last five to ten years are quite apparent now and hurting
marketing:

1. _Marketing communication is congested._ Too many communications
    that even with strong, analytical targeting fails to achieve, failing
    to break through and drive the ROI (return on investment)
    companies are expecting in a fragmented media.
2. _Marketing seems to have become a battleground._ Marketing has to
    justify its existence, even its survival, and getting cut in as a 'non-
    revenue' and 'non-essential' function.
3. _Marketing disciplines are fighting each other._ Functions fighting each
    other for diminishing budgets as the core effectiveness problems
    fail to be addressed in favour of cost-cutting efficiency. Whilst

consumers realize that anything can be a message medium, marketing and services fight for budget.

4. *Too many marketers are in love with one instrument*. Individuals focus on a tried and tested method at the expense of change.

5. *Many internal relationships and client–agency relationships frequently don't look like partnership*. And when functions and agencies work together they do not pull together because no one has aligned strategy, measurement and execution.

The comfort zone that marketing was enjoying as little as a decade ago, has gone.

MEASURING MARKETING EFFECTIVENESS

Companies are becoming impatient with marketing. This is reflected in articles by leading marketing gurus such as Schultz (2003) and Kotler (2004). It is often easier to establish measures and returns for their investments in finance, production, information technology, even purchasing, but much harder to understand what their marketing spending is achieving. As a result, there is a feeling that the marketing function is being pushed lower and lower in the corporate hierarchy.

To investigate these issues, the Association of National Advertisers (ANA), a leading US marketing trade organization, undertook a study in cooperation with consulting firm Booz Allen Hamilton (Hyde, Landry and Tipping, 2004) to discover whether marketing has become disconnected from companies' leadership agendas, to determine the causes of any dysfunction and to uncover the best practices of superior marketing organizations. Their research was based on an online survey of 370 marketing and other executives at more than 100 companies in nine industries. The industries represented were automotive, consumer packaged goods, financial services, health, manufacturing, professional services, retail, technology and telecommunications. This was supported by in-depth interviews with marketers across a range of industries.

Their conclusion was a surprise. The general belief was that the marketing function is more important now than ever before, but that marketers are having a hard time keeping up. Good marketing is regarded as being key to corporate success by 77 per cent of marketing executives and 78 per cent of non-marketing executives overall, with some variation by industry. In healthcare, for example, 86 per cent of executives regarded marketing as important, whereas in the automotive industry this fell to 59 per cent. The study identified three dichotomies which hinder the effectiveness of marketing organizations:

1. More than 75 per cent of marketers and other managers say that whilst marketing has become more important to their companies during the past five years at more than half of all companies, the agendas of marketing and the CEO agenda are not aligned. This is illustrated in Figure 2.1.
2. Higher expectations for marketing have driven nearly 70 per cent of all companies to reorganize their marketing departments during the same period. Despite such activities, the position of chief marketing officer (CMO) remains ill-defined in relation to other functions within the company.
3. Measurable outcomes are now expected for marketing programmes. Sixty-six per cent of executives in the study noted that a reliable return on investment (ROI) analysis is one of the

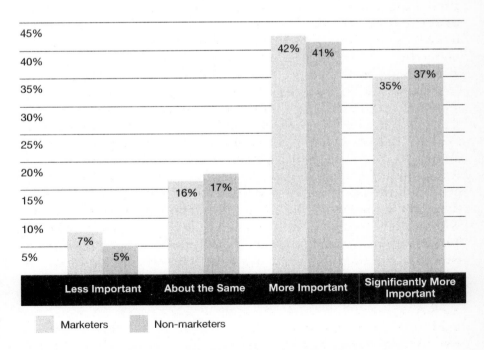

Figure 2.1 *The rising importance of marketing*
Source: ANA/Booz Allen Hamilton Marketing Organization Survey (2004).

31

marketing function's greatest needs. However, most companies are still using surrogate metrics, such as awareness, instead of ROI measurements.

To investigate further the reasons for the apparent mismatch, Booz Allen Hamilton sought to compare marketers' own evaluation of their focus and their contributions against those of company leaders. They compared the key priorities of CEOs, as identified in the US Conference Board's comprehensive annual survey in 2004, with the priorities of leading marketers in their study. Their findings, summarized in Figure 2.2, make interesting reading. According to the Conference Board, the top four chief executive priorities are:

- top-line growth (52 per cent);
- speed, flexibility, adaptability to change (42 per cent);
- customer loyalty and retention (41 per cent);
- stimulating innovation (31 per cent).

This is supported by a recent IBM Global CEO survey that pointed to 'profitable growth' and 'customer intimacy' as very high on the CEO agenda.

In the US study marketers seem to be giving some of these priorities short shrift. The marketing agenda seemed to be quite disconnected from that of the CEOs in some areas. Marketing's focus is still tactical. However, the pressure to measure marketing effectiveness is plainly on. In a UK IBM chief marketing officer survey, measuring marketing effectiveness came top of the list. The need for accountability and a feedback loop to support continuous improvement is essential, as marketing spend is typically about 6 per cent of company turnover and more than $250 billion is spent to produce and manage marketing output by the top 1,000 companies according to a Gartner study.[2] UK enterprise spends at least £40 billion per annum on marketing and communications. This expenditure is far from optimized. Our estimate is that the potential for improvement is in the range of £4 billion to £10 billion per annum.

In the IBM survey, senior marketing executives were asked to grade challenges as strong, medium or weak, with strong being a challenge of near-term significance to their organization. Over 70 per cent of respondents saw developing the capability to measure marketing effectiveness as a strong challenge. Only 3 per cent of the senior marketing executives interviewed felt that marketing effectiveness had little relevance to their brief. When asked to give their top three near-term marketing challenges, respondents again viewed measuring marketing effectiveness as the most significant challenge. Close to two-thirds of all respondents cited measuring marketing effectiveness in their top three, with over half of those respondents rating it as the most important focus area for their marketing department. More evidence of this interest is found in the number of studies and professional workshops on this topic in professional and industry marketing for associations.

Part of the underlying drive towards marketing effectiveness is based on the fact that many companies are realizing that they need to win the battle for high value customers. In other words, you have to focus on those 10–20 per cent of customers that make all the difference. The difference between a market leader, the number two and number three is often down to a company's share of a very small group of high-value customers. A brand leader always finds better ways to bond more closely with them. Building and managing those relationships is critical to maintaining or acquiring market leadership. This is where marketers need databases, data-mining customer analytics and campaign management. This also means beating the competition. It is not good enough to be effective. A company must aspire to excellence and to winning against its competitors throughout the customer management cycle. This requires close alignment of investments to business strategy and growth opportunities.

Measuring marketing effectiveness has not proved easy. The problem is, how can marketing show an ROI, based on some sort of acceptable cost–benefit calculation in the same way as some other corporate functions? The impact of marketing is difficult to track, especially its longer-term effects. The costs are usually clear, but benefits can be more difficult to articulate. To compound the problem, the definitions of measurement and what to measure can make this even more challenging. Does one measure all marketing? Does this include all customer touch points? Measuring effectiveness goes beyond executional efficiency. Limited progress seems to have been made in the last 10 years on revamping marketing metrics. In the finance area both the 'R' and the 'I' are uniformly measured in monetary terms. In marketing, various quantitative factors – such as cost per incremental volume – have to be balanced against qualitative factors such as product awareness over both the long and the short term. High-touch, relationship-based industries with differentiated products (such as financial services and automotive) tend to use awareness and image-related forms of measurement. Low-touch industries (such as food and most retailing), in which marketing

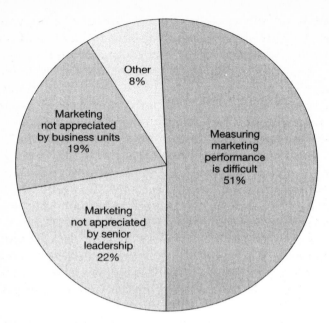

Figure 2.2 *Concerns with the marketing function*
Source: ANA/Booz Allen Hamilton Marketing Organization Survey (2004).

creates differentiation among commodity products, rely more on market share, growth and profit metrics. Although these forms of measurement are valid, they are harder to explain and sell to other senior executives, who typically come from backgrounds with different disciplines.

Having said this, some companies have actually managed to define a lead metric, such as churn rate in mobile telephony, and use this as a published marketing metric on their annual report.

Measuring effectiveness also involves understanding how well a company is executing against its business strategy.

IBM and OgilvyOne have designed a joint framework for effective marketing, the 'Marketing Effectiveness Matrix'. In this model, marketing effectiveness is assessed against three fundamental building blocks:

- direction;
- train;
- track.

Direction is about ensuring that marketing strategy aligns to the business model, for example through alignment of expenditure to opportunities, channel strategy, communications strategy and brand building or maintenance. It is amazing how often most of the ineffectiveness of a marketing strategy or marketing mix has been built in at the stage when direction is being set. The strategy says we are going over there, but spend implies we are going over here (in the opposite direction). This strategic road map is the fundamental starting point of the market planning process.

Train is about ensuring that everything that has been put in place is running smoothly, relevantly, consistently and efficiently. These are your operational and activity metrics. An example of this is the IBM Business Consultancy Services marketing scorecard, where various criteria are being measured at activity and business unit level across operational units.

Track is about ensuring that we have recognized and are applying best practices in all marketing activities, through processes, information, technology, organizational structure and measures. This means not only benchmarking internally and against competition, but also against best in class.

Various tools are available to marketers to help manage these areas. These would include assessment methodologies in CRM and integrated marketing, such as the Customer Management Assessment Tool (CMAT) offered by IBM and OgilvyOne's subsidiary, QCi Ltd

LET'S KILL CUSTOMER SATISFACTION BEFORE IT KILLS US

Why should we want to 'kill' customer satisfaction? What's wrong with it? Of course, the short answer to that is – nothing. Marketing is about identifying and satisfying customer wants and needs. What we need to think about more carefully is, once we have produced a satisfied customer, will it do us any good? Will that make the customer more loyal, will it complete the hoped-for progression from prospect through customer to advocate for our products or services? These are questions to which the answer is – probably not. In spite of the huge amounts of money spent on measuring customer satisfaction by companies, market research is failing to predict customer loyalty. Many customer satisfaction surveys are transaction-focused but fail to examine commitment to the brand and bonding. Satisfied customers will still shop around, for all sorts of reasons most of which have little to do with the products or services that they have been provided with elsewhere. Some of these may be to do with convenience, some to do with availability, others to do with policy. We have come across instances where a customer has almost begged a company to lower its prices to match those of its competitor. The customer was extremely satisfied with the service that the company had provided over the past year, in this case in financial services. The customer was told that their preferred company could not compete on price, as to do so was outside policy limits. It would seem that not every company is even interested in retaining its satisfied customers!

Most European companies now enjoy the 'benefits' of both national and European regulation to a greater or lesser extent. Companies in some sectors, often those that had been in the public sector until a few years ago, tend to be more heavily regulated. Let us consider what makes customers happy in (heavily) regulated industries, where the company might be under government pressure to show that it monitors what it does for customers. It basically has two choices. The first is some variant on the customer satisfaction theme, monitoring whether transactions and other contacts between customers and suppliers left customers more or less satisfied. Data must be captured soon after the transaction so as to be able to show the authorities that there is a consistent process for measuring and improving the situation. The other choice is to go 'back to basics' – to focus on what customer needs the industry aims to serve, to identify the promises made by the industry in terms of its ability to meet these needs, and to determine whether the promises were delivered.

The second choice is clearly to be preferred, not just because it is the ethical choice. Today we can use database marketing techniques to produce a more accurate picture of what happened at different stages of the customer interface. This will then help companies focus on where they need to improve or conversely withdraw from meeting the needs of some customers.

Let us take medical treatment as a specific example of a heavily regulated area. The patient comes to the doctor's office with some symptoms. Diagnosis takes place, whether by the doctor or, after referral, by a consultant. The doctor or consultant, together with the patient (in theory) makes a choice about the appropriate treatment. Some time afterwards, the treatment takes place that either does or does not produce the right result. If these data were recorded, we would be able to say whether the process had worked for the patient. This is much more important than recording whether the patient had to queue in the surgery. Obviously if the patient had to wait weeks to get an appointment either with the doctor or the consultant, or for any of the treatment, then the delay is clearly important.

Recording customer satisfaction is a bit like recording waiting time in the surgery, whether the receptionist was pleasant or whether the doctor made the patient feel confident in the diagnosis, irrespective of the success of the treatment. This might be misleading. If you set out to establish a rather questionable practice in cosmetic treatments, you might not be a very good doctor. On the other hand, if you handle the customer interface well using your undoubted social skills then you could probably continue in business for some time before your patients realized that some of your treatments did not produce the effects you had promised or perhaps did not work at all.

What is particularly bad about using customer satisfaction is that it can divert resources and management effort from the main aim of the supplier. It can even obscure whether the aims are being achieved. In services this applies to whether that aim is to make a patient better, to educate a student, or to provide good investment returns. In automotive, at the manufacturing end the aims are to provide a car that is safe to drive, has low maintenance costs and provides a safe, timely, journey from A to B. At the service end the aim is to help the customer get their crash-damaged car back quickly and in a safe state while providing an appropriate replacement car (our recent research shows that this is rare). One insurance company that integrated vertically to cut costs (by setting up its own repair workshops) found itself putting out unsafe vehicles to accelerate the speed of return of vehicles to customers and so reduce replacement hire. This resulted in safety issues and loss of customers. They sold off their crash repair business.

The wrong conclusions are often drawn from surveys in industries where the kinds of variables measured by customer satisfaction surveys are actually part of the core service, such as punctuality of trains and planes. For example, departing on time is much less important to customers than arriving on time. The marketing industry is struggling its way towards this conclusion. In practice, the term 'customer service' needs to change into 'customer experience'. Management must begin to take interest in the long-term experience, not just the immediate transaction experience. This is important because the longer the period of measurement, the more management must focus on whether the product or service actually performed for the customer is as promised to the customer. The longer the period of measurement, the more management must focus on whether the enterprise – with its objectives, processes, systems and staff – is really focusing on meeting customers' needs rather than keeping them happy in the short term.

The good news for marketers is that this is extending and deepening the focus on marketing as something which involves everyone with a role in delivering and supporting products and services – production teams, customer contact staff, researchers, branding and advertising people. It will bring them all closer together and encourage a more long-term concern with the development of customer insights. Such an approach has significant implications for marketing. If you really are going to meet customer needs, where the relationship lasts for some time and is based on an initial customer service followed by a long period of using the product or service – such as long-term medical treatments, education, cars, longer-term investments – you need a record of what went on at the beginning: the situation, the treatment, the promise. In some industries, such as financial services and health, companies must keep such records anyway, though sadly they are rarely used to show the relationship between initial needs, treatment and subsequent performance.

If an enterprise just adopts (yet another) customer satisfaction measure, the regulators will always be able to criticize them on their long-term performance. Worse, their own management teams will be focused on the wrong measure, a short-term measure. This will in turn make their long-term performance worse (both in terms of customer experience and as measured by the regulators). The need is to use measures which bring customers, staff, managers and even shareholders together, not ones that divide them. This will also have implications for data collection and systems design which we will discuss in more depth in Chapter 10. The customer databases must provide the equivalent of the medical diagnoses, recommendations, treatments and outcomes – relatively easy to write, but they can be very difficult to put into practice. So how do we begin?

SENSE AND RESPOND MARKETING

The problem is not to do with databases. It is because marketing is lagging behind customers. Today, it is possible to have a more even balance between supplier and customer, one in which each engages in a useful dialogue about their future plans. This could be called 'sense and respond marketing'. It may sound a little futuristic because it is so rare today, but it is starting to emerge. It is emerging in companies whose websites allow customers to tell them what they want and which communications they would like to receive, such as Amazon, ebookers and lastminute. Some banks gather intentions data too, often from their financial advice divisions. They then move it to their routine banking operations where it is used to manage customers. Much of this is still at an early stage.

That is because most marketers believe they can do better than customers. Their credo tends to be, 'We, the clever marketers, gather data from you, the customers. We analyse it, profile you and then tell you what you want next.' In its most advanced form it is trigger marketing, but the triggers are based on data about what the customer has just done (enquired, transacted, bought), not what they plan to do. Unfortunately, this doesn't work for many customers, who could be excused for thinking that what drives marketers is, 'We surprise you with our incompetence at guessing what you want next because we don't ask you what you want. Nor do we use this information to manage you in every channel, in every interaction.' Many customers refuse to give intentions data to large organizations because they know they will not use it well. At best they may fail to store it, at worst use it as an excuse to sell them the wrong product.

In sense and respond marketing, businesses 'sense' customers, who they are, what their actions are, what their thoughts and intentions are. The business then translates this information from sensing into a statement of targeting. This identifies which customers to deal with and produces a statement of customer requirements, what customers need, when they need it and so on. They then respond by giving customers what they want and what they will want, when they want it, at the right value. They do this now and for the future, through the right channels, both those currently used and those that will be used, customized where appropriate, while making a profit. They keep sensing to identify whether they have really achieved what they want with customers.

How might customers behave in such a world? They sense businesses, to find which business or organizations are likely (now and in the future) to offer goods and services which meet their needs. They seek to identify which businesses can use information about their needs properly, so as to meet their needs. They capture the details of the propositions that they offer, the channels through which they are available, their value, their pre- and post-sales service. They then use the information derived from this sensing to enquire, buy, give information, develop relationships about where they want to obtain and use their service. This contrasts with current practice, where most businesses use data about past customer behaviour and needs to predict the future. They are often responding to past needs, or poorly predicted future needs based upon simplistic generalizations. Just because you had a pepperoni pizza the last three times you came in the restaurant does not mean you will order one on your fourth visit. So customers talk about big companies in disparaging terms. They believe that they know nothing, can't be trusted with anything, and talk down to them.

Most businesses are poor at sense and respond, because their predictive models of customer behaviour are poor. They do not allow for inputs that allow the customer to tell them how they are feeling right now. Certainly, professional users of predictive analytics based on past behaviour of individual customers, such as time series or cross-section data based on similar customers, do better than those that use predictive analytics poorly or not at all. They look like best practice in sense and respond, but their absolute standards are low, as measured by targeting success. Nevertheless, customers rate these businesses well, though this is a relative rating because the relevance offered by most businesses is so weak. At least it is a start.

Sense and respond marketing requires faster, smarter use of customer information. It requires an 'on-demand' style, with a much faster, smarter response to customers, not just in day-to-day interaction but also in tuning marketing budgets (marketing resource management) and adjusting the total customer proposition (enterprise marketing management). In businesses where customer events such as business activities or professional and personal life-cycle events determine value, as in, say, banking or telecommunications, customers will tell suppliers what they are planning next and will supply these data routinely. At the same time, suppliers will routinely sense and respond to customers and will add these customer data to existing customer data to plan what to offer next. The offer will be alerted to the customer and the customer will be allowed to influence the way the offer is presented, in terms of timing, personal tailoring, delivery options and payment terms. This results in significant customer benefits as customers need to expend less time, energy and not least cost to get what they want. They also get more relevant products and services for their needs. Supplier benefits include more cost-effective marketing, higher market share and more profit.

Is it feasible? It may not be as hard as it looks because sense and respond marketing is based mainly on what companies do already in terms of systems and processes. It does, however, require much-enhanced data sets (past facts, preferences, expectations, intentions, plans), working at much greater depth, faster, more comprehensively (blending intentions and facts) and with better integration. The real change required is a change in the marketing mindset.

TAKING STOCK OF MARKETING

Let us consider the rise and rise, over many years, of certain grocery retailers and what seems to be the inevitable decline of others. What causes some to succeed where others struggle? Is it due to the respective capability of their data handling capabilities or the calibre of their marketing efforts? No, the finger can be pointed in only one direction: the quality of senior management. It is no use blaming marketing strategy, information systems or organization structure, although symptomatically these all have a part to play. However they are as it were, secondary factors. All of these are determined and implemented through the decisions and behaviours of senior management. It is senior management who set up (or even encourage) weak governance systems that cause great companies, be they limited companies or mutual organizations, to slide, crumble or even disappear. It is senior management who let projects and programmes slip and slide and sometimes fail.

Good senior managers, especially those who can manage large companies effectively by developing them, motivating their people, keeping achievements and rewards in balance, are hard to find. Much of what has been going on in marketing can be explained by the above. Let us see why.

One of the strongest conclusions of research into success and failure in marketing is that success requires business action, not just technology. Technology is a hygiene factor: you need it but it does not need to be the most sophisticated. A personal handwritten note or even just a smile at the right place and time probably has a more powerful effect on customers than any number of mailshots. Business issues are nearly always the sticking point, not systems. Sometimes these issues are programme management or implementation ones. The strategy is right, but harnessing the energies and time of people in different functions to deliver what is wanted proves too difficult. Sometimes they are strategic, if senior management have misunderstood the nature of the business model required for success. For example, they may believe that customers want a deep, mutual relationship, when they are mostly happy to cherry-pick.

There is no presumption (either way) about the relationship between process and using outside suppliers (from consultants to outsourced services). The trend has been towards outsourcing, not just of systems or databases, but of services. Again, successful companies know how to manage outsourced suppliers and combine them in a team, with each other and with internal teams, to deliver results. They also know that suppliers must be chosen for their ability to provide a broad range of services, not just systems and their ability work with the wider team.

Successful companies have also broken one of the oldest restrictive practices: the separation of market research and customer database management. They combine them into a true customer insight function. This function is charged not only with managing the main sources of customer information so as to produce results for the company, but also with thinking about the customer perspective. If the customer is giving all this information to us, whether anonymously, through personal details or through transactions and responses, what do they feel about it? How is it being used? Have they given permission for it? Do they see any benefits? This in turn is strongly linked to how different channels and media are used by companies, taking into account productivities and permissions.

Once again, good senior management breaks through the traditions about what channels or media should be used for what tasks, and sees them all as ways of managing how the company talks to customers and vice versa. A multichannel strategy is developed, changing as channels change their characteristics and media-neutral communications planning takes root. For companies who get this right, marketing becomes less intrusive and so risks less being a whipping boy of consumer groups and governments.

In well-led companies, marketing in its broadest sense is the shared responsibility of senior management. It is based on a clear and shared set of marketing ideas (not just a marketing function) that leads all aspects of marketing, whether it be branding, direct marketing, relationship building, selling or trade marketing. This helps to build the company's income, develop the right products for the customer base, retain and gather customers and so on. It also helps to prove the worth of this to the main board, to shareholders, to customers and other stakeholders.

FIVE STEPS TO ALIGNING THE MARKETING FUNCTION WITH THE CORPORATE AGENDA

Hyde, Landry and Tipping (2004) suggest five steps to begin the revolution of the marketing function:

1. Choose a marketing model that suits your organization in conjunction with senior leadership:
    - _Marketing service providers_ – lead a small corporate staff function and manage marketing services that offer centralization benefits such as media buying. They also coordinate marketing–service supplier relationships.
    - _Marketing advisers_ – tend to lead a corporate marketing function. They help to align marketing plans with corporate strategies, ensure compliance with corporate trademark and brand guidelines, and coordinate the sharing of best practices across the business.
    - _Drivers of growth_ – by contrast, work closely with the CEO in propelling the corporate growth agenda. They direct brand strategy, foster new business development and innovation. They also drive the marketing capability agenda based on ROI measures. They are empowered by the CEO to align marketing in the business units and their personnel, with the main corporate agenda.
2. Agree from the beginning on a 'marketing contract' with the CEO and continually check progress against it. If marketing metrics differ from organization to organization, if the marketing role varies from one company to another, marketing managers may have an indistinct understanding of their goals and authority. A leadership contract is an effective tool for establishing the decision rights needed to lead an effective organization. The key elements of the contract are:
    - _Agenda_. Whatever the objectives, marketers and the chief executive must be unified in approach and emphasis. Without the total support of the CEO, marketing cannot perform or produce.
    - _Controls_. Marketing may no longer have full control over all of the 'Ps', but it should have a strong influence. If marketing is charged with developing and executing a strategy aimed at, for example, realizing benefits from premium pricing, it ought to have some authority in making pricing decisions.
    - _Outcomes_. When considering revenue, earnings, market share, conversion rates, ROI or indeed any other aspect of

corporate and marketing performance, marketers and chief executives must agree on how they will measure success. If expectations are not clearly defined, CEOs tend to run out of patience.

- *Visibility*. In companies or industries where marketing does not have a track record, it is important to understand how to market marketing. In industries like consumer packaged goods, where marketing is prominent, marketers may face a different but equally difficult challenge to their relevance. Everybody is a 'marketing expert' and therefore they value the marketing function less. In either case, it's vital that the CEO visibly supports the marketing agenda within the organization.

3. Develop organizational linkages. The marketing role is a mixture of control and influence. There must be clear guidelines about how to market with – not through – other demand-side functions such as sales, R&D, and the corporate or business unit marketing departments. At one company, a blend of formal and informal linkage mechanisms includes weekly videoconferences among key stakeholders in any decision. It is critical to understand the boundaries of responsibility (what you own) and what you need to influence.

4. Drive a marketing capability agenda. Much more is being asked of marketing, particularly in the area of capability development. Moving the organization ever closer to a true basis for calculating an ROI on marketing capabilities is important. The approach must blend data gathering and evaluation, decision rights, implementation and outcome-based organizational adaptability, all focused on the goal of more profitable sales. If this can be achieved, it will provide marketers with credibility, support and increased leverage.

5. Take risks – come up with the big ideas. Sometimes you have to stick your neck out. Marketing must not only support current initiatives, but come up with some big ideas of its own that can really make a fundamental impact on the fortunes of the company. Marketers must learn how to foster innovation. Marketing cannot concern itself simply with brand identity guidelines, good television commercials and rising awareness scores. It is also about building new businesses, identifying new opportunities and leading integration across the organization.

MANAGING THE CUSTOMER JOURNEY

Managing the customer experience should be the focus of marketing, sales and service projects, particularly in companies with large contact centres or those using several different customer management channels. Customer experience management should focus on how to manage everything that contributes to the customer's experience of your products. These include associated services, the promotional campaigns through which they are offered and, if necessary, the brand within which they are provided. It also includes things that are controlled less directly, such as how the product or service is offered through or with third parties, how expectations are generated by the company, by media coverage (including PR), by other customers (through word of mouth) and even by competitors. It is an integrative perspective, crossing the boundaries of marketing, sales and service and of different channels of communication and distribution. It has a much broader scope than contact management.

This integrative perspective is too easily abandoned or lost. Even companies that seek to manage the customer experience through contact centres suffer from disconnects with direct mail, branch operations and so on. Still, a focus on the total customer experience, even just in a contact centre, is beneficial. It forces a strong focus on the customer. It is a reminder that, particularly in service industries, most customers experience not 'marketing' or 'sales' efforts as such, but those of operations.

For example, if you are the customer of a bank, a mobile phone company or an airline, your experience of the company is mostly of operational things. You make a call on a mobile phone. Have you got reception? Is it good? Can you get through? Does the call drop? (ie does the telecommunications network cause the call to cease even though the customer did not end it?) If it does, is it automatically restored? If lost, are you credited on your bill? If you tried to make a call and failed, is the call recipient notified by their company? If you are a busy professional, you might experience the operational practices of the phone company tens, even hundreds of times a day (several times per call). If you pay through your bank branch, did you queue? How long? Did you have to fill in a complex form? Was the payment made in time? If you took a flight, were there any nasty surprises on the price of the final fare? Did your tickets arrive in time, or did e-ticketing work? Did you have to queue? Did you have access to a lounge? Did the flight take off and land on time? Were the cabin crew any good? What about the food?

In the best companies, data on at least some aspects of customers' experience of operations are used routinely to manage them. Dropped calls are a predictor of mobile phone customer attrition and are used by some companies in an integrated way. That is, they are copied to a data warehouse to be mined along with other data in order to identify valuable customers who might be likely to leave.

However, these experiences are part of a wider experience, the customer journey. Here the focus is on time. A journey is a time slice through customer experience. Experiences are a sequence of events. There are many sequences or journeys, usually interrelated. The shortest include web visits, telephone enquiries or even opening direct mail. These may be part of a longer sequence such as product or service acquisition, themselves part of a product use journey. In the middle are contract-length journeys such as actual experience of a mobile phone company or car insurer for the contract period. At the other extreme are life-stage and lifetime journeys, such as the journeys many people have with life insurers, banks and retailers where customers tend to be loyal for long periods.

One of the longest journeys of all is the category journey – over the period for which the customer uses the category. The longer the journey, the closer the customer's feelings about it tend to be to their feelings about the brand. Many customers are intelligent enough to recognize the difference, but many simply assume the two are identical and take their business elsewhere. Hence the typical complaint of the loyal frequent flyer. Take someone who has years of intense flying, followed by years of inactivity. The airline downgrades them to the bottom tier of the frequent flyer scheme. The common complaint? Don't you remember I used to be Gold? The answer in many cases is, no. It is not on most airlines' customer-facing systems, although the data are there in the database. The customer interaction is being assessed, in an automated way, based as it were on the (current) trip, not on the lifetime journey.

Managing customer journeys in an integrated way is an aspiration which demands a big data integration effort over time and over different activities such as operations, marketing, sales and service. It is not always worth it, but it often is. It can be a significant competitive differentiator. Typically your market research will tell you if it is likely to be worth it and whether your best customers will reward you for it by staying longer and buying more.

Case study: the museum experience

A visit to a museum – with all its steps, beginning with the decision to make it – is always a powerful experience. The step-by-step analysis of this experience can help to identify those elements that affect the visitor's perception. It also provides useful directions to decision makers and experts.

IBM conducted a study of the 'customer experience' in museums – the interactions between the customer/user/visitor, the organization and its products and services. The study focused on ten museums, including the British Museum, the Musée du Louvre, the Metropolitan Museum of Art and Galleria Borghese. The analysis focused on how museums could improve the customers' experience so as to increase market share, wallet share and customer profitability. It examined user profiles and customer journey scenarios, services offered and channels used. Using five user profiles and 27 scenarios, the methodology compared both how the company's and the customers' value expectations were perceived and met.

The study identified best practices and improvement areas across the group. The study showed that museums are using the brand to increase customer demand, to define development strategies, partnerships and cooperation (best practice example: Guggenheim Bilbao). Other museums, such as the British Museum, are driving innovation through value chain enlargement and the development of innovative services focused on customers' needs, while the Hermitage Museum is a leader in developing new interaction channels based on innovative technologies to enrich user experience and differentiate the value proposition. This project opened the opportunity to provide a richer value proposition and increase demand, in partnership with the private sector.

THE BEGINNINGS OF MARKETING REVOLUTION

Unless it changes, marketing as we know it may not survive. In human terms, marketing is not at all well; indeed it is ill. Like a person who is experiencing symptoms, marketers know there is something wrong but don't necessarily know what the cure is. So at the moment, all that is happening is that organizations are feeling the pain. They sense that they need treatment, but they are not very clear what the treatment might be.

What marketing does today is largely seller-centric, helping businesses to sell more things, and this is not appropriate in all industries. The future will be buyer-centric rather than seller-centric. The marketing function must switch to enabling the buyer to buy more. By enabling the customer to buy, they may not buy from you but you may have a better, deeper relationship with them than before, although fundamentally different. It will take a long time for marketing to adjust its role in this way – perhaps up to 20 years for a revolution like this.

In the future, the customers will control the data. They will manage their own customer information. Customers will then make the information available to business when and how they want to. At the moment businesses hold vast amount of information about the customer, and they control it. In the future the customer will be in control. As a result, it will be important for companies to develop beyond the single view of the customer that they tend to take now, focused on the most recent transaction. They will need to use multiple channels so as to bring together a detailed view of a range of transactions. For example they will need to be able to draw together personal, family and secondary purchases (on behalf of the main customer) to get a complete picture of what the customer is doing. Such a change will necessarily take a long time and there will be problems with privacy and data protection.

Of course there have been some promised treatments in the past for this illness. Customer relationship management (CRM) is a good example of a customer-centric approach. As a result, a huge amount of money has been thrown at customer-centric marketing and customer management in the last five years. It was seen as a quick-fix pill. Unfortunately the illness is quite complex, and while the pill itself was not wrong, it needed to be taken with some other medicine. Superficially CRM seems to be a technology thing; indeed, one major database vendor actually took out an advertising campaign based on 'CRM in 90 days'. Buy a couple of million dollars' worth of hardware and software and the problems will go away.

Unfortunately they also needed to take an organizational pill, a people pill and a whole load of other pills at the same time, to fix their problem. Sometimes if you take the wrong medicine, it can have side effects that produce another headache. This brings us back to our earlier point. The very fabric of organizations, what they look like, how they are managed, where the powerbases might lie, depends on the decisions, inclinations and actions of the senior management team. Changing one part of the structure will not only fail to change the other parts but may well cause an imbalance. Thus the scale of revolution cannot be cosmetic nor can it be a silver bullet. Whilst there is nothing wrong with the CRM approach, just as in medicine, even with the best transplant team in the world, if the transplant is rejected by the body then the body dies. To compound this, the change is not easy. A global IBM CRM survey in 2004 showed that the most important factor differentiating companies that successfully implemented CRM projects from those that failed was change management and project governance. The survey went on to model projected success based on how these control levers were being balanced.

BEST PRACTICE AT WORK

So what have we learned so far? Perhaps a first observation is that best practice solutions work at four levels:

1. *How objectives are defined.* Clear business objectives based on core truths of the brand enable richer communication concepts. Most touch points can achieve a series of objectives – idea forming, relationship building, sales activation, help service, product experience. This requires working with marketing people to change how they define objectives, for instance in terms of outputs and relationship measurement.
2. *How touch points are seen and used.* Unprejudiced media concepts mean that all touch points can work harder. Marketers need to match touch points against all objectives and consider marketing in the broader context of customer experience.
3. *How communication solutions are viewed and practiced.* Richer communication concepts enable more creative solutions; better collaboration means faster, more effective working. The collective experience – marketing, call centre and so on – all needs to add up. Some of the best breakthrough marketing communications combine process and media in a new way.
4. *How data are collected and used to learn.* A common planning and evaluation framework across all touch points, disciplines and media enables shared learning. To work better, marketing needs a proper understanding of the audience common between disciplines.

Focusing on these factors helps improve customer relevance. According to Gartner, companies have not had a high success rate in ensuring relevance:

- 3 per cent relevance for sales:contact ratio for enterprise-initiated, marketing-driven, 'intrusive' contacts – the norm in most industries;
- 20 per cent for event-driven, customer data triggered, 'convenient' contacts;
- 40 per cent for customer-initiated, relationship-driven, 'appropriate' contacts.

We suggest that this could be up to 100 per cent if the customer tells you what they want (or will be wanting) and you comply. What this suggests is that if you get smarter in managing customers, the gains are significant.

NOTE

1. iPod is a registered brand name of Apple Computer, Inc.
2. As presented to an E.piphany user group in London, Summer 2003, by John Radcliffe, VP and Research Director, Gartner.

3

Customer insight[1]

A NEW APPROACH TO INSIGHT

It has become fashionable to name the person in charge of a newly merged market research and customer database department the 'customer insight manager'. 'Insight' is considered by some companies as just a new name for market research, perhaps enhanced by information from a customer database.

Consumer insight has two forms. Firstly, there are 'insights' in the everyday sense, flashes of inspiration, or penetrating discoveries that can lead to specific opportunities. Market research or customer databases can deliver these and often do. However, much bigger than this and central to what companies need today is 'insight' in the singular. We might define this as 'the ability to perceive clearly or deeply', a deep, embedded knowledge about consumers and markets that helps to structure planning and decision making. Everyone involved in marketing needs this form of insight. In a customer-focused organization (as many claim to be), it is something that almost everyone should have.

For this purpose, we need to think in a different way about how customers interact and relate to our company. Most if not all companies are concerned with the delivery of their physical performance or service. To borrow an established advertising phrase, does it do what it says on the tin? Did we identify a need correctly, design and deliver a good-quality product or service, make sure the customer got what they paid for in value for money terms? That is what we are supposed to do and we did it. Less often do companies concern themselves with how the customer felt about the performance. Indeed more than that, what was the network of emotions and interactions like as the customer went through the process of searching for, obtaining and consuming whatever it is that we provide? This introduces two important ideas. The first is the notion of a customer experience. The second is the notion of the customer journey. To market more effectively we need to understand both of these areas.

THE CUSTOMER EXPERIENCE

Customer experience can be defined as the blend between a company's physical performance and the emotions that evokes. These motions are matched and measured, intuitively, by the customer against their expectations of performance across all points of contact. These points of contact might be called the customer journey. They are the series of cumulative experiences in which a consumer 'touches' or interacts with an organization, that consistently align with their expectations to create loyalty, advocacy and attraction. The reputation of a company, its brand, is no longer built solely via the mass media. It is also built at customer touch points. Whenever customers come into contact with an enterprise they experience what it is like to deal with that organization and they form an opinion. The experience is the ultimate conveyor of value to the customer and a primary influence on future behaviour, so it is of great potential value to the enterprise.

How the customer experiences the brand at every interaction in every channel will be a new and lasting source of competitive advantage. A total of 84 per cent of CEOs say that customer experience is the main driver for value creation in CRM investments (IBM BCS Global CMO Study, 2004).The ability to deliver consistent, superior customer experiences has emerged as a differentiator in a world of increasing product commoditization. Companies cannot avoid providing an experience, so designing and managing it is an important role for marketing. A poor customer experience is a step towards customer defection, and of more than one customer if the experience is shared with others. However, a good experience can encourage a repeat purchase, and ultimately help to create loyalty. According to Forrester Research in 2003, 92 per cent of US executives rank managing the customer experience as critical or very important, but only 38 per cent do it.

Although integral to the customer experience, customer attitudes and perceptions have been largely neglected while organizations pursue more concrete operational improvements. A strong focus on customer experience is an opportunity to drive profitable growth, stronger customer loyalty and improved shareholder value, but requires stronger integration of customer insight, delivery channels, staff, communications and technology, but focusing as much on the emotional experience as on the functional dimension. Traditionally companies have focused on improving functional execution at touch points, many times within the silo of a particular channel. To be able to manage the experience, the company must collect and monitor 'soft' data, often considered irrelevant to the relationship or too hard to collect with existing processes and systems. There are various reasons for this:

- The way a customer feels about a company is determined by the experience they have each time they interact with its products, its services and the community at large.
- The way a customer feels will directly impact upon their commitment to and advocacy of that company's products and services. Watch out – 59 per cent of customers interacting with a brand across multiple channels will stop doing business with the brand after just one bad experience... in just one channel (Source: IBM IBV 2002 Study). According to Research International, brands delivering high emotional and functional benefits will typically experience retention rates of 84 per cent and cross-sell rates of 82 per cent, versus low-experience brands at average retention of 30 per cent and cross-sell rates of 16 per cent.
- Commitment and advocacy directly affect the bottom-line drivers of retention, cross-product holding and referral. In an Ogilvy study across 16,000 worldwide brands, research showed a direct correlation between customer 'bonding', value and brand leadership.

The general environment in which this takes place is illustrated in Figure 3.1.

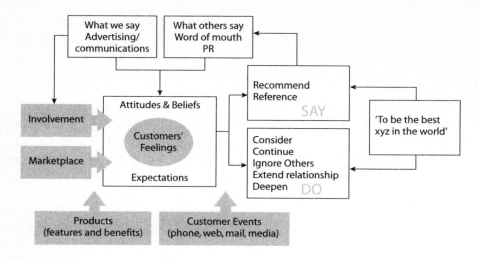

Figure 3.1 *The customer experience*

Each customer experience is delivered through the manifestation, in the customer's eyes, of a company's brand values and personality, products and propositions, service delivery and community inter-action. The unique combination of these elements creates a unique customer experience; unique since each customer will have their own individual perceptions. Therefore all these components need to be taken into consideration when marketing actions and touch points are being designed to deliver against a series of objectives. Some of these elements, such as promotional activities, seem more amenable to internal control and positive definition. Others such as word-of-mouth communication, the way that affects the company's reputation, accumulated previous experience of the company and previous experience of other companies (not necessarily competitors) are less easily controlled. The customer experience is a combination of product, service and the 'feel-good factor' generated by a range of stimuli (eg visual, tone of voice, smell, atmosphere, care and attention to detail) at consumer touch points such as salespeople, call centre agents, advertising, corporate events, debt collectors, receptions, product brochures and websites) and so on.

The customer experience is a step beyond customized service in the 'progression of economic value'. This is illustrated in Table 3.1. The experience, like product and service, must be designed and managed. Buying art for reception and staff areas, staging of themes at exhibi-tions, attention to the details of navigation on a website, a supportive attitude in response to complaints and ensuring easy visitor car parking – these are all part of the same phenomenon, creating a positive customer experience around the value proposition.

DESIGNING THE CUSTOMER EXPERIENCE

An IBM survey showed that 85 per cent of senior business leaders believe they could increase customer loyalty and market share by focusing their organization on integrated customer experience strategies and implementation. In spite of this 44 per cent of all experiences were described as 'bland or uneventful' (IBM IBV 2002). In designing and managing the customer experience, it is important to aim to _just exceed_ expectations in the areas that really matter to a consumer and _just meet_ expectations for the rest. Customer insights are vital here because they can establish which parts of the consumer value proposition and experience, at which points of the customer life cycle, or via which promotional channels, consumers value most. They can also help identify those elements which are merely the necessities that all suppliers are expected to provide and which are potential touch points (as opposed to actual touch points). Exceeding expectations can be time-consuming and costly, so must be done where it will have the most effect and where it takes you further into what might be called your business's 'halo', not away from it or into a whole new one, unless that is your specific choice. We will define 'halo' more fully later in the chapter.

Following an idea by Shaw and Ivens, the positioning activity for experience design is illustrated in Figure 3.2. Basically the aim is to maintain a balance between rational and emotional expectations in such a way that rational expectations are met and the emotional

Table 3.1 _An example of the evolution of customer services_

Product	Model
Birthday cake cooked by parent from basic ingredients	Ingredients sold as a product
Premixed birthday cakes	A service added to the basic product
Ready made and iced cakes	Greater value service added to the basic product
Parents buy a complete party experience including cake	An experience is built around service and product

experience is positive. Perhaps the easiest way to reinforce the point is to think of air travel. Most of the world's airlines fly similar planes built by one of the world's two leading manufacturers of commercial aircraft. They subscribe to the same global distribution systems for reservations and sales, again based on a choice from a small number. Their passengers arrive at, take off from and land at airports used in common with other airlines. So what is the difference? Why choose one rather than another? The answer has to be based on service, and notions of service are based on personal experience.

The major steps in designing the experience are:

- Confirm by research that the company's brand values and image are valued by consumers and are seen as different from those of competitors. Also, what do your staff and managers think, what do they believe the organization to be? Determine how this matches up to what the customers are saying.
- Develop customer insights to establish how consumers currently feel about the experience, and what they expect and value when interactions work and when they go wrong.

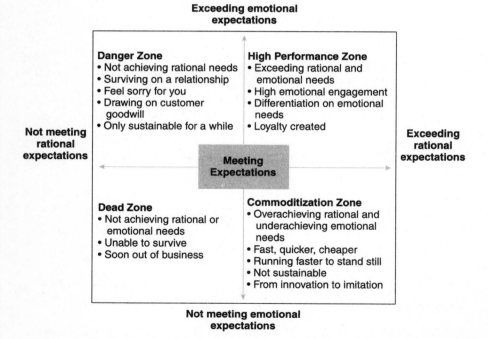

Figure 3.2 *Customer experience zones*

- Using a combination of touch-point analysis, consumer life-cycle interaction processes and mapping known relationship determinants, identify the key 'moments of truth' (MOTs) in customer interactions. Do this from a customer perspective (eg pre-sale, transaction, service, after-sale) as well as the company's matching business process (eg marketing, sales, service) across all interaction points. Try to figure out where the experience makes the most positive and negative impact on consumers. Map and score each interaction against key brand values and touch-point objectives.
- Establish the gap between desired and actual customer experience at the MOT's. Understand the footprint of customer experience today and the future state.
- Establish the employee experience at each MOT, and compare it to the customer experience.
- Design and pilot new consumer and employee experiences.
- Recruit, train, coach and provide incentives to staff to support the customer experience. Remember that according to the Vivaldi Brand Leadership Study, 2002 companies with high brand rating from _both_ consumers and employees have 320 per cent higher return on shareholder value over five years.
- Build the required experience for each segment into the consumer value proposition. Think about customer value tracks and which touch points potentially can contribute the most benefit and which carry the most risk (eg invoicing).
- Develop a measurement tool that allows you to measure far enough out to see if you are moving towards or away from your halo. If you want families to love their birthdays and to have more parties to celebrate, measure there, not just how they liked the cake.

The customer 'journey' described the way in which the customer moves from touch point to touch point along this path. This is shown in Figure 3.3.

This analysis framework is being used by a number of companies across industries to re-engineer their processes. Leading users of this approach today include examples from retail banking, insurance, government, and travel and transportation.

Assessing moments of truth during the customer journey

Let us see how this might work in practice. The management of customer experiences comes in two parts: strategic design and

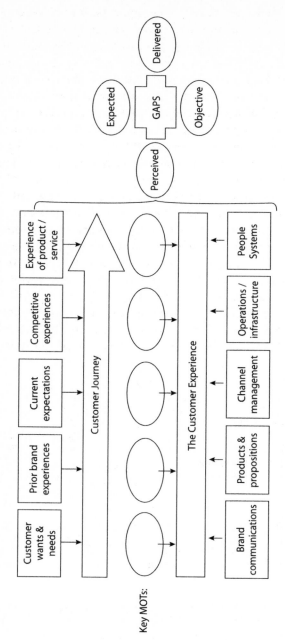

Figure 3.3 *The customer experience model*

continuous improvement. Continuous improvement is enabled via customer feedback or experience stories. Feedback allows the company to resolve complaints and to improve the day-to-day customer experience. It can have an immediate effect on business by reducing the level of defection and business at risk, while increasing the likelihood of favourable word of mouth. Feedback can cut customer defection alone by 2 to 3 per cent per year. There are several ways to collect feedback such as surveys, projective research techniques, complaints management, feedback calls, consumer surgeries, analysing telephone and web interactions, and user group discussions. The trick is to turn those data into knowledge which can then be used to build improvements into the customer relationship. Immediate improvements to the experience can be introduced in areas where short-term changes to procedures, processes and behaviour will bring a long-term gain. Where it is deemed appropriate to avoid 'knee-jerk reactions' to what might be a short-term condition (such as a change in competitor activity) then the measures are used as input to a strategic process to ensure that consumer investment and objectives are on track. Let us stay with the airline example for a minute. Figure 3.4 illustrates some of the touch points that might constitute MOTs along the journey for air travel. Some of these are positive and some negative. It must be remembered that the

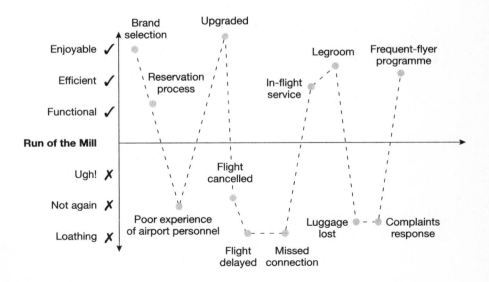

Figure 3.4 *Assessing moments of truth along the journey*

figure starts after the customer has chosen their preferred airline, so that there is in effect a positive disposition by the customer at the start of their 'journey'.

Thus the key task in developing customer insights is to understand which touch points are critical and then to manage those by ensuring that the product or service offered at each of these points enhanced the overall customer experience. Let us illustrate how one airline, used its analysis of customer experience touch points to create a new, more positive set of customer experiences (see Figure 3.5).

BUILDING THE BUSINESS HALO[2]

The customer experience is important in building up longer-term emotional 'loyalty' or commitment to an organization. Table 3.2 shows a development hierarchy for this bonding effect. The customer experience is the ultimate conveyor of value to consumers and is a primary influence of their future behaviour. A poor customer experience is a step on the path to defection and poor word of mouth. A good experience is likely to lead to retained business, recommendations and greater loyalty. Customers have the biggest propensity to recommend a company just after a major interaction. The more loyal the consumer, the easier it is at these times to encourage them to make recommendations. Companies that build emotional loyalty therefore create a big advantage over those who still only look at rational customer satisfaction.

The benefits of managing the customer experience are therefore fourfold:

Table 3.2 *From presence to halo*

Presence	I tried it before and I am familiar with it
Relevance	It's for people like me
Performance	It does a good job
Advantage	It does a better job
Bonding	It's my brand, I'm committed to it
Halo	It really does everything I want in this category, long and short term

Moments of truth	Getting to the airport	Check-in	Comfort until flight	In-flight comfort	Arrival	Getting to destination
Feelings	• Stressful • Complicated • Parking • Lugging	• Long, frustrating lines • Unnecessary (only necessary to the airline)	• Want/need to work • Want/need to relax	• Planes are uncomfortable by nature • Long time spent in a seat • Boredom	• Unkempt • Unshowered • Clothes a mess	• Traffic • Unfamiliar place
			Customer Experience →			
Service solution	• Transport to airport provided • Driver handles luggage	• 'Drive-through' check-in • Airline knows where you are	• Clubhouse with internet access, fax, library • Salon, massages, beauty • Sound room, driving range, skiing machine	• Full-sleeper seats • Mood lighting • Gradual dawn • Bar • You decide meals	• Arrival valet • 18 showers • Make-up & shave • Heated floors • Clothes pressed • Hot & cold breakfast	• Chauffeured delivery to destination • Comfortable ride door-to-door • Knowledgeable local driver

Figure 3.5 *Creating new experiences*

- More positive word-of-mouth recommendation from opinion leaders and others.
- Improvements in customer loyalty.
- Differentiation from competitors.
- Improvements in retention rates.

CUSTOMER RETENTION AND THE CUSTOMER EXPERIENCE

Keeping good customers (or those that are likely to become good) is important. It is not an especially new idea of course. Customer retention has a pedigree that goes way back to the era of classic direct marketing and branding. In many businesses, acquisition costs (including marketing, sales and administration) of new customers are very high. Yet despite this, much existing marketing focus has traditionally been on acquisition rather than retention. This may even be true in branded product markets, where a strong, pervasive brand supports high lead generation and acquisition rates. All this effort can be undermined by poor retention. The retention and development of profitable customers is a critical success factor.

In some industries, managing retention is particularly complicated because serving the customer is complicated and lots of things can go wrong. Complex customer experiences create special retention challenges. Today, customer experience management is the focus of many projects, particularly in companies with large contact centres or those using several different customer management channels. It is the 'child' of customer satisfaction. Most companies know that satisfaction measures don't tell them much – perhaps only that very satisfied customers are more likely to be loyal and to recommend them. Focusing just on service satisfaction leads to other important customer attitudes being missed, such as those relating to a brand or even a category. Category satisfaction is about how satisfied a customer is with a whole category of products (eg telephony, banking, and holidays). If you are a customer's main supplier for that category, a customer may be happy with you but dissatisfied with the category and so looking for change.

Total customer experience management focuses on how to manage everything that contributes to the customer's experience of your products, their associated services, the promotional campaigns through which they are offered and the brand within which they are provided. It also looks at things under less direct control such as how the product or service is offered through or with third parties, the expectations generated by media coverage (by PR), by other customers (through word of mouth) and even by competitors. It is an integrative perspective, crossing the boundaries of marketing, sales and service and of different channels of communication and distribution. It has a broader scope than contact management. The focus on the customer experience forces a strong focus on the customer. It is a reminder that, particularly in service industries, most experience is not of marketing or of sales efforts but of service operations.

As this analysis of customer experience shows, you cannot just tell customers, 'Stay or else!' The aim of the customer retention effort is to change how they think about you in order to secure their retention. One way of doing this might be to bribe them (as in a loyalty scheme or with discounts). Another, perhaps more effective way is to get them to regard your proposition or service as worth staying for, ideally by making sure that it is right for them.

Retention criteria and their measures differ in relevance and importance from product category to category, especially as there is so much variation in the relationship length and relative effect of switching barriers between different products. Finding the best definition and measures are vital to how well a company can evaluate its performance and link this performance to actions in the market. In the last few years trading conditions and the marketing environment have undergone some radical shifts in perspective which have affected all consumers. Since the millennium we have seen the end of the dot.com era, a stock market collapse and recovery, 9/11, economic stagnation in some countries, the expansion of the European Union, the emergence of China as a world economic power and a growing interventionist stance by the United States. These changes were particularly tough for the types of company for whom loyalty and retention are key issues, such as utilities, telecommunications companies, simple financial services (retail bank services, general insurance, credit cards, short-term loans and deposits, mortgages) and travel companies (airlines, packaged holidays). In these companies, even if they stayed profitable, hard questions were asked about the relationship between profitability and marketing, usually by finance directors.

In some companies, retention is excellently managed. Good, well-managed customers (those that bought enough) were managed efficiently and appropriately. So they stayed, perhaps bought more and didn't cost too much to manage. These customers provide most of the profit, so it is worth investing in managing them well and managing those likely to constitute the next generation of loyal customers too. This involves defining 'good customers', doing the data and analysis work needed to understand and manage them and their value today and tomorrow, devising timely, relevant product and service propositions to encourage them to stay. It also means ensuring they have a fair chance of being offered these propositions, perhaps by changing the systems and processes by which they are managed and so on. Other companies believe that all customers are worth managing better because they all contribute value. Before this can happen, data investments are needed, because existing systems and data do not tend to support improvements to customer management at the moment.

Customer loyalty and retention is now an area where companies battle fiercely against their competitors. Excellence in the data management, analysis, strategy and systems required for customer retention is becoming central to survival. In other words, better customer insights are needed if a company is to succeed in this area.

THE CHALLENGE OF THE NEW CONSUMERS

The challenge for marketers is magnified by changes in market demographics and behaviour.

> *For the past hundred years, the real division was between the rich and poor. For the next hundred it will be between young and old.*

> *(Foundation for the Rights of Future Generations 2003)*

Twenty-four of the world's 25 'oldest' countries are in Europe (the other is Japan, which comes in at number three). The UK fits neatly between 'mature' Europe and the 'youthful' United States. The United States is more youthful because it still accepts substantial immigration from countries with younger populations and because first-generation immigrant families still tend to be larger. Whilst the UK has one of the youngest populations in Western Europe with fewer over-sixties than Germany, France, Italy or Spain, it shares their demographic trends in population balance where the active workforce is shrinking and the proportion of the population aged 50 or more is moving towards 50 per cent of the whole. The 50+ group is the fastest-growing demographic group in the UK today. In 2005, it numbers about 20 million people. Meanwhile the UK population aged under 40 is in absolute decline, with the proportion of 10- to 19-year-olds falling by 9 per cent and the 30–39s by 12 per cent over the next 20 years. As a result, 'age dependency' has become a fact of life – over the next 50 years the ratio of people over 64 to the working age population is projected to grow from 25 per cent to 45 per cent according to the Future Foundation.

Where it comes to money, the UK's wealth, savings and spending power are now heavily concentrated within the 50+ group. They hold 80 per cent of all assets and 60 per cent of savings, whilst 75 per cent of all UK residents with assets worth over £50,000 are also aged over 50. This group controls 40 per cent of UK disposable income, making them a key buying group in high-profile sectors such as cars, holidays and technology.

However, the outlook is not rosy for everyone: many over-fifties face an uncertain financial future, with nearly 40 per cent dependent on state support for the majority of income. For those who have invested in private pensions, over half of retirees say their pension pot is worth too little given the impact of falling annuity rates and declining stock market returns.

The lack of recognition of this change from marketers to the 50+ segment has been surprisingly limited when the impact of population ageing on all aspects of family life is considered. Families are starting later. The average age for having a first child is now 31 (up from 28 a decade ago). One result is that a third of families with working parents still have children under 18 present at home. At the same time 60 per cent of over-fifties still have living parents, requiring them to cope with both parents and grandchildren at the same time! This increases the pressures on their time and also may change the way they take their holidays and spend the rest of their leisure time.

Finally, with 70 per cent of men and 65 per cent of women now working past 50 there are 1.7 million more over-fifties working than in 2000. This increases their income but also creates continued pressure on time-constrained older adults. It may change what happens as the economy's growth rate fluctuates, in terms of different regional and age patterns of unemployment or part-time working.

Implications

Actuaries have been considering the effect of these population trends for many years. As a result, planning for the long-term provision of state and private healthcare, pensions and other support vehicles is well advanced. However, by contrast, few UK businesses have considered how the ageing population affects short-term demand. Perhaps a good counter-example here is Camelot, that manages the National Lottery in the UK. After a successful launch it experienced lottery fatigue as seen in other countries. In addition the ageing population – its customer base – was eroding, resulting in lost revenue. The company turned the situation around and moved into growth again in 2005 by targeting product segmentation and innovation, alliances and more importantly by adapting its marketing to the young and their lifestyle (eg texting) to compensate for the ageing players.

What does marketing need to do to respond to this emerging opportunity? According to European Union statistics less than 10 per cent of marketing expenditure targets the 50+ audience despite this group forming half the peak-time TV audience and actually dominating radio listening. In the world of advertising, nobody lives beyond the age of 49! Whilst the need for better customer insights may seem obvious, it is interesting to reflect that although the over-fifties constitute 50 per cent of beer drinkers, advertisers still prefer to target their advertising at 18- to 24-year-olds in the belief that the over-fifties are unresponsive to advertising and that it is better to attract new drinkers to build brands. So much for customer retention.

WHY ARE CHANGING POPULATION DEMOGRAPHICS BEING IGNORED BY MARKETERS?

It is useful to consider why important customers are not being targeted by many marketers despite robust data that demonstrates their collective value to a category or brand. Given the hyper-competitive, mature markets within which so many businesses operate, this lack of commercial responsiveness may appear almost irresponsible (or at least wildly prejudiced!). There is clearly no single reason for this failure, but there are five possible explanations.

Is the spending power of the over-fifties overstated?

Whilst the over-fifties own the majority of assets and savings, the mature market is essentially 'asset rich' but 'cash poor'. In theory they could spend it, but the majority of these assets are locked up in housing and other long-term investments such as pensions and annuities. Despite the increasing take-up of equity release schemes by older consumers, no one knows how long the money will need to cover them for. With life expectancy at an all-time high – in most developed economies an average mid-seventies for men and just over 80 for women and still rising – people are more eager than ever to maintain their assets. Meanwhile concerns over deficits in corporate pension schemes have heightened the need for individuals to provide for their own financial futures. On the health side, many over-fifties now hold private medical insurance cover associated with their concerns about state health provision. The real winners from the post-war 'wealth bubble' could therefore be in 20 or 30 years time, when the inheritances from current, affluent over-fifties passes on to their children (although the increasing longevity of their parents means that these children will inherit several years later than in earlier generations). The implications for high-end asset management are likely to be significant. In the meantime, this wealth tends to be reflected in spending on 'little luxuries' for self-consumption and others. The fact that the over-fifties purchase a quarter of all children's toys and are the single biggest buyers of gifts at Christmas should come as no surprise.

The idea of a distinct '50+' mindset is no longer valid

The actor Jack Nicholson is reported as saying, 'Sixty-six-year-old guys were never like us. Today, we have good nutrition and positive attitudes' (*Daily Telegraph* 2004). What it means to be 50+ has certainly changed. Perhaps there is no longer a clear need to innovate, target and communicate with consumers according to their age? It might well be that for some over-fifties, more self-focused, hedonistic attitudes will emerge as they imitate the lifestyles of the young. A more relevant approach may be to talk to consumers based on shared values, attitudes and mindsets that cut across age boundaries. The key message here is to target individuals based on their self-perception, rather than your perception of them. When asked whether the term 'elderly' applied to them, 88 per cent of 60–64-year-olds said 'no', as did 52 per cent of 75–80-year-olds, according to private health care insurance provider PPP. Indeed in 2002 opinion poll company MORI found that 96 per cent of 60–64-year-olds and 82 per cent of 75–80-year-olds answered 'yes' to the question, 'Do you feel young at heart?'

Appealing to the over-fifties will alienate the 'mainstream'

Another possible challenge to 50+ targeting is that companies are worried that by appealing to older consumers, they risk alienating younger brand buyers and future category entrants. In addition, it might be thought that the over-fifties are perceived as unreceptive to innovation and change, not easily influenced by advertising and that they are not opinion-formers. Being seen to appeal to them could risk alienating essential younger audiences. Given the number of mature, that is, zero-growth consumer markets in which many businesses are now engaged, teenagers and young adults entering markets for the first time often represent one of the few certainties for future growth. Therefore companies may argue that establishing the maximum appeal to younger individuals could be considered a key to future success. It may be reasonable to conclude that failing to target older consumers based on this insight seems churlish. Maybe the real reason is that few businesses are comfortable with the idea of a genuinely segmented and targeted approach that allows you to appeal to both 20-somethings and 50-somethings, by harnessing different contact channels to deliver tailored messages? After all, who is the 'mainstream' these days?

Marketing is a youth industry

In 2003, management guru Peter Drucker observed in an *Economist* article that the new society will be a good deal more important than the new economy. In other words, social change will be more important to marketers than changes in patterns of wealth. One reason why businesses are afraid to appeal to over-fifties may be the very structure of marketing departments and the agencies that support them. Unlike other professional services sectors such as law or accounting, where experience is respected and charged out at a premium rate, marketing tends to be staffed by (relatively) young personnel who create brands, advertising and direct marketing messages largely for people like themselves. This is indicated most clearly by the Institute of Practitioners of Advertising's data about the age profile of today's UK commercial marketers. For the marketing departments that create and manage brands, they indicated that:

- 39 per cent of marketing directors are aged under 35;
- only 10 per cent of marketing directors are aged 50+;
- 70 per cent of brand managers are under 35.

Meanwhile for the advertising, direct marketing and design agencies that support them:

- 82 per cent of people working in marketing agencies are under 40;
- 51 per cent are aged under 30;
- of the 13,000 people in IPA member agencies, only 776 are aged 50+.

This is not to suggest that people who are outside a target segment cannot create compelling messages and marketing campaigns for that segment. It may be the pervasive culture of constant 'new-ness' within marketing which is the real driver behind the interest in eternal youth and a reluctance to market to a maturing population in a relevant way, even though it might be more profitable. Either way, the risks for UK business go far beyond the possibility of upsetting existing customers. In the near term, businesses may find that their traditional customer base has simply aged from under them. Alternatively, more sympathetic competitors could come up with more convincing ways of understanding, meeting and communicating their product or service benefits for older consumers. The problem may stem from today's marketers, but will they wake up soon enough to create the right solutions for tomorrow's customer?

Older consumers have become too marketing-savvy

Finally, there is the argument that businesses have tried (or are trying) to market to mature consumers, but that these individuals are too marketing-savvy to be seduced by targeted promises and proposi-tions. Much can be learnt by reflecting on the environment in which today's over-fifties grew up. The UK's first commercial television station appeared in 1954, airing the first advert a year later (when today's 50+ consumer was an infant). The growth of 'mass markets' and the term 'mass marketing' took place in the 1960s (when they were an impressionable child or teenager). The availability of low-cost video recorders, portable tape decks and then CDs occurred in the 1980s (when they had a young family). Finally, inexpensive personal video cameras, digital satellite television and widespread internet access since the 1990s have all reflected widespread marketing innovation that often took root with older (that is the 50+ segment) consumers, before being accepted as 'mainstream'. Today's mature consumers, especially those aged up to 70, are therefore the first generation to grow up comfortable with mass marketing. It is therefore reasonable to assume that they are also the first generation to become intolerant of and desensitized to the sheer number and type of marketing messages now being driven into the market.

SO, WHY DO MARKETERS NEED BETTER CUSTOMER INSIGHTS?

From what has been written, at almost every level, the implications for future business growth through better customer insight are significant. Many marketers are neither recognizing the importance of working in the context of a set of customer experiences (the customer journey) nor are they recognizing the changes in behaviour that demographic and consequent social change will bring about. Together, these factors will have several important consequences:

1. *Customers will make themselves increasingly less available to marketers.* More experienced, 'savvy' customers will begin to opt out (both in a legal and an engagement sense) from traditional marketing. As the legislation moves in their favour, more customers will restrict their brand interactions to a limited number of brands and contact channels. For the owners of the databases that power these contacts, opted-in, engaged customers will be key to future success.
2. *There will be increasing frustration (and hostility) towards the media and marketing.* The lack of empathy by their peers within modern media groups create frustration and even resentment amongst them. However much they currently dislike writing letters to their local newspaper or TV show, it seems likely that they will begin to campaign actively and visibly for fairer representation by the media and by marketing groups.
3. *Brand-building will become more difficult.* The growing proportion of mature customers will make it more difficult for traditional brand builders to succeed. This is not because they are unwilling to change brand preferences (as some marketers have suggested) but because they are demanding convincing reasons for change, not just temporary reasons for short-term brand switching.

4. *Businesses will face a corresponding employee backlash.* David Ogilvy (of advertising agency Ogilvy & Mather) once famously remarked, 'The customer is not stupid. She is your wife.' By the same token, today's alienated customer is often your employee (increasingly so as more over-fifties remain in the workplace). Businesses therefore need to wake up to the corresponding pressure from within, as their staff begin to ask whether an outward antipathy towards the growing 50+ 'underclass' is being reflected in the internal culture of their company at the same time.

Marketers have long been complaining about the difficulty of achieving relevant competitive differentiation through their products or services. The time delay between a market-leading innovation and becoming a standard industry requirement has shrunk from years to months or even weeks. If this unique opportunity for leading brands to finally get ahead is to be seized, companies will have to develop more penetrating customer insights. They will also need to develop the processes and systems to respond to those insights more effectively.

Developing better customer insights

Insight is not just about having some pieces of a jigsaw but all the pieces, joined up to produce a *quantified* picture that everyone, from senior management to those who actually manage customers, can see. Sometimes it will come as a flash of inspiration. More usually it will be based on hard work based on many pieces of research, database(s), financial and planning data, market and competitor intelligence, feedback from sales and customer service staff. It will even include customer complaints.

The following case study shows how important this insight is and how it results from combining evidence from customer databases and market research.

Case study: using insight to attack new segments

Tesco is the UK's largest retailer. Data from its loyalty card scheme, Clubcard,[3] revealed that families with babies who shopped for childcare products at Tesco spent much more than similar families who did not buy these products from Tesco, although they bought similar amounts of other products. Tesco's market research revealed that non-baby product buyers trusted the Tesco brand less for baby products than for the other products that they bought at Tesco. These customers preferred to take their baby business to Boots, the leading retailer of healthcare products, despite often charging up to 20 per cent more. Tesco therefore decided to modify its positioning towards mother and baby customers, partly by setting up the Tesco Baby Club. This and a number of other initiatives led to Tesco gaining share rapidly from Boots. It now sells as much in childcare as its nearest two competitors, Boots and Mothercare.

Few companies have this kind of insight. Consumer goods companies have historically built insight-hungry cultures. Most of their insight comes from market research rather than customer databases. They have fewer sources so it is easier for them to build a complete picture. In many other industries, particularly those with direct contact with their end consumer, so much information is available from so many sources (predominantly from large databases) that creating a 'joined up' picture is much harder. Few companies have a formal structure that brings all these sources together.

Source: Humby, Hunt & Philips (2003)

What 'insight' includes

'Insight' combines several ideas. It includes traditional marketing data such as:

- knowing who customers are;
- what they do;
- where they are;
- what they buy;
- what they would like to buy;
- what media they are exposed to;
- what media they choose to view, listen to or read.

Many of these behaviours on the part of the customer are not conscious. Most are conditioned by external factors, from the state of economy and society, to the way a product or service is marketed. Customers are not born wanting to buy a particular brand! So insight also includes more psychological areas such as:

- What customers think and feel.
- What their objectives and strategies are.
- How these influence behaviour.
- The experience that we (our organization and our competitors) give to customers.
- Their feelings about the experience.
- Whether they have told us what they think about it.
- Some idea of whether we have delivered against any promises made to customers (eg through branding, product descriptions or marketing communications).
- Whether we have fulfilled the role in their life that customers have allocated to us.
- Whether they have unresolved problems.
- Finally, it includes whether we are gathering and using customer insight properly – both in the legal sense and in the sense of allowing customers to delineate where their privacy begins and our insights should end.

Without a proper process to manage it, data collection is an expensive hobby. It can even be a destructive hobby. The quality of the process for managing it also counts. Thus it is important to decide how the insights are to be used, what operational processes are needed to use it, whether when your organization or your business partners are interacting with customers, and when you are planning to take action with your customers. Many studies show that this is often the main problem facing larger organizations in this area (for example see Stone, Woodcock and Foss, 2002).

The professional domain of customer insight

Professionally, the domain of customer insight stretches from market research, into database marketing, customer service, and any function that deals directly or indirectly with customers such as supply chain management. The relationship between market research and database marketing is often troubled. Database marketers need research to make their work effective. They also generate information that is useful to market researchers. However, sometimes market researchers feel threatened by database marketers, rather than encouraged to work with them. Much can be gained by using the information that database marketing generates. This includes the number and type of customers a company has, how they are contacted, who responds and how, what they buy as a result and so on. Knowing what to do with the numbers that normally result from a direct marketing campaign is a researcher's skill. The marriage between database marketing and market research can produce customer insight without a single market research project being commissioned.

Most market researchers, with the few exceptions where customer insight is properly organized and managed, have every reason to be confused by the inroads knowledge from customer databases has made into 'their' territory. However, this is an adversarial perspective. Both share a strong interest in gaining and acting on customer insight. Market researchers may well have been confused by the many revolutions that database marketing has gone through, certainly in the last 20 years or so. Fashions have come and gone. They are often linked with the great waves of technology that break upon the marketer's shore, particularly to those associated with advances in IT to manage large customer databases and with the technology used to interface with customers – from advanced systems for producing direct mail, to telemarketing systems and now the internet and mobile telephony.

Other developments have included direct mail or direct response marketing. Perhaps just as importantly, the disciplines of database marketing have evolved as their application has spread from the world of mail order into utilities, financial services, retailing and business-to-business marketing. Today, mobile telephones, digital interactive television and the internet have taken their place alongside direct mail, the sales force, ordinary telephony, stores and branches as important marketing media or channels. As a result, customer insight arises from many sources. It must also be fed back to many channels, if customers are to feel that they are being managed as they should be, using their information, irrespective of the channel they first used to contact a company.

From research, through measurement, to management

Organizations need customer insight for much more than supporting specific marketing or service decisions. Customer insight is an essential part of a mechanism that tells the organization whether it is meeting its customers' needs while meeting the needs of other stakeholders. These include owners (eg shareholders), business partners (eg distributors, marketing service suppliers) and staff – particularly those who have to manage customers, in stores or branches, contact centres, leisure and transport facilities. This use of customer insight is very important. Perhaps the best example is customer satisfaction surveys but we also include measurement of the effectiveness of marketing campaigns and other initiatives.

This area is controversial because despite all the science of market research and customer database analysis, customer insight is rarely used properly in this area. Much in the planning of marketing and management has not changed for years, although the rapid evolution of information and communications technology has changed many areas. Measuring customer satisfaction has become very big business. Many market research companies make much of their profit from it. Staff measurement and motivation systems are increasingly based on customer satisfaction targets. Despite this, surveys show declining customer satisfaction in most markets. Setting targets and measuring customer satisfaction does not make customers any happier, or more likely to repurchase. Much so-called customer insight purports to tell you what your customers want. In reality it only tells you what they have said, which can be a very different thing. If an organization focuses only on what customers say about its products or services, this can stifle creativity and limit innovation. Setting staff targets using information based on what customers are saying they want, can actually make the situation worse. Organizations are driven in the direction of their targets and measures. This is fine if the measures and targets are something which the business, its stakeholders and its customers truly want, but this is rare. Customers may say they want to be answered more quickly in call centres. In fact, they might actually give much higher priority to better value for money whereas they may be happy to make compromises in terms of rapid telephone access. The success of low-cost airlines demonstrates this.

The targets and measures being set in larger companies and public service organizations have become increasingly complex and controlling in the last few years. The notion that 'If you can measure it you can manage it' has spread like a cancer. This has led to large-scale customer satisfaction surveys, targets and league tables, yet a fall in customer loyalty and overall satisfaction. The focus has been on winning the league rather than offering customers the products or services they want. This focus has become internal, leading staff and the entire organization away from first considering the customer.

League tables and metrics induce stress. They focus mainly on cost reduction and control. Neither motivates staff. They stifle innovation and bold thinking, vital for success. Retention of good staff gets harder. Negative staff behaviour spreads. Perhaps the best example is replying quickly to complaints rather than resolving them. Organizations have targets for so many areas that are nothing to do with the organization's original intent. For a target to move a business in the direction its customers would really like, targets should relate to things customers and staff both want, to the real reasons customers buy its products or services, not to transactional factors whose only justification for inclusion is that they are easy to measure.

Health service organizations illustrate the point. The strategic intent is far removed from where it should be. A health service's reason for being is about helping new humans be born, keeping people as healthy as possible and, where this fails, healing and sustaining them and in the end, helping them die with dignity and minimum pain. For many health workers, measures are not related to any of these. Rather, the measures are process and transaction-based, counting beds, people on trolleys, queue lengths, waiting times and costs to serve, all important in achieving efficiencies but not delivering the service people need.

Wherever there is a fracture between the internal measures and the real reason a company or organization exists, there is stress because staff know they are not doing what they should really be doing. Short-term thinking dominates because the organization is only trying to hit the next target. Customers are unhappy because they can feel the organization's pain every time they deal with it.

Using customer insights to help customers

The answer to this apparent conundrum is to ensure that the customer insight process helps to change how we think about customers, staff and our organizations, rather than supports a counter-productive way of thinking about them. Once the purpose of the organization has been defined, it is possible to redefine what is measured. This may mean disposing of many internal measures, put in place to manage and control people. These might be called the 'head' measures. Marketers tend to be hyper-rational. Their actions and measures relate to things like:

- profiling and targeting;
- cost per contact and response rates;
- conversion rates and cross/up-sell ratios;
- campaign ROI and value of the customer to the company.

Such measures should be replaced, or at least balanced, by measures relating to what the business or organization aims to do for its customers. These might be called the 'halo' measures, and can be measured, but differently. 'Halo' might be defined as follows:

- It is what your customers see when you are the company they want you to be.
- It is what your staff and suppliers are proud to have when you are what your customers want you to be.
- It shines in every communication with your customers.
- It makes your customers welcome your communications and treat them seriously.
- It makes them opt in to your communications, not opt out.
- It appears when you create your future company around your customers' needs and your communication supports this.

The reason for this is that while customers may want to minimize cost or just get the best return, this is not always their aim. Depending on the product or service category, they may just want to feel happy, interested, safe, reassured, insulated from shocks. They may even want their suppliers to be their guardian angel (for the category).

A clear halo definition enables an organization to assess the effectiveness of its actions in relation to its stakeholders' expectations. Defining your organization's halo and structuring its objectives around this halo is the departure point for a revolution. It gives a clear, unambiguous destination for an entire organization. Put simply, if your organization wants people to have a good day, then the measurement needs to relate to whether your customers had a good day, not whether you picked up the phone quickly! If your organization aims to bring benefits to customers (a standard marketing objective), its measurements should affirm its desire to do so and ensure that it is on course for this aim. This is not a vision statement but a measurable affirmation of the aim of your organization. The measurement attached to it should be visible to all in the organization. Each person should be able to see where their part of the effort to meet the measurable affirmation is, and how close they are coming to their goal.

Implications for customer insight

This argument has clear implications for customer insight. The main one is that if you use performance measurement techniques which are based upon customer insights which preclude understanding whether customers really got what they wanted from your organization, then you are likely to be driving your organization, unwittingly, in the wrong direction. At a technical level, it means that any interpretation of customer insight that does not use insights into whether customers got what they wanted is likely to be misleading.

Case study: the halo effect at work in insurance

Motor insurance company A bought a smaller insurance company B. The management of the combined operation wanted to know why insurance company B was performing less well under their new owners. Company A always made good profits whereas Company B only made moderate profits, despite being known as an excellent employer and having a good share of markets known to be more profitable. Company A had focused on reducing costs in Company B, whose sales levels and profits were falling. Across both companies, complaints were rising, staff turnover was above 50 per cent in some key areas, and their public profile was being dented by media stories concerning the quality of their service when claims were made and vehicles repaired. The halo process was used to discover whether the cause of these problems was related to the direction in which staff were facing.

It turned out that staff in both companies were focused on very small areas of the business. This focus was intense and heavily targeted. The transactional focus of all the measures meant that the company was being managed by numbers and not a vision. The staff vision was now simply that of making lots of money. Not surprisingly this was the focus that customers felt when they made a claim. All staff jobs were divided into small parts, where each individual delivered only a small part of the overall service. This allowed the company to set targets for virtually every transaction, but no one could see the big picture. Research using the halo process allowed the company to put the disparate pieces of information together and show how it felt to be a customer receiving service from such a fragmented company. Once the company saw the result of breaking their staff's roles into such small pieces and setting each area of the business in competition with each other, they were left with a choice. They could take action and join the pieces together again by retargeting on bigger measures (what the customers wanted) and taking out some of the harmful transactional ones, or stay as they were.

The validity of this approach was confirmed when an insurance company got very bad publicity about the quality of workmanship from one of its own repair centres. It was targeting its repair shops on the speed of the repair. It had taken it as a given that the quality of the repair would be up to standard, but the need to meet time targets prevailed over the quality of the repair. Staff were paid bonuses related to the speed, not the quality of the repair. Clearly targeting needed to change to encourage safe repairs. If this business had been using good customer insight techniques, allowing it to understand what its customer really wanted, the problem could have been avoided.

When a customer buys car insurance there is a myth that everyone only wants to buy the cheapest and that the decision is price-driven. This might be true of those who have never claimed, but once someone has claimed, whether on their own or someone else's insurance, the service received when claiming becomes much more important. One of the key factors is the provision of a replacement car while the claimant's car is mended or replaced. To save money, many insurers do not give a replacement car as standard. Some offer it as a paid-for extra. However, this is often not discussed with customers as it takes the premium above a certain price point and highly targeted sales people do not want to jeopardize the sale. One insurance company that practices the add-on price found that its sales agents were not offering the feature. They then discovered that its claim complaint levels were rising, to such an extent that the agents handling claims received unprecedented call volumes. The majority of complaints were coming from claimants left with no replacement car. The company needed to modify how it motivated its agents so that they sold what customers really needed, rather than just a price.

Customer insight and marketing revolution

An essential prerequisite to marketing revolution is true customer insight. What do customers really want and how do they go about trying to get it? In some areas it would be better to spend more to achieve greater effectiveness (accompanied by greater cuts or switches elsewhere). Proportionate cuts and stiff targets across the board rarely produce the best outcome. Priority-based budgeting helps to re-base the budget, but care has to be taken that the resultant 'portfolio of spend' is balanced and aligned strategically to what customers want.

One example of success is e-enablement. E-enablement refers to, for example, web-based marketing as practiced by low-cost airlines or book retailers, where customers control the process, decide what they want and buy it. There are also many examples of situations in which up-to-date and accurate customer insight data is given to call centre or branch staff when the customer calls in (inbound marketing). Sales (and customer satisfaction) levels escalate. The proportion of contacts (compared with outbound marketing, when the supplier contacts existing customers) that result in both qualified prospects and sales can increase twenty- or fortyfold. This is because customers are being offered something they want as opposed to something they don't want!

Is this revolution? Well, the work that needs to go into cleaning and analysing the data and making it available via computers to the staff member handling the customer call, into training and motivating staff to want to meet customers' needs and to being sensitive to the immediate reason for the call, into devising compensation systems that don't lead staff to push at the wrong time, *is* revolutionary. It requires changing marketing emphasis and breaking down functional barriers (between marketing and service, for example). It requires customer-focused marketing to have a strong influence on branches and call centres and on websites. It affects product design as well, as you discover much more quickly what your current customers really want, now. The gain is revolutionary too: it is substantial.

However, each company must determine whether and what it needs to transform. Revolution costs money and takes much management thought, time and effort. It must start at the top. If your competitors get more value per customer than you do because they are using customer insight to meet their customers' needs, they may be under less pressure to recruit new customers. They know, better than you, which customers yield greater value if their needs are met, so they can be more selective about whom they recruit. They can concentrate their marketing on attracting potentially more valuable customers, leaving you with the rest. Over the years, the value of your customer base will decline relative to theirs. You will find it hard to meet your customers' needs while making profit. That is an insidious, cumulative, commercial poison!

This situation can be changed by a change of focus and attitude, particularly at the top of a business, if the change of attitude relates to a move towards or away from something that customers really want from your business or organization. The idea of pounding the numbers to squeeze an extra half of one per cent return is fading as customers wise up to smart communications and seek a real benefit from the product or service being offered.

The implications of this for marketing, customer insight and market research are clear. As in customer relationship management, companies are more likely to succeed if they understand that they are changing their model of customer management. They must make a conscious decision to use change management techniques and have people dedicated to managing change. This applies both to marketing in general and to managing efficiency, effectiveness and customer insight. If this change is not managed well, few insights will be gained and the company will fail to understand how changing the relationship between itself and its customers will improve the business.

A choice has to be made about how to use customer insight. You can use it merely to become slightly better at what you do now. Or you can use it to revolutionize your marketing and customer service. The revolutionary option is the more painful in the short term but it presents a better survival option than incremental change that simply fails to respond adequately to changing customer needs.

NOTES

1. This chapter is based on Stone, Bond and Foss (2004).
2. The concept of 'Halo' was invented by Alison Bond and is developed in Stone, Bond and Foss (2004).
3. Clubcard is a registered brand name of Tesco.

4

Revolution through strategic planning

A company that has decided to revolutionize its marketing through the more effective use of customer insights needs to be well organized. Instead of planning a few, 'monolithic' marketing campaigns, it will launch perhaps hundreds of mini campaigns which adapt fluidly to changing customer needs. The constant feedback loops provided by operational analytics demand that the company be able to revise, adapt and deploy new campaigns to highly targeted customer segments. Whilst this may sound challenging, designing an organization structure able to do this can be an even greater test of corporate will power.

To deal with these demands, some large corporations have become a collection of small, quasi-independent business units responding to market forces rather than a chain of command. They are more focused, flexible and responsive to customer needs and market requirements. Market-based definitions of businesses have shifted the focus toward more competence-based definitions of these units, for example from IT products to IT-enabled solution creation and delivery.

These more modular companies look for opportunities to link up selectively with other companies to utilize the specific skills, capabilities and enablers they require. Networking in this way allows companies to avoid the trade-offs between the needs of customers (for efficiency and a broad range of resources and skills) and the needs of companies (to manage their resources effectively and achieve economies of scale). Companies no longer have to choose between market efficiency and corporate effectiveness; a networked solution can allow both. What will this look like in practice?

ENTERPRISE AS A MOVIE STUDIO

The Hollywood studio operating model has been offered as a future model for companies in the networked environment. Jeremy Rifkin (2000) noted that Hollywood has a lot of experience with network-based approaches to organization. The entertainment industry has long had to deal with the risks that accompany products with a truncated life cycle. Each film is a unique product that has to find a quick audience if the production company is to recoup its investment, making a networked approach to doing business a matter of necessity.

Every film production brings together a team of specialized production companies and independent contractors, each with its own expertise, along with the talent. Together, the parties constitute a short-lived network enterprise whose lifespan will be limited to the duration of the project. The major studios still exercise control over much of the process by their abilities to partially finance production and to control distribution of the product. In the film industry, the key to maintaining effective control has always revolved around controlling access to the distribution channels. 'By holding on to their power as national and international distribution networks, the majors were able to use their financial muscle to dominate the film business and to squeeze or to use the independent production companies' (Rifkin, 2000: 27). Rifkin also reports on an article by Joel Kotkin writing in _Inc._ magazine, where he claims that, 'Hollywood [has mutated] from an industry of classic huge vertically integrated corporations into the world's best example of a network economy... Eventually, every knowledge-intensive industry will end up in the same flattened atomised state. Hollywood just has gotten there first.'

In order to survive, modern forms of enterprise must possess more dynamic and fluid control structures than many of their forebears. Yet many management practices are still predicated on the notion of a monolithic structure which is more or less centrally controlled.

Managers assert their control over this organization through the exercise of power and authority distributed by some form of hierarchy. It is presumed that under this scheme of arrangement various devices, either for enforcing control or for manipulating consent to authority, will be employed to translate strategic intent into operational performance. Such an approach is far less effective for new, dynamic forms of enterprise. Here, the links between processes, business units and important stakeholders are far more difficult to identify and define. In a fluid organization, epitomized at its most extreme by the virtual organization, problems of strategic planning are at their most acute. Such organizations may suffer from difficulties in maintaining internal integration, which in turn may reduce their ability to innovate and to survive. In these circumstances, the strategic posture adopted by the corporate core must be designed to diffuse the desired corporate culture, to enable effective strategic planning.

MANAGING RELATIONSHIPS

Many of the anxieties expressed about fluid forms of organization or the behaviour of stakeholders are rooted in issues to do with perceived or prospective imbalances of power. The redistribution of power in an uncontrolled manner may lead to outcomes which are not considered desirable by the controlling person or group. One of the most successful and long-serving chief executives of recent times was Jack Welch, former CEO of GE. GE has a spectacular corporate record for growth and profits. It is one of the very few corporate giants that has survived in the world's top ten for more than a century. Yet Welch used to be known as 'Neutron Jack'. His style was supposed to be similar to that of a neutron bomb, killing all the people but leaving buildings intact, as he ruthlessly downsized and restructured ineffective business units.

Yet such managers and chief executives are simply doing what they are paid to do. No revolution can take place without leadership and no leadership can take place without vision. Vision implies an idealized concept of the organization. This may mean breaking the current mould and moving to some future state in a non-linear fashion, unrelated to the here and now. Such a change is very difficult to implement if it disturbs the present power balance, institutionalized perhaps by current flows of information and the normative effects of culture. Indeed so robust are many processes, so embedded within an existing power distribution pattern, that they can be very hard not merely to alter but also to recognize. We shall come back to this in Chapter 11.

In Chapter 1, we referred to the problems faced by successful, large companies in facing change. The problem is that they avoid change and adopt innovation reactively in response to their external environment. In these companies, senior managers are predisposed to interpret their business situation as being stable and predictable, regardless of apparent evidence to the contrary. Eventually the environmental mismatch between the belief and the reality ends in tears, as has happened to several of the world's major IT companies in the last decade. The essence of the strategic process is to determine where environmental fit may be lost and where and how it might be regained.

In some ways, large organizations face the problem that there is an inverse relationship between detailed operational knowledge, authority and power. This is not a new problem. The Romans used to worry about it. How do you manoeuvre a very big business? How can a supertanker be made to spin like a dinghy? More seniority brings with it greater authority but also greater distance from the many and varied challenges faced by different parts of an organization. Companies driven from the top by those divorced from many operational issues are bound to face difficulties. The major issue to be addressed in large organizations remains that of designing flexible, responsive structures and resourcing them adequately. This must be done in a manner that retains coherence and apparent synergy without imposing over-rigid rules, unresponsive to change.

STRATEGIC POWER ISSUES AT THE ORGANIZATIONAL LEVEL

The end of strategy?

There is no shortage of management theories to assist with this problem. Over the last 30 years or so management writers have offered many remedies for creating flexible and responsive organizations. They have included, for example, management by objectives (MBO), matrix management, decentralization, one-minute management, management by walking around (MBWA), competitive strategy and total quality management. Such theories seek to address variously organizational structures, management behaviour, management styles and customer relations. They are sometimes associated with techniques such as life-cycle management, zero-based budgeting, value chain analysis or currently, process re-engineering. It is difficult to understand quite what governs the fashion for each of these ideas. Some sort of life cycle can be discerned as each proposition moves from the status of an idea, to a cult, to a panacea, through to disenchantment and repudiation. As in marketing, the problem of identifying the duration and stage of each idea in relation to its life-cycle stage is unresolved. It may be that disillusion and lack of commitment are linked. When reported outcomes do not seem to match expectations the onset of disillusion begins. The best example was the 'excellence' idea of Peters and Waterman (1982) after some of 'America's best-run companies' ran into trouble.

Could it be that strategic planning has also moved from the point of popular acclaim to disenchantment and repudiation? In the search for acceptability (and lucrative consultancy contracts) new management ideas are often oversold. Strategic planning has been fashionable for a while. Indeed the Chinese general and strategist Sun Tzu (1971), for example, made reference to a director of strategic planning in his original text written some 2,400 years ago. Even Henry Mintzberg (1994) himself is of the view that strategic planning has entered the stage of disillusion and repudiation. In fact, he appears to conclude that strategic planning does not work!

The role of strategic planning

Mintzberg's central point, by which he argues for the demise of strategic planning, is that the planning procedures designed to suit mechanistic structures, especially bureaucracies (which is the form adopted by most companies) are ineffective integrative mechanisms for other forms of organization. Instead he proposes three possible distinct forms of structure for strategic planning. The first, which we all know about, is a bureaucracy. The company has a formal structure, a power distribution reflected in an organization chart, and defined roles and responsibilities. The second is an adhocracy. The best example of an adhocracy would be a project team. A group of people drawn from across the company to do a specific job. When the job is done, the project team may be disbanded but others may be formed to deal with new problems. The third form is an ideocracy. An ideocracy is an organization which exists because its participants believe it exists.

Virtual organizations may be the most obvious example but so too are multi-businesses, strategic alliances and networked organizations. The integrative mechanisms for an ideocracy are information and culture. Plans and behaviours are modified on the basis of exchanges of information based on beliefs about the predispositions of other stakeholders. In other words, the company, its customers and it suppliers exchange information and use that information to make plans.

The idea is not especially new but it is a considerable extension of earlier thinking about organizations as political contrivances. It also has deeper implications for strategic planning. The end of strategy occurs when there is a mismatch between planning roles and organizational form. In other words when forms of planning used in bureaucracies are applied elsewhere. They are too rigid, especially for adhocracies and ideocracies. So how can strategic plans be developed in fluid, customer-responsive companies whilst maintaining some sort of coherence and internal integration?

Strategic planning as glue

The answer lies in the plans themselves. They must act as the glue which binds the many business units together. Strategic plans are developed by the corporate apex or the hub of a network. Goold, Campbell and Alexander (1994) coined the term 'strategic parenting' to refer to this activity in an enterprise made up of many businesses. Sub-units or processes may or may not be able to function independently and therefore from a planning perspective the similarities between a monolithic multi-business, a virtual organization, a network of companies or a strategic alliance are close. The idea applies not only to large enterprises but to small and medium-sized enterprises determined to lever advantage by positioning themselves pivotally within a network of other service providers. The example of small Japanese companies and their relationship to the Zaibatsu springs to mind (Oh, 1976).

The potential of the strategic process for creating or destroying value is enormous. A poor acquisition, or the appointment of an especially able general manager, may result in significant losses or gains of value for the enterprise. Strategic integration is therefore particularly central to survival and to establishing and maintaining a competitive position. From this perspective, the choice of integrative mechanisms between business or service units needs considerable care. The choice hinges on how the strategic process may add most value to the total enterprise.

Increasing business unit value

Case study: RTZ

RTZ is a big, international mining conglomerate, organized like a bureaucracy. It allows for a considerable degree of decentralization but product and market decisions, capital spending, pricing and the appointment of key personnel are all made centrally. This relationship with the various business units is potentially fraught. Questions arise such as how the partial efforts of managers in the centre, concerned with many businesses, could add value to the focused efforts of managers in sub-units who concentrate on one alone.

In RTZ, businesses move ahead through periodic, major capital projects. The investment required to bring a new mine into production is massive and the decision to proceed may affect the success of the business for decades. Value is provided strategically through a capital project submissions procedure that acts as the focus for planning. The company has particular expertise in computer-based modelling and conceptual mine planning. Project submissions are worked up within the operating companies in collaboration with the centre. Information services in the centre provide expertise in areas such as mine planning, strategic and commercial evaluations, financial analysis and planning, and macroeconomic modelling. RTZ has been at the forefront of analytical techniques for capital expenditure evaluation since the 1960s when it started working with DCF analysis, and it now specializes in weighted risk rates. Creativity is focused on financing packages and funds are made available to units on an internally competitive basis. The trick is to fund all 'good' projects. Integration and value are therefore added through information services. The modelling they provide for business units cannot be matched elsewhere.

Maintaining integration through the provision of functions or services that cannot be matched elsewhere is no easy task, especially if this is based on information alone. Information services are relatively easy to duplicate. Clearly a corporate staff incurs overheads of its own and is further removed from the customer interface than any of its subsidiary business units. Hence there is a danger that individual units will regard the centre as out of touch or interfering. Service provision must go well beyond the supply of market research or financial management better than a specialist organization. If this were all, then value added could be maximized by outsourcing. Strategic planning is therefore an obvious area where the centre may make a binding contribution. As a part of the enterprise disinterested in the politics of individual business units, the centre is better placed to make decisions which will maximize the position of the enterprise as a whole.

Case study: Shell Oil

Shell Oil, an Anglo-Dutch company, is one of the world's largest corporations with operating units around the world. It employs over 10,000 managers of over 70 different nationalities between some 100 operating companies. It trades in the technically complex area of oil, gas and chemicals in a business that requires periodic, substantial investments which invariably commit the organization in the medium to long term. It therefore needs excellent information services to provide technical support and some means of maintaining a coherent internal culture. Not only are its own managers influenced by their indigenous culture, but commercial conditions in different countries provide challenges of their own.

Perhaps unsurprisingly, Shell has been described as the largest consensus-seeking organization in the world. There is a great deal of decentralization and local control. This internationalization may have been fostered by the company's roots with the need to design a management structure split across two European countries at the time of writing in 2005. (This situation may have been resolved by recent reorganization at Shell.) However, the culture is also formalized in the form of agreed principles which are imposed strategically on business units through a Statement of General Business Principles. These principles aim to provide a code of conduct designed to act as consistent reference point for the standards of behaviour which the company expects of its managers, wherever they are based.

Information services stem from a relatively small central office of some 700 people, spread between London and the Hague, which provides high-quality technical expertise that can be brought to bear throughout the world. The balance between centralization and decentralization is reviewed on a situational basis. In the case of exploration where decisions about future investment require careful analysis of large data sets or, in the case of chemicals, where competition is research based on a global scale, there is much central involvement. Mission critical intelligence is therefore concentrated. So-called downstream operations such as marketing and refining are more decentralized. Thus the centre is better able to assess markets, technologies and products than any of its units. Strategically, Shell also creates value through its corporate ability to maintain good relationships with local governments, communities and partners throughout the world. This is coupled with an ability to reinforce local managers with international experts. Its particular form of matrix structure thus allows it to redeploy functional specialists and key personnel when needed.

The downside of these centrally provided services seems to be that they can experience difficulty in moving away from what might be regarded as their core business. Shell was not outstandingly successful in areas such as metals, mining, consumer products, coal and nuclear power. Very often this requires business units with different cultures that do not sit well with the corporate core. This is a problem that needs thinking about since the operational analytics needed for a full marketing revolution depend on large-scale, fully integrated information services able to network multiple databases so as to have the best possible basis of advanced data mining.

Case study: ING Direct — how strategy, structure, marketing and systems interact

Whatever you hear about the service level retail customers get from their banks, one thing is clear. Though customers switch their current accounts less often than they should, or than they think they should (based on cost and service comparisons), they vote with their feet when it comes to finding value and convenience. This underlies the success of the world's fastest-growing pure direct bank, ING Direct.

ING Direct was designed to give consistent value to customers. This meant avoiding playing the 'best rate table game' – a vicious and unethical game similar to the games played by music and film companies to become 'top of the pops' at the right time. In savings, banks play it by being top of the table occasionally, through special offers, but not providing the best return over time. ING Direct combines good, steady value to customers, a low net interest margin and no fee income, with good profitability, by keeping operational costs very low. One key to this is account opening via internet or call centre, not branches. ING Direct's rapid growth (and profitability in its fourth year) is achieved through simplicity. It is lean – a small head office and small management teams in every country. Controlling size encourages managers to think of the company as a small one – one that encourages them to act and take accountability. Only about 10 per cent of its people are not directly involved with managing customers – handling enquiries or processing applications. Each new business unit aims for profit in its fourth year.

A small management team is only possible if the business is kept simple. But simple does not mean stupid! ING Direct prides itself on recruiting the best people internationally, and moving good people to get new operations going. It uses best established practice in all functions. Its internal watchword is 'proudly stolen', referring to how people learn from each other. For example, directors of each function meet twice a year with their colleagues from all over the world to learn what works and what doesn't. They aren't mandated to use the same approaches – the emphasis is on learning what works and then making their own decisions.

The company has also learnt from the successes and failures of its competitors. Its strategy is to focus on big, mature markets, starting with an attractive savings product. This means customer acquisition costs much less than the hard sell needed by banks offering less value. Account numbers grow quickly. Average deposits are high – sensible savers look for best steady returns for their funds. Only about 10 per cent of savers switch for short-term special offer rates, but ING gets customers who know better. The mechanics of account opening may seem complex (setting up direct debits from your current account), but they work for ING customers, who include a large number of better-off, older individuals. They are not deterred by internet or telephony.

New products are not rushed. ING Direct knows what it wants to sell, but prefers to wait until customers start asking for more, as they already are asking for more in the UK. Each geographical market is entered cost-effectively and quickly, with good preparation, using experience from entering other markets. The aim is to build brand awareness and mass presence quickly, to ensure low acquisition costs. ING Direct's offer to customers is ease, convenience and transparency, with no tricks. Funds are invested at low risk, to ensure low capital consumption. ING Direct has avoided the product and channel proliferation of many other direct banks – this results in no differentiation and no clear value to customers. 'Share of wallet' takes second place to customer value and profit. However this has not stopped it fielding a broad product line in its most advanced markets. The significant absence of a current account is not due to inability to make it profitable, but rather to being able to use its capital better elsewhere.

Its IT strategy and management are particularly interesting. Senior management is closely involved, and a clear strategy is used. IT supports a simple business model and processes. IT is business case driven, not technology push. In other words, structure follows strategy. It uses standardized components and business solutions, only from proven, best-of breed technology. It is flexible and future proof, ie designed and built to facilitate change. Strict change management disciplines are followed, and there is a strong emphasis on areas such as knowledge management, multi-vendor management, regional and global governance, security, business continuity and operational excellence.

Is all this sustainable? There will be ups and downs as conventional banks dip in and out of the market. However, for many customers – particularly the most valuable – there is no substitute for ING Direct's low-cost, customer advocacy model. Over many years and spread over many countries, the returns look good to shareholders too.

HOW STRATEGIC PLANNING ADDS VALUE

If strategic planning is to achieve better results through the use of information, three things are clear. First, even in tightly coupled organizations the balance between central and local control must be carefully judged. The management of information services is one method of sustaining that balance whilst maintaining cohesion. Second, the strategic planning process must add value in some way. This can only be achieved really through attaining insights which are not accessible to other business units. Third, the strategic planning process must focus on creating an enterprise culture in which those insights can be exploited. The competitive position is fundamentally related to such a capability. A thorough understanding of what the culture might be and how it is deployed is critical.

Information services might be seen as the integrative mechanisms of culture. This implies a rich information environment which is concerned with much more than units of data or information. The expertise of the people who control strategy planning is a part of this environment. The extent to which they have the confidence to use information as the basis for empowering business units, secure in the knowledge that culture will maintain cohesion, is critical. Fluid forms of organization are therefore fostered strategically, through information services and culture. Thus at business unit level, locally derived, contextually relevant solutions to limited strategic problems can be chosen by managers empowered to make their own decisions on the ground as the situation evolves.

Strategic planning and culture

Management groups sometimes do things simply because they exist. Let's face it, managers like to 'do things'. Whilst this may be true, there is in fact some evidence that strategic planning can do more than provide work for idle hands.

Pekar and Abraham (1995) offer some encouragement. Using a sample of *Business Week's* top 1,000 companies, chief executives were asked to rate themselves in terms of the sophistication of their strategic management processes. The findings were meant to measure the progress of strategic management in the United States. Results were considered in four areas: evaluation (which examined strategic focus), SBU differentiation (which emphasized core capabilities relative to the competition), resource allocation (which sought to relate compensation and budgets to strategic priorities) and value creation (which looked at the effort devoted to new business development). Pekar and Abraham found a surprisingly strong correlation between three-year average ROI and the extent to which companies rated themselves as sophisticated strategic planners. If ROI is taken as an important measure, then the 67 per cent difference between those firms that rated themselves at the top and the bottom of the scales is significant.

What seems to be at the heart of this difference is not so much the perceived relative competence in strategic planning skills at each end of the scale. The study seemed to find little variation between the competences claimed by both sophisticated and unsophisticated firms. Rather, the explanation seems to lie in the effectiveness of their strategic planning, in conditions of increasingly severe and aggressive global competition. Weaker companies seem to have a much lesser grasp of their own entrepreneurial vision – their corporate philosophy, their understanding of where competitive advantage might lie and the alignment between organization structure, corporate vision and corporate culture.

Successful strategists seem to be those who can, in Tom Peter's words (1996), put the 'wow' back into strategy. By this he is referring to organizations such as Microsoft, Asea Brown Boveri (ABB), General Electric, IBM and PepsiCo that are able to maintain internal integration, yet allow for considerable fluidity in organizational form. A characteristic of these firms seems to be to encourage innovatory approaches by small teams which are then given considerable scope for action. In other words, first you need strong decentralization between multi-business units. Second, you need a CEO who encourages dissatisfaction with the present situation. Where we are now just is not good enough.

Strategic planning frameworks and culture

Many strategic planning frameworks have been proposed over recent years. Core competencies (McFarlen and McKenney, 1983), the five forces model (Porter, 1980), critical success factors (Boynton and Zmud, 1985) and business process re-engineering (Hammer and Champy, 1993) provide some examples. Each of these and other frameworks requires extensive use of information services either in performing analysis or in enabling change. These services are used to maximize the speed of diffusion, to add information value to products, to enable process customization, to increase differentiation, to maximize delivery speed and, of course, to collate and analyse data.

It seems obvious therefore that the information services (IS), the organization and application of data management services, must be fully integrated with the strategic management processes. Surprisingly, this is often not the case. Even where companies are involved in changing the shape of their enterprise at a strategic level, information services are often disregarded. McKiernan and Merali (1995) studied 200 acquisitions by British companies in the mechanical engineering, banking and insurance sectors. To their surprise, they discovered that IT/IS issues do not seem to figure either before or after an acquisition. In over 50 per cent of cases, the acquirer did not have information about the target's IT/IS strategy, nor its potential for alignment with business strategy. IT/IS issues were not even considered at pre-acquisition stage since this was, 'not important to business strategy'. It would seem that the importance of an information infrastructure has yet to be properly recognized by many organizations.

Organization culture

If the alignment of IS between organizations is disregarded, what about the second key strategic integrating mechanism, culture? This question was looked at by Hall (1995) in a variety of strategic relationships. These included not only acquisitions but also partnerships and alliances. She proposed a categorization of national and corporate cultural styles based on the two-by-two matrix so beloved by business schools. This uses the dimensions of assertiveness and responsiveness to categorize organizational styles culturally. This describes the preferred behavioural approaches of corporate executives in negotiations, which in turn yields important clues as to their strengths and weaknesses. It also provides an indication as to which business units are likely to be able to relate to each other and where they might conflict. Sometimes the cultural void between two organizations is so wide that the prospect for effective strategic cooperation is not tenable. Hall gives the example of negotiations between a European and an Asian organization. The European firm moved immediately to an exercise in financial analysis. The Asian firm, which cooperated with the exercise in a bemused manner, regarded the exercise as tangential to more important matters such as the need for shared values and a common philosophy.

Failures between business units in the same corporation, caused by cultural differences, can be avoided. Whilst it is ineffective for one partner to attempt to impose its culture on another, it is possible to resolve cultural differences and accommodate them. If this does not happen, a failure of management has occurred rather than anything else. This can lead to disaster. The proposed merger between the Leeds Permanent and the National and Provincial Building Societies in 1993 illustrate the point. This merger would have created the UK's third-largest building society. When the merger failed, the *Financial Times* (30 October 1993) reported that the two societies had 'found too large a gulf in their management cultures'. It also noted that there were major discrepancies between their IS structures.

Strategic planning is an important part of this conception. If they are to succeed, organizations must find ways of adding value to flexible organizational forms through strategic planning. Information services are a key enabler of this process. To add value to strategic planning, IS designs must recognize organization culture. In order to maintain shape, direction and cultural integrity, IS must be deployed as an integrative mechanism. Although considerable lip-service has been paid to such a notion it is evident that many organizations continue to disregard its importance, which may account for some strategic planning failures. Although a variety of organizational forms may be successful, even within the same environment, they must be imbued with a shared cultural perspective. From this basis, information services may then support a coherent, effective strategic planning process which adds value.

STRATEGIC REVOLUTION THROUGH CONTINUOUS IMPROVEMENT

Peter Drucker (2001:35) once wrote, 'The customer is the foundation of a business and keeps it in existence. He alone gives employment. And it is to supply the customer that society entrusts wealth-producing resources to the business enterprise... Because its purpose is to create a customer, any business enterprise has two, and only these two, basic functions: marketing and innovation.' Innovation must be continuous and pervasive. The network business allows research and development to extend beyond traditional boundaries which adds even greater force to the argument for the need to integrate part of the network into a system. The innovation process will therefore need to draw on an eclectic range of sources to stay ahead of the competition (Chesbrough, 2003). Business planners must not only share their needs across various business units but also actively solicit inputs and proposals from external research providers as well. Internal projects are then used to fill in the gaps. In other words, the strategic planning process is used to draw together the threads of innovation, for new, customer-driven products and services, into a coherent whole.

As an example of innovation at work, by 2005 about 200 of IBM's researchers were designated as 'services research-consultants'. Their role is to help companies do everything from targeted electronic marketing, through mining data for retail operations to analysing statistics on auto warranty claims. This is part of a trend where the large companies with research capability will take on more of the burden of innovation, especially in services. Product and service innovation is important for revolutionized companies. Research and development can yield insights and early warning of new directions that the company may have to take to meet tomorrow's emerging customer needs.

Organizational culture is an important aspect of innovation. Innovative companies are services led. The traditional bureaucracy will succeed as long as it can operate in a stable environment. When next year is like this year, so that this year's tested rules will work next year, then the outcome will be good. By contrast, marketing revolution requires solutions that are unique and often highly customized, requiring a responsive, confident culture capable of coping with change. This does not suit everyone and, indeed, it does not have to do so. Many people are more comfortable in work situations that they consider to be stable and unchanging. This is not a problem. Companies can have more than one culture. In the fluid organization, comprised of many interlinked business units, several cultures may exist. What is important is that the key people in the organization who have a large say in determining what the dominant culture should be, influence and shape that culture in critical areas such as marketing.

SUMMARY: REVOLUTION AS A JOURNEY

In any change, a choice has to be made between 'big bang' – let us do it right here, right now – and a gradual progression. Each approach has its merits and risks. Some companies focus primarily on revolutionizing the sales force with new processes, skills and systems. Others aim to revolutionize through acquisition, acquiring business consulting firms or hiring key individuals. Acquisition can provide quick access to specialist resources although managing mergers and acquisitions brings challenges of its own. However, acquisition can help revolutionize organizational culture either by hiring a key person or by establishing a new business unit to act as a kind of change agent. The important thing is that the need for revolution is recognized and that the strategic planning process is formally reorganized to enable the revolution to occur.

A customer revolution is taking place. Managerial capitalism is being replaced by the networked businesses. New business designs are emerging to satisfy the needs of customers for exceptional value and the 'Hollywood studio' model is one that lends itself to strategically managing this change.

Organizational culture is an important determinant as to whether the strategic revolution required will be allowed to work. Of course this must be led from the top. CEOs are responsible for organizational form and above all for strategic planning processes. They must nurture the right culture. The extent and speed of revolution depends on many factors and differs between companies. In Chapter 11, we will look more carefully at the processes needed to manage this change.

5

Revolution through segmentation

Today, customer segmentation is no longer a simple, or static, marketing technique; it can be of central importance to the way successful companies run their business. A senior manager in one of the top five US financial services companies noted that, 'Segmentation results are used across the whole organization; segmentation is critical to many departments in our organization.' However, the commercial world is full of strategists creating blue-sky segmentation approaches that never see the light of day, in terms of practical application. It is relatively easy to create intellectual ways of splitting up customers that look very aesthetically appealing. It is much more difficult to make them work. When they do, they can be a very powerful tool. In a leading health products provider, the chief marketing manager reported that, 'Customer segmentation has enabled us to make educated business decisions (strategic and tactical) that have significantly increased company sales.' Segmentation is therefore an important strategic planning tool. In a 2003 study of segmentation practice, the IBM Institute for Business Value Analysis reported that a leading hospitality company used segmentation as part of its strategic planning process. 'Segmentation data are used in developing and refining the business case in support of new product and service ideas.'

Unfortunately very few marketing directors have grasped the point that segmentation is strategic. If segmentation is to be applied effectively then the approach must be integrated across the whole of the marketing effort. It is no good confining the exercise to marketing communications. If customers are to be segmented and treated differently then the whole firm needs to know about them and to change what they do accordingly, in areas like customer service, purchasing, new product development. In other words, segmentation is a company structure issue. In fact, segmentation is even more top level than that. It is about identifying what business you are in, what benefits you are trying to satisfy and then pinning down how these customer benefits might change with different groups.

Can marketing be revolutionized with segmentation? Yes, either by being creative in developing powerful ways of splitting up the market, or through better implementation than anyone else. Creativity springs from customer insights and is just one reason why the messages of Chapter 3 are so important. Segmentation is a vital weapon in the revolution armoury and is built on customer insights. To illustrate how effective this can be, we will draw on extensive research carried out by IBM's US based Institute for Business Value. In its study, the institute interviewed 15 executives and surveyed over 120 companies to find out first hand how companies benefit from customer segmentation.

WHY DO COMPANIES FIND IT HARD TO IMPLEMENT EFFECTIVE SEGMENTATION?

The term 'segmentation' was first coined by Wendell Smith in a _Journal of Marketing_ article in 1956. His idea was simple enough: split up your customers and treat them differently. You will then be able to present different customers with products and services more relevant to their needs. In the private sector, this means that the incremental income must of course exceed the investment you have put into the segmentation exercise, since the data analysis and refinement of marketing promotions raises the costs of doing business. In the public sector, the emphasis is on service-level efficiency and 'customer' satisfaction. For instance, the UK's Customs and Excise (before its merger with the Inland Revenue) segmented its corporates into small businesses and large companies with different approaches and levels of service. Academics, marketing analysts and marketing managers have devised the increasingly complex tools and techniques that can be used to cluster customer data. However, analytical elegance is one thing, commercial practice quite another.

Practitioners are more cautious. Faced with a presentation from their marketing strategists with a precisely defined but hard-to-target set of segments, they say, wait a minute. Just because we could do this does not mean we should. Segmenting involves organizational change, and this may reduce the chances of successful deployment of segmentation. Another problem is that up till now, many segmentation ideas have been based on marketing research and one of the difficulties has been of finding a way of translating a research market segmentation pattern into practice. For these reasons a well-developed, industry-revolutionizing segmentation is rare. Managers may wonder if segmentation attempts are worth the effort and the risk; but segmentation may at last be an idea whose time has come. New advances in database technologies are providing better capabilities for companies to link the insights derived from their customer databases to effectively segmented marketing campaigns.

THE PROBLEMS WITH TRADITIONAL SEGMENTATION

Batch-based segmentation

The basic approach to segmentation has been understood for many years and has been explained in most serious marketing texts. For want of an appropriate enabler (in the form of powerful database technology) companies have not been able to develop the capability of linking segmentation with channel management. For most companies, the result has been to turn to a batch-based segmentation of customers according to needs revealed by out-of-date market research or offline analysis of customer databases which are often out of date by the time they are finished. This is not to imply that batch-based segmentation is wrong. Done well, it makes a big difference to the relevance and timeliness of the proposition put to customers. However, for many customers the broad nature of the segmentation and the time delays associated with the analysis has meant that they have been receiving the wrong offer, at the wrong time, based on an inappropriate creative message, in a medium not of their choosing or through the wrong channel. In fact recent research from OgilvyOne and IBM shows that many companies are finding it hard to manage customer relationships effectively, as complexity based on growing channel choices increase. At the same time, customer expectations both in the form of service and of product differentiation are increasing.

Leading companies have realized that this poor performance not only damages their relationship with customers. It also damages their brand. For a brand is not just a product, it is an experience. For some products, the brand experience is confined to what happens when the product is picked off the supermarket shelf or when it is consumed. The proportion of short-term brand benefits of this sort is falling and their importance continues to decline as our complex service economy continues to develop. Whether in financial services, travel, leisure, health or even in public services, the experience of the brand is increasingly conditioned by the relevance of the treatment the customer experiences at many different touch points with the company. Customer relevance therefore demands more than batch segmentation. It demands a combination of good data management prior to contact and careful, systematic analysis. In practice this means with real-time analytics, using data given during the current interactions, which modify and update existing batch-based models.

The days of pure batch segmentation are over. Customer-facing systems, whether in branches, contact centres or on the web, can now use the latest information on customers, including information gathered during the very transaction that the company or its customers want to complete. This information is used to tune the relevance of the offer. Some leading-edge companies such as Orange, HBoS and HSBC are using these techniques already. Nor does using customer data intelligently necessarily mean using it simply. Better insight merely means that the result for the customer may appear to be simple. They receive the right, timely offer so that they can more easily buy what they want. This apparent simplicity derives from the analysis itself, deciding which proposition to offer based on insights. Evidence is mounting, in areas as far apart as mobile telephony, banking, book and CD buying, that immediate relevance brings results.

Problems with demographic segmentation

Kennedy and Ehrenberg (2001) have studied segmentation techniques extensively and are sceptical about some of the claims made. They point out that few if any lasting analytic success stories have yet been claimed in the segmentation literature. Almost all the studies are concerned typically with analysis techniques and methods. The issue of results is usually not even mentioned. Based on studying significant commercial data they found that, contrary to popular belief, it is hard to find demographic differences between people who prefer different brands within a category. So there are few demographic differences in reality between Visa and Mastercard users, between BMW and Mercedes drivers, or between Nescafe and Kenco coffee drinkers. However, they are optimistic about the lack of brand segmentation for brand positioning, targeting and the other marketing functions. It makes the marketer's job much simpler. Marketers can operate in a large pool of unrestricted data. Whilst there are more competitors in an unrestricted data pool, there is also more scope and more need for what they call 'plain' marketing.

They urge simplicity and warn against a tendency to restrict targeting too narrowly based on demographic analysis if the differences between segments are not obvious. The temptation is to believe that sophisticated techniques like structural equation modelling or conjoint analysis will reveal differences more imaginary than real. In this case the marketer is mesmerized by the apparent sophistication of the analytical techniques being used. After all, there is no point in using advanced statistics to stumble across the fact that it is cat owners who mostly buy cat food or even that some only buy dry cat food. Sometimes a simple analysis of small data subsets will tell marketers all they need to know about demographic differences.

They conclude that demographic-based segmentation is often not employed very effectively in marketing terms, even where it does occur. For example, results from Target Group Index Data on the UK retailer WH Smith reveals that males are slightly more likely to shop in this high street stationers than with competitor retailers – 6 per cent more male buyers than the competition in fact – but what should WH Smith do about this? Probably not a great deal, seems to be the answer. Similarly, just because BMW gets a lot of its new customers each year from Mercedes, this may not be as significant as it seems if it gets still more customers from the mass market. The mass market is, after all, much larger and brand migration between luxury cars is not only to be expected but probably balances out.

Segmentation is inherently strategic

Piercy (1998) provides a useful discussion of the all-important link between segmentation and strategy on the one hand and segmentation and capability on the other. Both dimensions must work. Apparently attractive segmentations of the market, generated by technically sound market research, may be useless if they are incompatible with internal competences, the internal organizational structure, or any notion of competitive advantage. For example, there may be little point in retailer Marks and Spencer identifying a series of clothing segments based on females in their late teens/early twenties if the company is at a competitive disadvantage in these particular segments.

So the place to start is at the corporate strategy level. Segmentation proceeds form a definition of the business that you are in, in which markets you want to compete and what the internal core competences might be. The approach is illustrated in Figure 5.1.

The key now is to focus on what the customers want from the company. This may allow a useful benefit-led segmentation to be developed. Tip-Top Holidays may identify adventure, relaxation, keep-the-kids-happy and cultural stimulation as possible benefits. Yet each of these is a distinct and separate benefit and requires a different customer proposition. Can each segment be offered a distinctive package that is competitive? Is Tip-Top competent enough in each area to offer several distinctive customer propositions profitably?

The next issue to consider is the compatibility of segments with the organization structure. Segments that cut across distribution

Figure 5.1 _Applications of segmentation_
Source: IBM Institute for Business Value (2003).

channels, customer service organizations, or sales force geography may meet with stiff resistance. For example, if Tip-Top is currently organized around routes and destinations, with each department fiercely defending its own turf, then how is it to make a success of a benefit-led segmentation, even if that is strategically the clearest way to go? Powerful forces within the organization that enshrine existing practices will militate against the success of the new segments. The same kinds of problems arise at the operational level.

Case study: Sony Corporation

In early 2002, to understand and serve customers better, Sony reorganized itself both internally and externally, by customer segments. There were three main elements to its revolution:

1. *To organize and structure by customer segments so as to live and breathe the customer*
   - Reorganizing by customer segments enabled the company to target products and services more precisely, according to customers' life-stages, preferences and needs.
   - The change affected leadership positions and go-to-market strategy across all divisions: marketing, product development, retail merchandising, advertising and customer loyalty programmes. For example, instead of products being marketed by product managers, executives were asked to champion and manage customer segments.
   - Beginning with the new fiscal year, Sony planned to create and report a virtual profit and loss account that reported on its $8 billion customer business by customer segments.
2. *To create a division focused on customer segment marketing*
   - The new business unit provided segmentation research and analysis which was used to drive marketing communications.
   - The new customer segments included: Affluent, CE Alphas (early adopters), Zoomers (55+), SoHo (small office/home office), Young Profs and DINKies (double income, no kids, aged 25 to 34), Families (35 to 54) and Gen Y (under 25).
3. *To create new generations of products based on latest 'Gen X and Gen Y' customer needs*
   - New approaches to the generation of products were designed to meet the needs, wants and preferences of each customer segment.
   - New products were showcased and marketed based on how they enhanced the lifestyles and experiences of specific customer segments.

BEING CREATIVE WITH SEGMENTATION

One way to create competitive advantage is to be creative. This is true with segments themselves. So segmentation continues to attract creative thinkers inside organizations, often attracted by the clean slate of different opportunities. Consider, for example, the following novel market segments in contemporary society:

- *Anti-marketers*. These no-logo advocates will dislike any marketing-speak that refuses to acknowledge what they see as their business-savvy approach to buying. They are most likely to be attracted by direct appeals to common sense such as 7-Up's,[1] 'Image is nothing, thirst is everything' campaign.
- *Collaborative individualists*. These are people who create their own bespoke communities that may have little to do with traditional structures. They are much more reliant on their social, career and cultural interests. So they do not allow old-fashioned structures to get in the way of individualist aspirations, but at the same time they want to feel part of a community. They are looking for products and services that make their lives easier.
- *1960s rebel, sixties granny*. Imagine a woman born in 1945. She would have been 20 in 1965, rocking to the Beatles at Shea Stadium. She would have two children by 1975, just at the onset of the punk era. And she would probably be a grandmother by 2005. Her kids would be 30, the average age for family formation in many Western societies today. Many of these 1960s rebels are now retired. Their own children are independent adults and they collectively have more disposable income (by far) than any other segment. Propositions directed at this group need to break the mould entirely in terms of previous approaches to the over-sixties. This is a lively, active and energetic segment with money to spend on new experiences.
- *Choice dislikers*. These are conservative people and there are a lot of them emerging. They are increasingly put off by the choice explosion in most customer markets. They think the switch from a state or private monopoly to choices from a myriad of private suppliers, in areas such as utilities and telecommunications, was a disaster. They are completely put off by the complexity of buying a mobile phone or a computer. They would rather the world just stopped for a few years. They have a desire for simplicity and a DVD recorder player with perhaps 50 different functions, backed

by a 30-page manual and driven by a range of software menus, all controlled by a remote with over 20 buttons to press is not for them.

There are significant strategic and managerial hurdles to jump before a company is in a position to follow Sony's lead. Much hard work is needed to develop the analytical tools and restructure the corporation but taking on the complexity will bring its own rewards. IT and database technology have improved to the point of providing a sound basis for successful implementation. New technology also brings to the fore a new type of segmentation. Customer value segments allow companies to cluster customers according to how much they are worth.

VALUE-BASED SEGMENTATION AND CHANNEL OPTIMIZATION

Segmenting customers according to demographic profiles is often ineffective. People may buy the same product for different reasons or different products for the same reason. Over-simplistic analysis can lead to major marketing errors. Take the example in Table 5.1 of two mothers in apparently similar situations but with very different needs and attitudes.

Table 5.1 *Needs and attitudes of similar life-stage and demographic customers*

Basis of Segmentation	Customer 1	Customer 2
Demographics	• Female • Early 40s • Married • Household income £85,000	• Female • Early 40s • Married • Household income £85,000
Life-Stage	• Two children • Working mother	• Two children • Working mother
Needs	• Menu-planning advice (low-fat and value orientated) • Cooking club	• Ready-to-eat products • Pre-cooked entreés • Home delivery service
Attitudes	• Value shopper • Prefers low-fat foods • Enjoys cooking	• Convenience shopper • Prefers organic foods • Does not like cooking

Companies need to understand which segmentation characteristics are meaningful differentiators. Customers which may appear to be alike will exhibit very different shopping behaviour since their internal needs and attitudes might be very different. However, marketing practitioners are often frustrated by the sheer difficulty in gathering and using data about motivations in a practical way. Customer databases allow companies to relate segments very directly to profitability, using value-based segmentation. As _Fortune_ magazine observed, it is amazing how many executives do not have the least idea just how profitable or unprofitable individual customers or customer segments might be. Yet segmentation is the vehicle by which companies know and manage their portfolio of customers. Figure 5.2 illustrates how a customer portfolio might be divided and what the implications are for managing different customer groups.

To make full use of this kind of value-based segmentation, companies need to track transactions as a matter of priority. By tracking customer purchases, variables like recency of purchase, frequency of purchase and product value can accurately be pinned down. This is second nature to direct marketers; in fact it is the bread and butter of their trade. What they and many marketers fail to realize is the _sheer power of this approach when combined with a company's route to market_. This is the most easily gained benefit from value-based segmentation. To grow revenue, compete effectively in the market

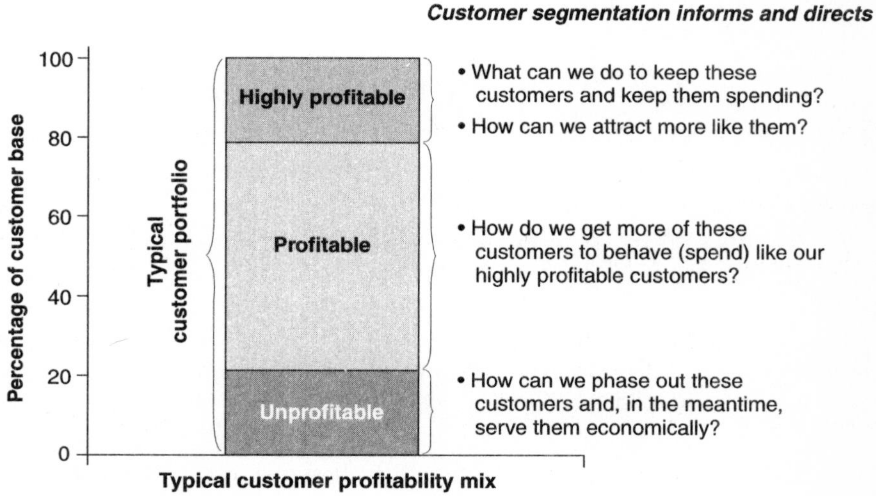

Figure 5.2 _Segmentation as the basis for managing the customer portfolio_
Source: _Fortune Magazine_, 'Will this customer sink your stock?' 15 September 2002.

and provide better services, a key winning strategy is to move resources into differentiated processes. That is to say, move resources from processes which rarely lead to differentiation in practice (though in principle they could certainly do so), such as human resources, finance, procurement, IT, customer service (typically costing 32 per cent to 47 per cent of sales spend) to business processes such as sales, marketing, product development and account management. Increased spend in these areas can increase the company's market competitiveness and allow it to differentiate its proposition and the way that proposition is delivered. In a typical company, these differentiated business processes represent 13 to 28 per cent of sales spend. These are the actions that will most quickly boost profit and share price. They should be a priority area of focus for CEOs and marketing directors.

One very effective method for putting this approach into practice is to use value-based segmentation to optimize channels. The key concept of optimizing channel spend through value-based segmentation needs to be looked at from two directions – within channels and across distribution channels. In some cases, customers are segmented according to value based on an analytic model. Customers of different values are then given a different channel coverage strategy. This sort of segmentation can results in major productivity improvement.

Multi-channel optimization is the biggest opportunity for most businesses. There is huge value to be unlocked. The reason for this is that customers prefer different media for the different types of customer journey that they make. These journeys might relate to buying different products, receiving service rather than sales or buying add-ons rather than the main product. At the same time, even when two customers are buying the same thing, they may each prefer to do so through different media. For instance, some people prefer to book their holiday through a travel agent while others will use the internet. Some customers will walk into their bank to discuss a mortgage but will prefer to make an inter-account transfer online. Since the transaction cost associated with these channels is vastly different, this opens up opportunities for companies to migrate customers to the lower-cost delivery channels while increasing commitments and services. When managed well, this is a win–win situation for the customer, the company (and of course its shareholders).

The business case is compelling. Using real data from companies but masking the provider to protect our source, in one telecommunications company for example in 2004, value-based migration was associated with a fall in attrition rates (customer loss) by 64 per cent, while customer satisfaction increased 20 per cent. At the same time sales staff were reduced by 44 per cent yet market share increased by 35 per cent. In a second case, a banking example, 25 per cent of customers shifted channels, while at the same time customer satisfaction ratings went up by 84 per cent and unit transaction costs reduced by 42 per cent. Of course you cannot spend percentages, but translated into an applied example, the numbers are significant. Imagine a company with 5 million customers, a transaction cost of $2, a single channel to market, a sales turnover of $1 billion and a market share of 12 per cent. Applying channel optimization based on value segmentation and using the strategies and technologies already available (in other words, without taking any innovation risks) impressive gains could be easily achieved. If the sort of benefits cited in these examples were to be duplicated, transaction costs would fall to $1.16 (down 42 per cent), sales turnover would increase to $1.35 billion, and market share would rise to 16.2 per cent. The lower transaction costs would produce cost savings of $4.2 million alone. It does not need much thought to understand that this will result in a higher share price.

Multichannel optimization is not an option that can be ignored. Market leaders are doing it. Companies that do not will remain less profitable and less attractive to investors. The factors driving this change are:

- *Rising customer expectations.* I am used to being able to manage my account over the internet from my bank. Why can't I do it with my utility bill?
- *Increased variety in channel use.* I would like to make arrangements for my personal loan in a branch, where I can talk to someone, but I want to manage the repayments online.
- *Allowing customers to manage relationships.* It is more convenient to give customers choice. Perhaps this week they will want to do their grocery shopping in-store, perhaps next week they would like a delivery to their door, maybe they would like to buy individual ingredients and a recipe book, maybe they would like to choose a recipe from an online service and have the store put together the grocery order.
- *Strategic competitive advantage.* Managing channels also manages profits. The transaction costs for an airline which allows passengers to book directly online, issues no tickets and even permits seat allocation online is massively lower than when each of these transactions is handled face to face or by telephone. This

is so potent a saving that some companies (especially airlines) now charge a premium for customers who do not use online services. If your company can establish greater customer intimacy for these services by mining better insights from its customer data, this achieves the double benefit of adding value whilst reducing costs. The unique relationship with the customer that results provides a more or less unassailable competitive advantage. For example, imagine a restaurant shopping for a utility provider to supply electricity. Price might not be the primary consideration. Perhaps reliability of supply coupled with 24/7 maintenance support for key items of equipment is crucial. A competitor who does not have the same insights and so chooses to compete on price is simply lowering margins without improving recruitment.

- *Channel costs.* The benefits of a reduction in channel costs of up to 40 per cent for each transaction are self-evident.
- *Customer view.* Allowing customers choice and flexibility in their choice of channels provides two benefits. First, if the company shares the reduction in costs with the customer through lower prices and better service, there is a direct gain. Second, by having the customer identify themselves at different touch points, it allows the company to 'recognize' the customer and to improve their insight and understanding of customer needs wherever they may transact their business.
- *Synergy.* For instance, one UK government department said that taking advantage of developments in new technology in one area allowed it to carry out government business more effectively in another.

REAPING THE BENEFITS OF SEGMENTATION-BASED, MULTICHANNEL MANAGEMENT

Like all real segmentations that change the way companies do business, adopting this new approach requires a careful consideration of all the areas both within and outside the company that might be affected. Revolution necessarily means difference and the impact of these differences must be carefully considered, especially where they will touch the customer. The critical success factors are shown in Table 5.2.

In the United States, Nextel is well on the way to reducing its customer care costs by using multichannel management based on

Table 5.2 _Critical success factors for effective segmentation management_

CSF	Risks
Commitment of the senior leadership team	Resources might be withdrawn at too early a stage as investments mount.
A clear ownership of services across channels	Loss of direction and turf wars as customer purchase patterns settle into the new channels.
A channel strategy that covers new and existing channels	Existing customers do not feel comfortable migrating to new channels or believe they are forced into working with the company in a way they find less comfortable.
Detailed modelling and investment appraisal, with clear migration targets	If a business plan is not developed with measurable, clear business targets, senior managers will find it more difficult to establish a return for their investment. The migration period will be long (in corporate terms, this means between 12 and 18 months) so that some short-term goals act both as progress milestones and show where early benefits are being achieved.
Organizational change management	If the impact of the organizational change is not thought through then internal 'buy-in' may be lost and the change may encounter more resistance and be less effective.
Integration of activities	Without seamless integration between channels, customers might encounter problems which reduce confidence. The problem is easily illustrated by situations where customers have to repeat information about themselves or their needs as they are passed between service departments.
Getting the marketing basics right	The dotcom boom went bust in many cases because companies failed to put in place a working infrastructure. Customers suffered from inferior products, poor delivery times and billing errors.
Professional change management, particularly scope control and clear accountabilities and deliverables	It is useful to have an external change agent both to boost confidence (people tend to have more confidence in consultants even if they give the same messages as their own managers) and it is useful to have someone to 'blame' for the painful parts of the change who does not have to face the music internally.
A clear roadmap for implementation	Without a road map, confusion results.
Ownership of data integration, data about customers and about what is happening to them in their relationship with you	Somebody needs to be responsible or you can end up with a database that contains a huge number of customers with a birthday on 1 January 1990!
Detailed control of the complexity of the business solution	Without a project manager, oversight of the process will be lost.
A partnership model to make it work, whether particular aspects are insourced to specialist groups, or outsourced to specialist marketing, service or systems partners	When part of a process is outsourced, a line manager within the company needs to be appointed to ensure that decisions are made within a consistent frame of reference. This is not the job of the project manager whose responsibility is to the process, not the performance.

segmentation. Table 5.3 shows how this has improved the service levels from its customer care representatives and also strengthened its competitive position. This shows that despite achieving significant cost savings, performance has either been maintained or improved. In fact, in the area of follow-up calls where additional customer value can be provided and where higher satisfaction levels are often derived, their competitive performance is much stronger.

Value-based segmentation can be very powerful, but what about the variables used to determine value? The variables to model and segment will vary by business. The dynamic interaction of these variables as shown in Figure 5.3 needs to be monitored.

Different industries find different variables important. Financial services companies may do better to segment by profitability, adopting a one-to-one approach to serve individual needs. By contrast a hospitality company might find behavioural segments more useful, paying close attention to frequency and type of purchases.

TIME-BASED SEGMENTATION

Another area where innovative firms are refining their segmentation is through targeting by time. Time-based approaches are currently rare but they are becoming increasingly important. This is clear and obvious in markets such as car insurance whose customers follow steady annual patterns of renewal. However, for many other firms time-related variables are critical because they highlight how customers and their buying phases might change. They allow a company to address the question as to when customers should be targeted, and refine the segmentation with this additional dimension. Thus the parameters of the offer include an additional element such as:

Table 5.3 Benefits of multichannel segmentation management

Customer care representative	Nextel (%)	Industry average (%)
Has correct information	91	93
Can clearly hear and understand the customer	95	94
Representative understands customer needs	89	89
Representative gives their name	96	94
Asks if they can assist with other matters	96	92
Makes follow-up call	20	12

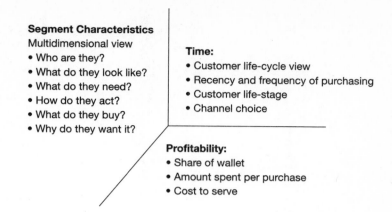

Figure 5.3 _Dimensions of segmentation_
Source: IBM Institute for Business Value (2003).

- Which characteristics will create a distinctive segment at a given point in time?
- How often will a customer buy?
- For how long will a customer buy?
- What point has the customer reached in their repeat buying cycle?
- What is the customer's propensity to buy at this moment?
- What emerging needs will the customer have over some future period such as a week, a month or a year?
- How will the potential profit from customers change over time? An unprofitable customer at the beginning of an executive career may be someone of high value in five years' time.

Figure 5.4 illustrates how buying patterns for three example customers might vary, and the sort of questions the company will need to answer in responding to differences in buying pattern.

There are real opportunities to be a first mover in this area of segmentation. In 2003, over 50 per cent of companies were tracking their customer profiles once a year or less. As a result many are missing opportunities. Of course, these opportunities vary by sector. Asset managers should consider highly dynamic segmentations, while for a distribution company a bi-annual review of customer purchase patterns may suffice. Table 5.4 illustrates the differences in approach that might be used by companies in three different industry sectors.

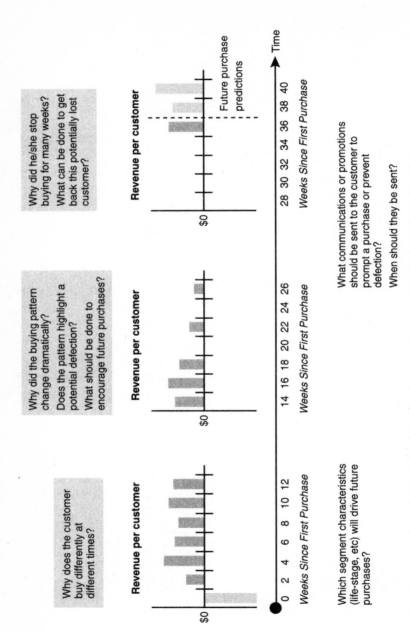

Figure 5.4 *Changing patterns: company analysis and interpretation*
Source: IBM Institute for Business Value (2003).

Table 5.4 *Frequency of analysis for time-based segmentation*

	Nearly real-time (daily–monthly)	Regularly and often (monthly–quarterly)	Less often (quarterly–annually)
Industry	Financial services: top five US asset manager	Distribution/retailer: international leader in pharmacy products and services	Distribution – consumer products Leading consumer products company
Purpose of segmentation	Increasing share of customer's wallet Migrating customers to higher value	Identifying attractive new offerings Customer retention Migrating customers to higher value	Determining optimal positioning Identifying new offerings for different segments Increasing share of wallet within growth segments
Nature of customer interaction	Through necessary, regular and frequent interaction with customers across multiple touch points (branch, online, ATM)	Through in-store and online shopping for products that are both necessary and nice to have	Through focus groups and customer surveys
Type of data collected	Individual customer data collected at each customer interaction Demographic data purchased from a third party	Individual customer data collected with loyalty cards Data about customers as a whole collected from sales data Demographic data purchased from a third party	Customer data collected in focus groups and customer surveys Data about customers collected from sales data Demographic data purchased from a third party

Case study: Luminar Corporation

One company that has successfully implemented strategic and operational segmentations is the fast-growing UK-based leisure corporation, Luminar. It employed two principal techniques for operationalizing its segmentation strategy, using data from its loyalty cards to refine its branding platform.

1. *Develop a strategy based on segmentation*. As a leading UK developer and operator of themed bars, nightclubs and restaurants, Luminar has many brands, each targeted at different customer segments and different needs. These include:
   - *The*, a new, stylized bar;
   - *Jam House*, a blues jazz concept;
   - *Life*, a trendy club bar;
   - *Jumpin' Jaks*, a Deep South concept bar;
   - *Chicago Rock Cafes*, provides the 3 D's: drinking, dancing and dining;
   - *Liquid*, a nightclub with computer graphics that can be changed to set the scene (seascape, tropics, forest, etc).

   The CEO recognized that the entertainment business is all about market segmentation, trying to work out what people want, where they want it and how they want it. The entertainment business is very competitive and volatile so the only way to grow the business is to match segments to what they want.

2. *Grow revenue by tracking customer patterns:*
   - The group collects customer data using its loyalty cards. When customers sign up for loyalty cards they provide initial demographic data. Subsequently they are rewarded in the form of discounts for answering questions about their drinking habits. Data are collected throughout each evening in each club so that the company can fine-tune its products or pass on the information to suppliers.
   - Luminar then uses online transaction data in real time along with historical loyalty card data and text messaging, to capitalize on current and changing trends. Advertising screens linked to point-of-sale systems payment systems steer customers from low-margin to high-margin beverages. The text message system is used to offer discounts and promotions to coax customers from crowded locations to quieter sites, thus evening out peak loads on resources. They also collect data on 14- to 17-year-olds at their under-18 clubs and non-alcoholic club nights so that contact can be made at a future point. When they turn 18, they get a phone call from the club to say, 'Now you are 18, you're legal', (the legal minimum age for buying alcoholic drinks in clubs in the UK).

Segmentation analysis can also be used to identify potential gaps in existing markets as the basis for developing new products and services.

Case study: Marriott Hotels

Marriott International has a robust segmentation strategy that enables the company to gain a deep understanding of needs and wants of both individual customers and segments of customers. Segmentation data are used to identify service gaps between brands that represent opportunities for brand improvements and chances to introduce new brands. There are two main strands to this process:

1. *Make brand improvements and product extensions based on segmentation findings*. Brand improvements result when a group or segment of customers expresses a specific need for new services provided at a current lodging brand.
   Example: Through customer research Marriott found that customers of Fairfield Inn[2] were looking for bigger rooms and more amenities. As a result, Marriott launched Fairfield Suites[3] to meet these needs.
2. *Develop entire new markets, based on knowing what customers want*. New markets are pursued when a group or segment of customers desire a totally new set of services that are not aligned with a current brand
   Example: Through customer surveys, Marriott determined that the company was not meeting the demands and expectations of elite travellers. This was a contributory factor to an eventual decision to acquire the Ritz-Carlton group.
   Example: Fairfield Suites customers desired additional amenities such as lobbies with carpeting, fireplaces, crown mouldings and breakfast rooms. These additions revolutionized the brand to the point that it was attracting new customers. Marriott then converted Fairfield Suites into Springfield Suites[4] (a new brand).

These approaches are open to all companies; the winners will be those who can implement the ideas most effectively. It is often the effectiveness not only of the data management that makes the difference but also of the extent to which the results of this analysis can be exploited and put into effect that separates successes and failures. Since data are often held on multiple databases, the technical complexity of merging different records sets to obtain a cross-customer view of all transactions and touch points often presents technical difficulty. For example, Mr Smith may sometimes identify himself as John Smith or J. Smith, or may undertake transactions through his purchasing office, his wife or even an agent. Thus records relating to the same Mr Smith may be held under several individual or company names. One major insurance company noted that 75 per cent of the segmentation effort is in database merging; data comes from multiple, disparate databases. If the segmentation analysis takes a total of eight weeks, it might spend five of those weeks merging data to create a single record for each customer. Only then are they in a position to conduct cluster and other types of analysis needed to segment their customers.

THE FUTURE OF MARKET SEGMENTATION: DATA FUSION

The difficulties of traditional segmentation using market research are encouraging companies to revolutionize their market segmenting using customer transaction data. These two methods are not necessarily mutually exclusive. It may well be that the future lies in a marriage of the old and the new. This is known as data fusion. The search to bring together the worlds of marketing research and database marketing has been going on for some time now. Indeed, as far back as 1994 data expert Peter Sleight pointed out that various parties were looking for areas of synergy between market research and lifestyle information. More recently database specialists like Experian and Taylor Nelson Sofres have begun to link together geo-demographic, lifestyle and purchase information data products. These can then be merged with client databases to give a multi-layered view of the customer.

Many of these data services are still at an early stage of development in spite of pressure from market leaders to develop them more quickly. Some companies have been relatively slow to recognize the potential power of a fusion between research and database data. However, there is no doubting the potential power here. While database marketers understand what their customers are buying, how much they spend, how often they buy and so on, a fusion of their data with market research gets them closer to understanding why their customers buy. The factors leading up to the purchase decision are revealed more clearly for large numbers of customers. This is an exciting development for the future. In Chapter 12 we provide an example of an outstanding success in this area from British retail giant Tesco.

OPPORTUNITIES FROM IMPROVED SEGMENTATION

Data-driven segmentation fusing market research with operational analytics is an increasingly important development. Companies

Table 5.5 *Areas of opportunity for segmentation-driven revolution*

Operational issue	Key findings	Segmentation opportunities
Turning segmentation into action	30% of companies surveyed found making segmentation actionable to be difficult; 36% found it difficult to measure	Develop clear strategies and plans for each customer segment that identify specific, appropriate offerings and service levels for each one
CRM	Only 17% of companies with CRM installed make use of the customer analytics capabilities	Implement customer analytics capabilities to help realize value of CRM investment and improve revenue through enhanced customer acquisition, retention and migration
Time-based segmentation	Over 50% of companies surveyed track customers' changes once a year or even once every few years	Track customer changes frequently to capitalize on changes early, before competitors do so
Better precision in targeting	Two-thirds of companies surveyed believe segmentation is important or highly important to marketing effectively	Improve the performance of traditional marketing efforts by enhancing segmentation capabilities to refine segmentation findings and identify new product and market opportunities Companies must interpret results in business terms and action them
Using attitudinal as well as behavioural segmentation	Only 20% of companies surveyed incorporate attitudinal data to know why (motivations behind) customers buy	Make use of predictive modelling techniques. To see real benefits segmentation must go beyond simply running the model
Developing an integrated marketing approach	Only 30% of companies surveyed use segmentation integrally (100% of the time) in business development or strategic planning; in customer service, finance and operations this is as low as between 15 to 19%.	Expand uses of segmentation to strategic planning, finance, customer service and new product development to realize full potential

which take advantage of this new technology and embed the operational capabilities that it offers into their marketing process can gain significant first-mover advantages. These are summarized in Table 5.5, which is drawn from a study carried out by the IBM Institute for Business Value in 2003.

Those firms who can commit at CEO level to drive these techniques into all parts of their business may reap the rewards. Before they start they should clearly understand the implications of what they are doing. There is nothing to be gained from technical elegance to create segmentation patterns that are theoretically sound, maybe even actionable, if they do not add to the sum of knowledge or if serving those segments would push the company outside its core business. It is even worse if those same sound segments do not fit within the service envelope that the existing structures of the business are designed to serve. The successful players in this area will be ones who plan from the outset to design and implement a value-driven segmentation strategy. This proceeds from the design of strategy, the development of a business infrastructure, then implementing segment-based techniques within the operational realities demanded by the business. Linking attitudes and motives to customer transactions may be the best way to refine segmentation patterns. Whatever segments are identified, the power of the customer database must then be harnessed to operationalize them.

NOTES

1. 7-Up is a registered trademark of Dr Pepper/Seven Up Inc.
2. Fairfield Inn is a registered brand of Marriott.
3. Fairfield Suites is a registered brand of Marriott.
4. Springfield Suites is a registered brand of Marriott.

6

Revolutionizing the company by living the brand

A great deal has been written about branding. Branding is one of the things that contemporary marketers actually do understand better than the rest of the company. This chapter will not revisit all the basic theories of branding. While it is useful to review the basic approaches to branding, the main area of interest is how powerful brands can revolutionize internal cultures. Changing the internal culture of a company will help to make people proud to be members of it. Developing the right brands and involving people in building those brands can set people thinking. This is what branding is all about. Not just following the rules. There are several excellent texts on branding and branding theory – see for example Kapferer (2001), Ellwood (2002) or Pringle and Gordon (2001). The aim of this chapter is therefore to present thought-provoking examples of experiences with brands, big and small. Focusing on revolution, we will show how the people of the organization and the brand can feed upon each other in a virtuous circle, creating energy and motivation for effective market-led change.

WHERE DOES BRANDING START?

Branding starts with segmentation. The starting point is to take a long hard look at the long-term profit potential of each customer segment. Based on the ideas that were presented in the previous chapter, it is important to remember that, useful as it still is, traditional segmentation can run the risk of leading companies into creating brands that have weak long-term potential. Time-based segmentation may be much more useful. Targeting a brand at a fad-conscious youth market can be tricky and expensive. Even more so if changing customer demographics mean that both wealth and fashion are increasingly focused on the over-fifties. Thus major revolutions in the marketplace need to be identified and tracked. These trends might start with a TV programme or a book. In 2005 in the UK, a celebrity chef called Jamie Oliver attracted a huge amount of public and political attention by running a series of programmes focused on children's school lunches. His campaign was so powerful that within months he evoked the kind of political response which other, more serious campaigners had failed to achieve over many years. More or less immediate increases in funding for better meals were magically produced from the public purse. However, the campaign also had the interesting side-effect of changing the eating habits of a wider section of the population, raising interest in general in healthy eating. This could be a trend to track. In passing, he also showed what could happen when a brand backfires. Oliver took to task a processed food product called 'Turkey Twizzlers', a brand belonging to food company Bernard Matthews. The brand became associated with unhealthy food products.

Brands are becoming increasingly narrow as customers seek to satisfy their needs in more individualistic ways. Examples are easy to find in more or less any product segment, but to illustrate the point easily it is only necessary to consider the vitamin supplement market. Today it is possible to buy branded vitamins that are positioned differently for men and for women. Vitamin A is vitamin A, but in marketing terms, a powerful brand might enable a company to capture one segment of the market which might otherwise be lost. A competitor dominating the general vitamin market could easily lose a segment (that of, say, women) to a cleverly created alternative brand. Brands target specific segments and allow a company to position itself both against the competition and against itself. Multiple brands allow a company to operate in many different segments and levels within the same product category. Again there are many examples.

Detergents are mainly manufactured by two dominant global players, both of which control a number of brands which position their detergents in different segments. This can be expensive to maintain, with different packaging, promotion and tiny product variations. Back in 1999 therefore, Unilever decided to fight against market fragmentation by instituting a brand consolidation programme. It eliminated hundreds of brands in search of economies of scale. Among the discarded brands were such successful names as Elizabeth Arden cosmetics and the Diversey cleaning and hygiene business. The strategy was praised by some analysts at the time but it proved to have short-term benefit. Five years later, Unilever's sales had stagnated, while primary competitor Procter & Gamble, with its niche branding strategy, enjoyed healthy gains.

THE BRAND UNPICKED

What is a brand?

In spite of all the material written about brands, many companies particularly in the business-to-business sectors get product management and brand management mixed up. If someone tells you a brand is a logo or name, ignore them. This is the sort of misunderstanding that leads to trouble. A much better definition is that brands are the sum of all associated images of the company or product, that reside in the customers' mind. Hence brands are by no means in the sole control of the company. Any company which runs into trouble will confirm this, such as Enron, Arthur Andersen, Equitable Life or Parmalat. It is true that some brands, usually packaged goods, can be built largely by clever advertising and big budgets. In service and business sectors, this is not so easy. The total brand image of, say, Disney would be a complex amalgam of lots of things such as childhood memories, films, visits to DisneyLand, attitudes to the United States, a recalled newspaper profile of Walt Disney and so on.

A brand is a promise of a benefit. This can be functional – what does the product or service do for me? Or it can be symbolic – can this brand help me say something about myself? Clearly then, products and brands are different. When Nestlé bought Rowntree it paid over £3 billion for £700 million worth of tangible assets. The remainder was the goodwill price of brands such as Kit Kat. Carlsberg is a powerful European brand of beer which uses the strap line, 'Probably the best lager in the world'. This may or may not be true. It does not matter.

What matters is that consistent, witty and clever advertising over many years has built an impression of quality in customers' minds. The actual product is less important than the impression. The creative theme has been so successful that Carlsberg continues to develop it.

Why are brands important?

Attractive brands allow companies to charge higher prices. Stella Artois[1] beer is 'reassuringly expensive'. Not only does Stella Artois cost more than competing brands of lager, but it makes a virtue of it. The business model is straightforward. The incremental revenue from higher prices must be greater than the incremental costs of creating and promoting the brand. Products come and go, but brands stay longer. These days product life cycles are shorter than ever. In markets like game software, product life cycles are extremely short, as little as three months. Brands, on the other hand, stick around. They take on a life of their own because they are owned by the consumer.

Brands allow companies to attack or defend markets. The easyGroup has expanded from easyJet to easyCar and many other markets including Cinema. The brand is the key platform to launch into these markets. Some companies are primarily the brand that they sell. Virgin is a good example. The brand is used for many products and services, some of which do rather badly in terms of products and services (such as Virgin Trains). Yet the power of the brand, which is viewed in an overwhelmingly positive light in the UK thanks to the popularity of its CEO Richard Branson, allows the company to prosper where others falter. A strong brand can also save a company when defending a poor situation. IBM fell back on its base platform of security and reassurance when in trouble in the early 1990s with the mantra 'No one ever got fired for buying IBM' coming to its aid.

Branding tricks of the trade

- A *Harvard Business Review* study (Blasberg and Vishwanath, 2003) suggests that what did distinguish brand winners from the pack were innovation and aggressive advertising. This was true across different sectors.
- Do not make the mistake of thinking that because you have heard enough of the messages yourself, from within the company, your customers will feel the same. Just when you are sick of repeating yourself might just be when your customers will start to internalize your brand. Keep going.

- Do not believe the myth that business customers are different to consumers. Business customers will respond positively to entertaining, emotionally charged advertising. One research study estimates that 80 per cent of the buying decision for IT managers is symbolic (what does this brand say about me/us) rather than functional (which brand offers the best features).
- Consistency is everything. While BMW has varied its creative style, it has kept the same theme, superior driveability, through all its advertising since the 1960s. Meanwhile the MG Rover group, which failed in early 2005, has chopped and changed its promotional theme, leaving customers unsure of what Rover was supposed to represent.
- It is better to underclaim and overdeliver. Both Skoda cars and Ronseal paints are testament to this.
- Entertainment helps get attention which helps build brands. This is clear and explicit in alcoholic drinks sectors where the likes of Bacardi, Heineken and Fosters use humour and glamour. But it is also true in business and service markets. Barclays Bank used Samuel L Jackson to tell amusing stories.
- Create attractive reasons to make a product into a service. Branding can be used to reposition a product. Harley Davidson, a US manufacturer of heavy motorcycles, clearly ran into difficulties when high-performance motorbikes from Japan offered better value and more speed at lower prices. Whilst the Japanese were able to wipe out the existing European motorcycle industry in the 1980s, Harley repositioned its brand as a fashion accessory, a statement, which worked so well that it was used not only on motor cycles but on other accessories such as clothing. Harley Davidson is perhaps the only brand that people tattoo onto themselves – now that is loyalty! Harley riders greatly value being placed in touch with other Harley riders, and their owners' group runs club events and socials. This would not work in the same way for a bank.
- Open up your company to interested customers. You can literally do this if you are a brewer or a heritage brand with a museum. Look for other ways to open up if you are an insurance company. Websites that help make what you do more transparent will help.
- Look for ways to turn your brand into a 'story'. You can do this internally and also externally. Myths and legends, heritage and history all help build a rounded picture for staff and customers. Companies can also future orientate this by capturing people's

imagination with interesting goals or new horizons. Both Virgin Airlines and easyJet's founder Stelios Haji-Iannou created political storms around their 'fights' with British Airways.

THE ANATOMY OF A POWERFUL BRAND

Brands are multilayered, like the rings of an onion as illustrated in Figure 6.1.

Brand DNA

At the heart of a brand is what is trendily known as the brand essence, or brand DNA. This is the brand's basic identity, that central heart of the brand without which the brand would cease to exist. It is a mistake to think that this essence is the sum total of all the attributes of the brand. A better way to approach this issue is to ask customers if the brand would remain intact without that particular attribute. For example, is Perrier without its large bubbles still Perrier? Is a Harley Davidson without the characteristic thrub-thrub of the engine still a Harley? Fitting a smoother, quieter engine could be a mistake for Harley. On the other hand, Skoda like to run a

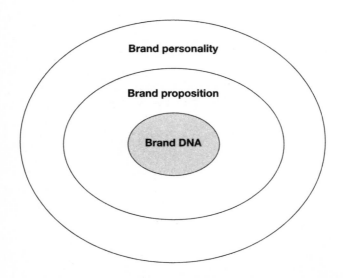

Figure 6.1 *Brand DNA*

campaign listing the attributes of the many varieties of engine available for their cars, ending with the query, 'Looking for an engine that will make your trousers vibrate at 50 metres? Sorry, wrong showroom.'

It is very important to identify your brand essence. The DNA analogy is important too. It implies that this attribute should pervade everything the company does. The DNA of Guinness beer, for example, is Irishness. At its heart is a strong link with the image of the country of origin, Eire, which in its own right has a powerful brand worldwide (see Figure 6.2).

Guinness was started up by Arthur Guinness in 1759 at St James Gate in Dublin. This is now the site of the largest brewery in Europe, a place where tourists can visit and have a free pint or two of the black stuff. Guinness has allowed a number of myths and legends to accumulate around the brand, linked to its Irish roots. In Ireland, Guinness was long thought to have healing properties. This was actually linked to advertising with the 'Guinness is good for you' strapline, until stopped relatively recently. One in every two pints of alcohol drunk in Ireland is reputed to be Guinness. For young people, a 'holy trinity' of drinking was followed by young men: Harp lager, followed by Smithwicks[2] beer, followed by Guinness when they finally grew up.

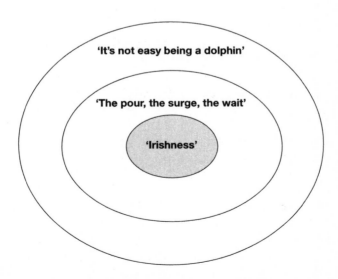

Figure 6.2 *Guinness: the brand*

BRAND PROPOSITION

A brand is a promise of benefits. The proposition is this promise, an explanation to the customer of what they are going to get for their money. These benefits are both rational and emotional or symbolic. The rational aspect refers to functional benefits of the product, service or company. UK-based Ronseal is a fantastic functional brand. It specializes in wood protection products and its adverts carry the strapline, 'It does exactly what it says on the tin'. This has been so successful that the phrase is now part of everyday parlance. The adverts celebrate and draw attention to the precision of what is said on the tin: '5-year wood stain protection, meaning it stains and protects wood for 5 years'. There are no complex messages, no cleverness or irony, just matter-of-fact sentences delivered in a matter-of-fact manner. A brilliant functional brand.

Guinness has a series of natural advantages including, most distinctively, its black colour. It also has a unique taste, promising a refreshing change from lager or ales. Guinness advertising heavily reinforces the long time it takes to pour a 'proper' pint of Guinness using the slogan, 'Good things come to those who wait'. Crucially, its advertising creates a series of image-based symbolic benefits. Guinness has positioned itself as an 'intelligent person's drink'. By drinking Guinness, customers can appropriate these symbols onto themselves.

Another great functional brand is Intel. Intel was one of the earliest companies to set itself manufacturing microprocessors and semiconductors in Fairchild County California (Silicon Valley) in the late 1970s. Its first Intel products were labelled rather than branded, the 8088, the 8086, the now famous x 86 families of microprocessors. Then Intel recognized the power of branding (and the difficulty of patenting numbers). So Intel and Pentium were born. Intel managed to brand, and make interesting, computer chips. Of course chips are always going to be of interest to computer specialists but the long-running 'Intel Inside' campaign is one of the most successful in advertising history. With this, Intel jumped over the heads of equipment assemblers to appeal directly to consumers. Its secret was to reassure business and individual customers at a time when they felt great uncertainty about buying something as complex as personal computers, as brands in that product category proliferated. People wanted something they could trust. Intel's appeal was to offer them a solution: look for the 'Intel inside' sign. With a catchy five-note jingle and consistent advertising, a great functional brand was built.

The best brand propositions are based on core competences. Positioning and differential advantage are based on the solidity of core competences. A core competence is what we do better than anyone else. Volvo, whose core competence is safety technology, used that as the basis of its branding proposition. Who else could sell cars with a slogan, 'Boxy but safe'? Volvo has successfully externalized this core competence to brand itself as a 'safe car'. It is, however, possible to become too well known in an area of competence. Safety has become so closely associated with the Volvo brand that by 2004 Volvo was struggling to convince car buyers that it could make exciting products too. By then, everyone 'knew' that Volvos were safe, but so were many competing products and safety buyers were now looking for something a little different.

BRAND PERSONALITY

If your brand was a famous person, who would it be? What clothes would your brand wear and what sort of people would it hang around with? The personality of a brand is the personalization of that brand. What tone of voice does it adopt? What sort of people use it? If the brand proposition is what the company offers, the brand personality is how it behaves. This is especially important in business and service sectors, but brand personalities are also something that can be created by clever advertising.

Guinness is a classic example of this. The tone of voice of their adverts is highly distinctive, clever, quirky, with a strong sense of humour. The ads set puzzles for you to solve. The idea being that if you solve the puzzle you are the kind of person who is clever enough to drink Guinness. So, actor Rutger Hauer tells you, 'It is not easy being a dolphin'. The customer is left to work out why. The answer (of course) is because dolphins cannot drink Guinness.

BRAND REVOLUTION

Corporate brands are becoming more important

The area of interest here is corporate, as opposed to product, brands. There has been a medium-term trend towards corporate brands in Western markets for over 10 years and this is set to continue. In Eastern markets corporate brands have always dominated and this has spread west. So in a sense we are following an established trend here, but the main reason for concentrating on the company brand is that it is at this level that revolution takes place. The East versus West dichotomy is important here. It is no accident that Toyota is a more powerful brand than General Motors worldwide. Toyota commands higher loyalties, higher prices and higher resale values than GM. In describing the Japanese approach Macrae (1996) noted that while Japanese firms work on a loyalty model, Western firms talk about loyalty but actually work on a transaction-by-transaction model. Japanese brands like Toyota, Sony or Toshiba personify continuity, trust, status. According to Kapferer (2001) brand identity in Japan derives from looking inwards and codifying one's own set of strong values.

These brands are based on something more solid and stable than the Western-style product brands which are often creations from an advertising agency and nothing more. These creations may be clever, witty and attractive and may last for years, but at the end of the day they are images, all smoke and mirrors. In order to sustain these nowadays agencies are relapsing into the familiar irony in which they acknowledge that consumers no longer take the brands at face value. They assume that everyone will suspend disbelief, as in any other form of theatre, and go along for the ride. No doubt this will continue for low-involvement, low-importance categories such as soft drinks, alcohol, everyday foods and so on. In high-involvement products, and especially services where the purchase is seen as being close to personal core values like pensions or health, there is much more consumer interest in the company behind the product.

FROM BRANDS AS MIRRORS TO BRANDS AS WINDOWS

Indeed Kapferer argues that the role of brands as differentiators is diminishing. Instead there is an increasingly important role of brands as 'sources'; that is to say, the role of brands as sources of credibility, authenticity, guarantee or ethics. This trend to brands as sources is given momentum by a number of forces. Distribution is now more heavily concentrated between fewer companies in most developed economies; retailer power has therefore forced brand concentration. Greater awareness of the power of loyalty (or maybe more accurately the profit potential of cross-selling) has nudged firms towards company-level databases of customers. Global business-to-business relationship building continues to grow and hence company brands predominate. Lastly, the increasing power of the media in raising anxiety and heightening perceived levels of risk must not be underestimated. Brands have always been risk reducers, but nowadays trust and reassurance are harder than ever to earn and easily lost. Face-value trust cannot be assumed. Corporate transparency is demanded more and more. The recent history of Equitable Life, a personal assurance company more than 100 years old and of impeccable reputation when it ran into trouble with its life assurance policies and difficulties in other financial areas (especially pension funds) in the UK, has left the public with a profound unease in dealing with financial services firms. The pressure is firmly on the brand at corporate level to demonstrate and earn trust.

HOW THE (BRAND) WORLD HAS CHANGED

The transition to corporate brands has been fuelled at least partly by the movement in the most advanced consumer economies to services and knowledge based economies. Middle class socio-economic groups, normally high spenders on consumer goods and services, now own lots of material possessions. Market saturation has been reached in many areas. Interest and appetite in simply buying more and more products is starting to flatten out. With this has come a rising interest in self-fulfilment in ways other than the materialistic. Spiritual, ethical and moral dimensions have started to become more important. With this comes a heightened scrutiny of the behaviour and practices of global suppliers.

The pride factor

So, given the increasing interest in the authenticity of corporate brands, it makes sense to look internally, inside the company. This brings us to a central idea, the power of pride. Proud employees make for a very powerful source of energy that can be harnessed in a virtually unstoppable way. Figure 6.3 illustrates the virtuous circle that can be achieved. Strong brands energize and motivate; in turn motivated employees build strong brands.

A great deal has been written about how employees might respond to a raised sense of involvement, higher corporate values, social

Motivated employees
build stronger brands

Brand

Employee

Strong brands make a proud team

Figure 6.3 *The virtuous circle of brand-building*

responsibility and just generally making the world a better place. Of course at one level this is easy to understand. CEOs always seem to be caught unawares by the not so surprising fact that employees are not really engaged or passionate about taking the company from, say, 34 per cent to 35 per cent share of market next year. 'Changing the world' in some way, maybe making it a better place, is understandably a better motivator.

This is all very well but is not easy to do convincingly, especially if your company makes and sells machine tool parts or something that is difficult to link to a sense of global values. For many, perhaps most firms, linking themselves to spiritual values is simply not credible. Instead, creating an atmosphere of achievement closely linked to rewards, of team spirit and of close communication can work well. In small companies, this sense of team work and pride is easier to detect. When the workforce clearly enjoy each other's company and make sure that having fun whenever possible is high on their list of priorities, a sense of engagement emerges. All members of the team share in the success of the company. None of this is rocket science. Nevertheless it does give off positive energy to customers, a sense that the firm is enjoyable to do business with. That is their brand and it feeds upon itself. As people tell them that they are fun to deal with, so they begin to see that maybe they can formalize this into a view of themselves that makes them feel good and is something they can badge.

Energy is created when a company can identify its own strong, personal vision and how this translates into something exciting for the consumer. When in-house teams are totally committed to this vision the virtuous circle starts to build up momentum. This is particularly true of challenger brands. Do Avis really 'try harder'? Well, they are certainly setting their stall out, directly challenging their own people, with their brand. Challenger brands by definition are trying to change the status quo, to shake up the market, to promote alternative ways of thinking. This generates its own excitement, within and outside the company. In the example of Disney, each employee is treated as part of a crew. The entire organization from the most senior manager to the cleaner is focused on the customer experience. Employee training reinforces brand values and attributes such as clean theme parks so that every employee 'walks the talk'.

Pringle and Gordon (2001) also talk about corporate life as theatre. They call it the corporate drama. Coming into the office each day contrasts more and more with the pleasures of everyday life. Successful firms create a sense of drama at work, a corporate story, in which everyone is an actor in a real-life play. Internal marketing keeps people up to date with what is going on and how much each team's work is affecting the big picture. This sense of involvement in unfolding events keeps staff engaged day to day.

Mobilizing and energizing people

It is amazing how the task of mobilizing and energizing people is still done badly, even after all the many studies and seminars that have taken place in the last 80 years or so concerned with motivating staff in big companies. One insurance firm in the UK recently underwent a brand makeover and implemented an internal change programme. A big bang approach was used with away-days, a conference hosted by senior management, redesign of building decor, videos of recent advertisements with employees as heroes and so on. Three months later there was little or nothing left of the buzz that had been created. Staff were particularly cynical about how the board had gone missing and were never seen. Senior management had distanced themselves from operating managers and the workforce. The sense of team work and commitment had been lost.

Orange is a good example of brands that people are proud to work for. Right from the start, Orange was determined to be different to its competitors such as Vodafone. The strongly themed advertising by its agency WCRS was based on the idea of a wire-free future. Orange never talked about mobile phones or showed a phone in its advertising. The advertisements were always beautifully photographed with huge space and tranquillity. Orange's people were asked to buy into a strong vision of a different world, and this became Orange's positioning. 'In the future everyone will have their own personal number that goes with them wherever they are so that there are no barriers to communication. A wire-free future in which you call people not places.' Orange made a virtue of clear, jargon-free communications. As a result it built high levels of trust – important for a technology company in a highly competitive market, where expansion often meant that the placing of its relay antennas, essential for the excellent performance of the network, might run into opposition from environmental groups.

Ellwood (2002) talks about the concept of 'flow'. Here the focus is on employees' personal development and how this is linked to the brand. His model of flow describes the optimal balance between the size of the challenge we can master, and individual abilities to achieve a goal. An athlete who controls his fear to win a race can feel euphoric about the balance achieved between a challenging objective attempted and the achievement. Too great a challenge leads to anxiety, too low a challenge leaves us bored. A good CEO encourages their staff to stretch themselves, within their own boundaries. Martin Troughton of award-winning agency HTW pays for his staff to visit London's galleries and museums, asking that they bring back ideas and lateral thinking into the agency. Creating a sense of flow is about encouraging employees to live their lives well and improve their personal capital. It is this that they bring to the 'party' at work.

Done well, this sense of linkage between people and their brand allows them scope for their own decision making. They know what the brand is asking them to do. Given the chance to offer something for short-term gain but which may not be right for that individual customer, the brand must be strong enough to guide employees to do the right thing. In some cases such as in the case of the pension mis-selling scandal, this failed.

Sometimes senior managers in large organizations have problems with what Pringle and Gordon call 'distance'. This is very understandable given the pressure on board members in wall-to-wall meetings all day. Nevertheless it is very dangerous to stay isolated from the operational front line for too long, especially if you are trying to change something, like service delivery. If the brand depends at least partly on your people, senior managers must find the time to interact with them. Once again, the buck stops on the desk of the CEO. At the end of the day, the CEO is the brand manager, they are responsible for the brand. Ellwood describes how in its troubled years,

Philips undertook a customer day in January each year. All employees worldwide would pause together to share best practices and hear from CEO Jan Timmer about focusing on customer benefits. In the UK, one popular TV programme featured senior managers going back to the shop floor for a day. The CEO served customers, packed and despatched products, dealt with complaints and did other day-to-day jobs for a week. Participants invariably had lots of reality-check messages for their senior colleagues at the end of the week. Instituting this as a regular practice, say once every year, might ensure that CEOs stayed in closer touch with the way some of their brands were actually delivered.

Another problem that often arises is the way in which messages are disseminated in some big companies. Strategies are often kept secret, long after the competitive confidentiality issue has passed. How can you deploy a secret strategy? Secrecy in this case refers to poor communication. Keeping people in the dark irritates them and is bad for morale. Worse, nature abhors a vacuum. Rumour and supposition replace fact and the supposition is invariably more negative than the reality. There is a tendency to assume the worst.

CUSTOMER-CENTRIC BRANDS

Rust *et al* (2004) pointed out that whilst managers often talk about customers, in reality they are often more concerned with brands. They cite the example of General Motor's very successful Oldsmobile[3] brand. There was clear evidence that, after a long period of outstanding success, by the 1980s the brand was dated. Instead of making the tough decision, from 1985 onwards the company invested substantial amounts of money in trying to reposition the brand through a new advertising campaign. However, its market share continued to fall and by the end of 2000 the company had no choice but to close the brand down. They raise the question as to why the company spent so much money trying to revitalize the brand when it could easily have taken the path of least resistance by steering its younger customers to other brands in the GM stable, or even launched another brand. Why nurture the brand and not the customer? The answer, they suggest, is that in large companies brands are fiefdoms, little centres of power that are nurtured in turf wars. The brand is the basis of budgets, the route to promotion.

Another source of frustration within marketing is the lack of attention given to qualitative and quantitative research by senior colleagues. Marketers learn to listen to the findings of their research. It is frustrating when corporate distance gets in the way. Big companies can get very remote from their customers. Even experienced organizations take their eye off the ball. Contrast the behaviour of Johnson & Johnson with that of Coca-Cola. In the United States, faced with a blackmail threat to its Tylenol brand when someone suggested that they had poisoned some of the product on pharmacy shelves, Johnson & Johnson did not hesitate to withdraw all product from across the United States for checking. In the short term it cost the company millions of dollars but in the long term the positive effect on the corporate brand name was enormously powerful. J&J had 'walked their talk'. They really did care about their customers. By contrast, Coca-Cola reacted very slowly when 200 school children felt ill after drinking Coke in Belgium. The company reacted slowly and in an apparently unconcerned manner. The effect was very negative as Coca-Cola targets its advertising towards young people.

Big company brands are not alone in losing sight of the customer. Surprisingly, the technology behind customer relationship management can sometimes be used to keep the customer at a distance rather than bring them closer. Indeed not only has it replaced face-to-face contact with more remote communication, but it has provided another, sneaky form of revenue. Until early 2005, customers in the UK chewing their nails with frustration as they waded through menu after menu of IVR (interactive voice response) machines, then listened with resignation to mindless background music interrupted by the occasional, 'your call is important to us' message, did not realize what was at stake. Companies were making £180 million per year from the premium-rate phone lines used to connect to their call centres. Nor were customers pleased when they received their phone bills. Once through to the call centre, frustrations can increase as powerless call centre agents find themselves unable to deal with the customer's needs. Either they are not allowed enough time or they are not given enough authority to deal with the call. The lack of any genuine empathy with consumers is exacerbated by the use of remote technology and not empowering the employee.

Many countries have hundreds of thousands, sometimes millions, of people employed in call centres, mostly taking inbound calls from customers. This is the pressure point where the finance-driven operations mentality meets, and usually wins, over the 'let's delight our customers' mentality of marketing. As we have noted earlier, this is due to the relative weakness of marketers in most boardrooms today. So the company ends up with bored, poorly paid, disheartened employees dealing with frustrated consumers. This unsatisfactory interaction is the brand. Perhaps part of the issue here is that not all companies have yet realized that the brand experience is made up of many touch points. How customers are treated when they phone into a call centre will affect their perception of the brand, positively or negatively.

There will always be tensions between the need to keep interaction costs down and the desire for a satisfactory customer experience. Whilst forecast lifetime values and allowable costs of interaction can be computed, does this really mean that everything is so ratcheted down that employee morale is destroyed, staff turnover is high and consequent customer attrition rates are increased? Are customers really that price-sensitive? In many cases customers will happily pay a little more for a higher-quality service. Those marketers prepared to buck the trend and innovate stand to win. A South African bank switched the incentive base of their call centre agents so that they were rewarded on the time spent on the phone. Average call time went from 2 minutes to 15 minutes, costs doubled, but revenue went up fivefold.

BRANDS THAT ATTRACT POST-MATERIALISTIC CUSTOMERS

Investing in quality can also pay off for the brand in other areas. In the UK the Cooperative Bank, a relative newcomer to the financial services sector, chose to position its brand along ethical lines: it became the 'ethical bank'. When surveyed in 1998, 90 per cent of its employees felt proud to work for the Co-op. In 2003 the bank ran a long-running series of adverts aimed at taking the high moral ground with customers unsettled by competing banks' rather dubious record in investing. At the absolute heart of the Co-op's brand, like all brands, was trust. In order to have the credibility to claim ethical status the Co-op Bank had to spend a lot of time, hard work and money divesting itself of any links with questionable companies. At the end of the day this paid off in two ways. First, the brand had a unique, differentiated appeal. Second, its ethical investments proved to be highly profitable for its customers.

The rise in interest in ethical practice has been marked, in particular in the 'green' and environmental arenas. According to futurologist company The Future Foundation, about 40 per cent of customers say that they are influenced by ethics in their purchases, a rising trend. This has yet to translate into mass purchase behaviour. FairTrade, an organization that labels products to encourage customers to buy from third world or environmentally friendly sources, finds it difficult to push its market share over about 2 per cent. Nevertheless the early signs are encouraging and the trend is upwards.

One reason for this could be that many companies' ethical credentials do not stack up. A number have been caught out, with high-profile damage to brands like Nike and McDonalds. Others, like Tesco, seem to have recognized the green wave early and used it positively to promote green values. Even so, many farmers struggling on wafer-thin margins take a rather more jaundiced view of the major grocery retailers. Many customers are also sceptical about the credentials of global multinationals as generous and good citizens of the world. Golden goodbyes to executives who have demonstrably failed to do a good job, while many front-line staff are paid on minimum wages, send a different message. In human behaviour, people believe what companies do more than what they say. Wal-Mart was taken to court in 2004 by female staff being allegedly paid less than male colleagues doing the same job. Meanwhile Wal-Mart's staff turnover is over 20 per cent per annum, compared to only 8 per cent at their rival CostCo.

Perhaps the lesson to learn is that big business now operates in a less forgiving, worldlier-wise environment. Corporate behaviour is under public scrutiny more than ever before. A promise or a claim about ethics and standards made in a headline-grabbing way is easily undone if actual practices demonstrate the opposite. Connectivity between policy and practice is everything if the brand image is to be convincing.

HOW TO REVOLUTIONIZE THE BRAND

Kick-starting the process of revolutionizing brands

The first thing to do is to complete a thorough customer and competitor audit, designed to answer the question, 'What business are we in?' Intensive workshops of cross-functional groups of employees are also important. People need to be encouraged to think in marketing, not product terms. It is important to understand whether you are selling sausages or sizzles. For example, through this sort of process, Revlon understood that although it was selling perfume, customers were buying hope. Hence Revlon defined itself as being in the hope business. How do companies identify the drivers for their brand? For example, when British Airways decided to remodel its first class and business class cabins to provide flat beds for travellers, the decision was important and expensive. Where can trade-offs be made between features and attributes? For example, one fast food company discovered that customers were more interested in speed of service than convenience of payment. It therefore abolished credit card payments for its drive-through service to accept cash only. This increased speed of service (and customer loyalty) without losing any apparent benefit.

The technique used to identify these attributes is based, once again, on operational analytics. Using an approach similar to that described in Chapter 3, companies use conjoint analysis and structural equation modelling (also known as pathway analysis) to quantify the broad relationship between brand benefits and product attributes. Starting with customer research, focus groups are used to develop questionnaires which then probe up to 250 different brand attributes. The tangible and intangible attributes that are then uncovered are then linked to loyalty behaviour using factor analysis. The ensuing mathematical modelling allows the company to identify, in quantified terms, the relative impact on customer behaviour of each brand preference. This is complex (and expensive) but it has the overwhelming merit of being another technique that allows a company to measure, in money terms, the impact of brand initiatives on customer loyalty. This also simplifies the problem of making touch-point trade-offs. Do we trade off a faster check-in against, say, bigger baggage allowances?

Having completed this audit the company is now ready to move into branding. The secret here is to encourage people to think in terms of brand stretching. What new markets could the brand succeed in? Again this exercise must be done very thoroughly with both qualitative, exploratory research and quantitative studies that attach money to outcomes. The whole essence of brand revolution falls out of a combination of a thorough audit and brand stretching.

ENSURE EMPLOYEE COMMITMENT AND BUY-IN

Once the key brand attributes are identified, it is vital to get employee commitment to the brand. Rallying people internally and externally around the brand should be one and the same thing. Businesses that work well understand this. There is no chance of pulling off brand revolution without a strong brand and without a realistic programme aimed at introducing genuine change. Board members might well agree changes which are transmitted to middle managers who receive them without enthusiasm. These are then passed on without commitment to work teams who promptly ignore them as just another initiative that will soon be forgotten. This kind of cynicism is corrosive, leading to lowered energy levels, a lack of focus and an inability to react quickly when it does matter.

Starting with a strong brand and high trust between board and staff, any change is much more straightforward to introduce. Employees of Ben & Jerry's ice cream or Virgin Atlantic airlines are proud to work for their companies to start with. They will commit to change because they want it to succeed. At the time of its huge corporate losses in 1993, IBM people got behind the changes introduced by the new CEO. IBM used its values and e-business concept to re-establish the brand through all its communications and business strategies, both internally and externally. The entire organization was realigned around the concept of e-business. The brand revolution was further driven through the aggressive consolidation of marketing agencies by the creation and enforcement of brand guidelines to ensure consistency and image control. This approach is also used by companies ranging from Boots through Nestlé to Dior. It was employee commitment that achieved the most impressive brand value recovery in the history of brands, from 248th to 3rd worldwide in a matter of years. If employees feel that they work for a big faceless corporation, the only way to get genuine, emotional buy-in to a new way of doing things is through demonstrable strong and determined leadership.

BRAND BENEFITS FOR EMPLOYEE RECRUITMENT

People like to work for 'big brands'. Indeed one of the secrets of success for many franchise businesses is that they allow small businesses to look like big ones. This gives confidence to both staff and customers. Working for a small, local car hire company may not seem to offer much security. Working for Budget Rent-a-Car is a totally different proposition.

The founder of Honda was once asked how he originally decided that Formula 1 motor racing would be a good branding tool. He replied that he did not think that way at all. His reasoning was that engine technology is a core competence of Honda and he wanted to recruit the best engineers. Formula 1 was a very good way of attracting staff. Great brands come from core competences. Great brands then attract great people, who further strengthen the brand in a virtuous circle. The point is that you do not start by considering how to communicate the company's products or services as a great brand. It is essential to build on solid foundations, then brand performance will be sustainable. The story of Skoda, one of the most remarkable brand revolutions of recent times, is an illustration of how an apparently destroyed brand can reinvent itself, brilliantly, around the talents of its people.

Case study: brand revolution in action – Skoda Automotive

What do you call a Skoda with a sunroof? A skip. Why do Skodas have heated rear windows? To keep your hands warm while you push it. How do you double the value of a Skoda? Fill it with petrol. Thanks to the incredible turnaround of one of Europe's oldest brands, you do not hear these jokes much any more. These jokes were the star turn of the early and mid-1980s, when Skoda reached its lowest point. It is gone from these depths to ranking number two in the UK on the JD Power survey of quality and performance in 2005, with almost the highest customer satisfaction rating in the industry. Indeed the baby is so successful that it is even worrying its parent Volkswagen that Skoda sales may attract buyers from VW's other marques. How did it turn around so fast?

If you take a trip to Prague Airport you'll find out how proud they are of Skoda in the Czech Republic. Skoda is one of the world's oldest car marques and started making motorbikes before 1900. Before the Second World War, Skoda was one of the premium brands in Europe, best described as the equivalent of Mercedes in Eastern Europe. But after the war Skoda's factory fell under communist control and unfortunately this signalled a distinct and steep decline in quality and investment in the product. The nadir came in the 1970s when only Ladas in Europe had lower book values (the cheapest used Lada was available for £10!)

The turnaround in Skoda's fortune started with its takeover by VW in 1992. Investment began but they knew they had a long way to go to reinstil trust in the brand. VW understood that it would have to be patient. Brand myths have a life of their own and the negative Skoda brand would lag well behind the reality. The starting point was the product. VW told Skoda to concentrate on two areas, innovation and product quality. The jewel in the crown of Skoda's manufacturing facility was assembled at Mlada Boleslav, 40 miles north east of Prague in Bohemia. Opened in 1996, the Octavia facility was built to exploit the 'fractal' manufacturing concept, based on small team working and just-in-time principles. 'Fractal' refers to the way in which the main assembly plant and its suppliers physically intermesh.

Employees are encouraged to take leadership for quality. They are grouped into 25 teams of between 8 and 12 employees where each member has equal responsibility for producing work that is free from error and for overall quality control. Interestingly, management and assembly workers have close contact because all admin functions are housed in glass-walled offices in the centre of the plant. Skoda's cost and price advantage over European rivals is secured by the low labour costs in the Czech Republic. Skoda itself pays its workers well above the local averages.

Skoda's innovative product designs have stemmed from Belgian Dirk van Braeckel who has been the top stylist since 1994. Thomas Ingenlath is now Skoda's chief designer and was responsible for the design of the Fabia world rally car. 'To become a Skoda designer, people must possess something extra', says Ingenlath. 'If a student came up with an idea that might be too crazy for someone else, it may interest us. We like unusual people and we can offer them the opportunity to develop their craziness.' Ingenlath believes that it is vital to understand the company's history to understand the brand. He explains that there is a balance to be struck between keeping true to the brand heritage and at the same time pushing the creative boundaries. Ingenlath's attitudes illustrate the self-confidence within Skoda's workforce. Ingenlath talks enthusiastically about the Czech heritage of Skoda but also explains the design essence of Skoda, the front grille: 'You can tell it is a Skoda when you look into its face.' The grille belongs to the long history of the brand; a 100+ year-old company has authenticity.

The Skoda brand front line is its dealerships. In the UK these are franchised, as in much of Western Europe, but Skoda exerts considerable control of service quality standards. Prices for different types of service are fixed and freely displayed behind service counters. Skoda dealers make a point of delivering every standard of personal care, quickly getting on good personal terms with their local customers. They know and understand the link between repairs and repurchase. Look at Skoda's loyalty figures. Over 80 per cent of Skoda buyers go on to rebuy. This compares to mass market averages below 40 per cent for the big players.

Skoda's advertising has itself been singled out for praise. The company has played a long-term game, understanding that revolutionizing a brand which plummeted to such depths that it became a national joke is not an overnight job. The ads started where the customer was in the late 1990s, deeply mistrustful and unwilling to be seen in a Skoda. They played on this in a gentle and humorous way. Dominic Mills of Campaign magazine explains. 'In the latest campaign, a new employee's first job is to attach *Skoda* badges to cars rolling down the production line. After a few Fabias, he gets the hang of it. But when the Superbs appear he stops, convinced they can't possibly be Skodas. The alarm sounds and the line is reversed. The end line appears. It is a Skoda too. Honest. It is classic Fallon, classic Skoda: beautifully shot and acted, charming and it makes its point.'

The advertising is designed to confront the issue of customer embarrassment with the brand head on. Agency Fallon, working with direct marketing specialist

Archibald Ingall Stretton, created the $6 million launch for Skoda's Fabia small car with ads carrying the self-effacing tagline, 'It is a Skoda. Honest.' This has pervaded much of its advertising since 2000. A direct-mail piece to Skoda owners was designed to look like a letter from a fellow Skoda buyer, with favourable press clippings attached. In _Advertising Age_, Britt reported on two ads in 2002 which featured potential customers who know a Skoda makes sense, but are still too embarrassed to own one. The tagline: 'It is a Skoda, which for some is still a problem.' In one of these ads, a customer hurls himself out of the car and runs into the woods when the salesman pulls over to let him drive. In the other, a woman about to buy a Skoda sneaks out of a dealership when the salesman fetches coffee. Direct marketing featured heavily in the 2003 launch of the new executive Superb, targeting the company manager who draws up the list of company cars employees choose from. One print piece listing Skoda's features reads, 'Damn. If there are still people hoping to find a reason not to buy the Skoda Superb we have some bad news.'

In the end, Skoda's story is an illustration of the power of brands, both good and bad. Skoda now enjoys over 2 per cent share of one of the most competitive car markets in the world, selling over 35,000 units per week. But a February 2000 study found 60 per cent of respondents insisted they would never buy a Skoda even though the cars themselves scored incredibly highly on JD Power & Associates' customer satisfaction surveys. Out of over 160 marques tested in the JD Power survey, Skodas regularly feature in the top ten, alongside Honda and Toyota. See Glover (1999), Britt (2002), Mills (2003).

THE ESSENCE OF THE BRAND

Brands were originally created in order to be able to differentiate what we offer from what the competition offers. We 'branded' it to avoid confusion and aid the choice of purchase. Branding increasingly became the basis of differentiation and the focus of competition. The problem is that, like any strategy, sooner or later everybody used branding. This is not the end of branding but the birth of a revolutionized branding.

A strong brand should fulfil three basic objectives:

- _Information_ – because it should tell us something about the product offered that is intelligible and decipherable. What is the basic value, or of what does the product or service consist?
- _Differentiation_ – because what it tells the customer should be perceived as different by the purchaser.
- _Seduction_ – because this is the raison d'être of any brand. The first two are in the service of the third. In the end a brand has to tell us

something that customers consider to be interesting and they are therefore seduced.

Numerous brands have reached the first stage; few have reached the third. This is because communication has been confused with brand creation or management. As a result, many customers have ceased to believe in the so-called traditional brands – the brands that have become stuck with classical management models, or brands that talked to their consumers from a pedestal, with a certain arrogance. Even global brands which have lacked sensitivity to detect small local opportunities. To revolutionize the brand it must have five characteristics:

- *An emotional as well as a real offer.* A good product or service is a minimum prerequisite to compete. However, if the brand is to be clearly differentiated, it will certainly have to have an emotional part that distinguishes it from the rest. A brand is made up of a good basic product plus a good dose of magic. For example, think of a Haagen Dazs ice cream or a cup of Blue Mountain coffee from the Jamaica Coffee Shop.
- *A feeling of community.* The true success of a brand is based on creating a shared experience for a group. This customer portfolio is the most valued asset of any company. Harley Davidson has achieved this, as has the Apple computer corporation.
- *Resonance with the values held by the consumer.* Customers are increasingly well trained and informed in today's world and we are less and less willing to buy a symbol-brand. Brands such as the Co-op bank show that socially responsible companies can achieve a direct, emotional connection with the consumer.
- *Communication that goes further.* Only the brands that communicate in a different manner manage to impress, to go beyond the medium being used to position themselves in the minds and hearts of people. Guinness and Carlsberg are examples of brands using a creative appeal that breaks the barrier of indifference to advertising messages that most people erect.
- *An obsession with small details.* An insignificant detail can have a tremendous impact on the perception of the product. Operational analytics can be used to model brand attributes and discover which are most likely to affect the customer and how changes to those attributes will impact on the bottom line.

Brands that are appreciated listen to the customer, enhance the customer experience. The communication should become a dialogue not a monologue. New technology transfers part of the power to the customer so that they can give their opinions, make a counter-offer, or even make judgements on the decisions of the big brands.

As Ollé and Rui from the Esade Management School put it, Actimel does not sell fermented milk but the ability to strengthen your defences against external aggressions; a VW Beetle is much more than a compact car; a Palm Pilot[4] is almost like a Game Boy[5] for adults; a Hallmark card is the possibility to communicate a feeling; Evian is the purest, most crystal-clear water in the world; Disney sells you eternal youth. Tell me how much magic your product communicates and I will tell you whether you have a powerful brand.

NOTES

1. Stella Artois is a registered brand of Interbrew.
2. Smithwicks is a registered brand of Guinness.
3. Oldsmobile is a registered brand of General Motors.
4. Palm Pilot is a registered brand of PalmSource Inc.
5. Game Boy is a registered brand of Nintendo.

7

Customer relationship management

MARKETING AT THE HEART OF THE NEW CRM AGENDA

We have seen in the preceding chapters how the increasingly powerful consumer is creating pressure that is forcing a radical change in marketing – a real *marketing revolution*. Those changes in marketing are also placing marketing at the heart of CRM. This repositioning is being driven by three factors:

1. *Marketing as an organizational competence.* Marketing is becoming a competence rather than a department. Effective marketing now needs enabling processes, speed and scale, technology support and less push, more pull. This is no longer being provided through just smart people or a single function (eg Tesco). Doing this requires the classic CRM strategy approaches like the change wheel (see Figure 7.1 below) and process design skills, as well as industry specific experience.
2. *An increased focus on communications execution.* Marketing expense is now a huge percentage of operational costs – 66 per cent more

than IT. Few companies have systematized their execution or evaluate their activity against ROI (return on investment). This leads to expensive and slow execution and an inability to prioritize activities. Marketing needs defined, best-practice working and system support. The development of new best-practice marketing methods and partnership between companies such as IBM, Unica, Aprimo and Ogilvy are creating new answers.

3. *Insight-based interaction with consumers.* As broadcast messages lose their reach, are filtered out and become increasingly costly, and consumers expect dialogue not monologue, relevance becomes critical to communication as contact is increasingly by choice. Marketing needs to integrate more closely with operations and manage the data and processes that enable communications.

This new CRM agenda sees marketing as 'top' of the corporate agenda – for revenue growth. CEOs around the world are looking to grow revenue profitably and to build a more responsive, customer-

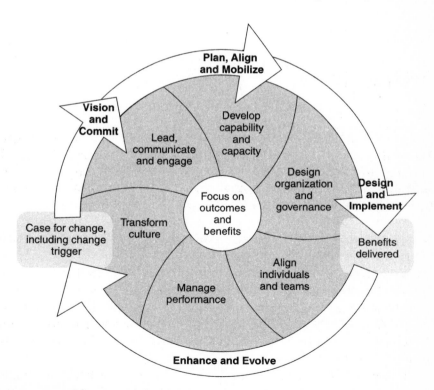

Figure 7.1 *The change wheel*

147

focused organization. Research shows a strong correlation between business performance and the way a company manages its customers. This is why far from being 'yesterday's fashion', the implementation of CRM is again a top item on today's agenda for many companies.

'CRM' is one of those marketing phrases that takes on a life of its own depending on the vested interests of the writer. Consultants will promote it as a philosophy and strategy that will solve their client's headaches, academics focus on its relationship-building aspects, others use the term interchangeably with direct marketing. CRM is important because rarely in history has so much money been spent by so many companies on improving their marketing. The sheer size of the budgets has concentrated the minds and attention of CEOs on marketing as never before. This is highly significant. The size of the investment has forced senior managers to focus on what marketing departments and marketers actually do. Here is both an opportunity and a threat for the marketing profession: can they meet the challenge? The good news is that a growing amount of research and real case study evidence indicates that CRM works – done right it can make a major impact on business performance. The same research has for the first time identified and quantified the differences between success and failure in the use of CRM. So the conjunction of circumstances offers marketing a unique opportunity.

DEFINITIONS OF CUSTOMER RELATIONSHIP MANAGEMENT (CRM)

CRM is a business strategy comprised of process, organizational and technical change whereby a company seeks to improve the management of its own enterprise around customer behaviours. It entails acquiring and deploying knowledge about customers and using this information across the various touch points. This should result in increased revenue and operational efficiencies. The idea of revolutionizing your business using CRM is deceptively simple. Instead of pushing products at an amorphous mass, the market, you start with customers. You manage relationships with them, meeting their needs with your services. In other words you go from product push to customer pull.

Small firms often do this as a matter of course, but as companies grow and start creating departments, it all gets much more difficult.

This is because the natural thing to do is to organize around things you can control, products, rather than things you cannot, customers. So why all the fuss around customer management? The answer is that done well, CRM can be a huge force for positive change in the organization, realigning it to a philosophy of customer orientation that is profitable. Gamble *et al* (2003) offer this definition: 'CRM is an enterprise wide commitment to identify your named individual customers and create a relationship between your company and these customers so long as this relationship is mutually beneficial.'

ELEMENTS OF CRM

Figure 7.2 summarizes some of the key elements of CRM.

As companies start down this journey they hit on a number of philosophical questions such as, 'Who owns the customer?' ie, which department. The answer is everyone and no one. Successful customer-oriented companies put the customer at the heart of all their business processes. This means that CRM must be espoused both by the board and by employees. Another stumbling point is, 'What part of the relationship do we have to manage?' Again the answer is the whole relationship. Imagine a human relationship where you only manage the 'dating' and pass on what happens next! From a business

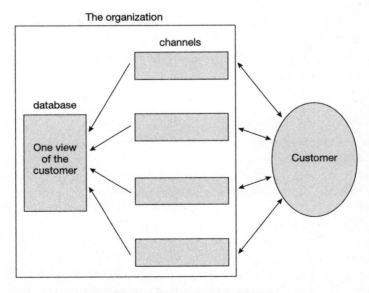

Figure 7.2 *Key elements of CRM*

149

point of view of the customer this means acquisition, retention, cross-sell, up-sell, channel effectiveness and customer experience management and win-back. Of course that encompasses the whole of sales and marketing. It also includes customer service, field service support and brand management. More than that, it extends beyond the firm because of the need to integrate with the supply chain or product fulfilment. If this seems too difficult, it is worth noting that some companies such as the packaging company TetraPak or Federal Express already define customer management in this way from a business process point of view. The complexity and difficulty of getting this all right, both from a business strategy and a technical point of view, is perhaps greater than many managers accept. Perhaps one of the key challenges for marketers is the marriage of marketing, technology and data needed to make this real. Fortunately there are several company alliances that are now tackling these very issues that can be called upon to help.

At the heart of CRM is the notion of 'managing customers' over time. A customer database captures individual customer details at the first sale. This begins the relationship with that customer; subsequently we need to treat them differently over time in order to generate repeat business. Another early consideration for CRM is the idea of improving the interface with customers. A choice of channel options is possible. Each organization aims to present a unified, consistent face to the world no matter which channel is used; hence the customer database must be independent of any one channel. This is harder than it sounds, with big firms taking three or more years just to realign themselves around these principles. A few years ago if you rang up a bank or an electricity supplier to order a new service, then walked into their retail outlet the next day, there was little hope that your order record would be known about, or that staff would be able to help you. Companies that have successfully installed CRM systems will allow 'live' processing of customer enquiries irrespective of the channel chosen – retail, telephone, internet, sales force or whatever. Given the low level of service standards often found in practice, this channel-free 'customer management' may be a source of competitive advantage.

Recent work by the Future Foundation suggests customers want a two-tier approach to company contact. CRM creates a 'skin' that surrounds the organization allowing people to navigate as far as they can themselves. The second tier then offers people-based help if they need it (see Table 7.1).

CRM has without doubt had huge impact in the last 15 years, with billions of dollars spent on it worldwide. However, it's been far from

Table 7.1 *CRM approach steps*

Critical area	Activity
Corporate governance	CRM strategy and value proposition
Organizational alignment	Business case and ROI
Budget process management	Change management
Capabilities and risk assessment	Implementation road map
Development of metrics	Process change
Customer data integration and data ownership	Prioritization of company initiatives
Customer needs analysis	Internal stakeholder assessment
Technology implementation	Senior executive and opinion leader buy-in

a smooth ride. Many companies have not achieved the return on investment they expected, and many CRM projects have been aborted or left to die a lingering death.

THE UNDERPINNING PRINCIPLES OF CRM

As long as 50 years ago, writers like Theodore Levitt in his seminal paper about marketing myopia pointed out that 'the purpose of business is to get and keep a customer'. By turning our attention to customers we can clarify how a business makes money, illustrated by Figure 7.3.

CRM theory explicitly recognizes the economics of customers over the lifetime of their contact with the business. Acquisition is expensive and usually loss-making; it is hard to attract new customers. High retention rates are usually crucial for long-term profitability; repeat customers usually cost less to service and buy more. This is not always so, but the core principles remain sound. The point about CRM is that it focuses the business on managing these economics, eventually leading to a changed mentality: measure profit by customer not by product. Sadly this self-evident truth can be hard to find in practice. The problem lies not just in departmental politics but also with technology and data. According to Forrester, while 98 per cent of companies recognize the value of an accurate single-customer view, only 2 per cent claimed to have built one successfully. Think of the task facing, say, a retail bank. It needs to manage data acquired from literally around the world, run its day-to-day applications and remain compliant with complex, internationally varied regulations. To do this cost-effectively is not simple. It is only today that

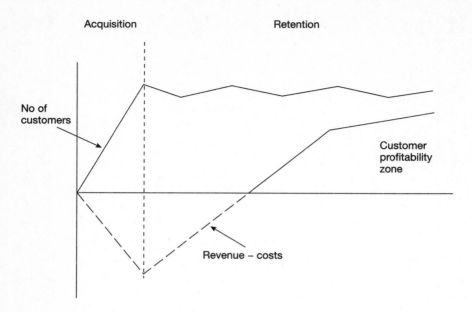

Figure 7.3 *Customer economics in CRM*

applications and data technologies are enabling leading companies to build a virtual, single-customer view and establish lifetime value figures. This was not possible, for instance, in retail banking even as recently as 2003.

Why is loyalty profitable? Fred Reicheld (1996) of consultants Bain & Co. has set out clearly the link between loyalty and profitability. Table 7.2 illustrates the point.

The table examines the relative profitability for a company that improves its retention rates from 90 per cent to 95 per cent over seven years. The retention rate is the percentage of customers at the start of the year, who remain with the company at the end of the year. The figures compare the situation of 100 customers over a seven-year period. Each customer costs an average of £30 to recruit. Each customer that leaves has to be replaced, at cost to the company. Each customer is worth £10 per annum in gross margin. Net present value calculations are ignored for the sake of simplicity.

In other words, a 5 per cent increase in customer retention leads to a 45 per cent increase in cumulative profit over the seven-year period. Reicheld found that a small increase in retention rate had a hugely disproportionate effect on profit in every sector examined. Most spectacular of all was the credit card industry, where a 5 per cent increase

Table 7.2 *The importance of customer loyalty*

90 per cent retention

	Yr 1	2	3	4	5	6	7
100 customers recruitment costs	3000	0	0	0	0	0	0
Replacement costs if 10 leave each year		300	300	300	300	300	300
Margin @ £10 per customer per year	1000	1000	1000	1000	1000	1000	1000
Cumulative margin	−2000	−1300	−600	+100	+800	1500	**2200**

The final cumulative profit of 100 customers at 90% retention is **£2200**

95 per cent retention

	Yr 1	2	3	4	5	6	7
100 customers recruitment costs	3000	0	0	0	0	0	0
Replacement costs if 5 leave each year		150	150	150	150	150	150
Margin @ £10 per customer per year	1000	1000	1000	1000	1000	1000	1000
Cumulative margin	−2000	−1150	−300	+650	1500	2350	**3200**

The final cumulative profit of 100 customers at 95% retention is **£3200.**

Source: Tapp (2004).

in customer retention led to a profit improvement of 125 per cent! This highlights the importance of acquisition costs on profitability. One major financial services company found the average acquisition cost per customer for loans was £280. Acquisition costs per customer in credit cards are typically £50 or more. In insurance they are often over £100. Clearly, the more customers that can be retained, the less costly acquisition activity.

Mature satisfied customers give more referrals. Referred prospects in turn convert at a higher rate than prospects recruited 'cold'. In addition, most loyal customers buy more from you when they get to know you better. They are also less price-sensitive. Customers of a car dealer may start with a basic car service but loyal customers may move on to valeting, warranties, hire cars and so on as they get to know more of the dealer's business and to trust them more.

These rules are not inviolate. Reinartz and Kumar (2002) actually found little or no evidence to suggest that customers who purchase steadily from a company over time are necessarily cheaper to serve, less price-sensitive, or particularly effective at bringing in new business. Sometimes short-term customers are very profitable but not worth chasing because they would not come back. Sometimes long-term customers are basically unprofitable. Table 7.3 illustrates the characteristics of some of these less profitable segments.

From a CRM point of view Reinartz and Kumar's work is not bad news by any means. There is probably still some truth in their assertions about loyalty. The point is to manage each customer according to their profitability. A data-mining strategy using customer transaction data is a sound approach that helps to identify who is profitable and who is not.

Customer management is not just about profitability; it is also about market leadership. Nowadays, to win the battle for market share and become market leader you have to win the battle for high-value customers. You have to win that segment of customers, be it 2,000, 50,000 or 100,000, that make all the difference. A study conducted by OglivyOne analysed 16,000 brands all over the world. What they found is that in every market and every category, brands do not differ that much when it comes to the occasional buyer or when it comes to the average buyer. The difference between a market leader, the number two and number three is down to a very small group of high-value customers. A brand leader always finds ways to bond better with that small group. When very few customers decide on whether you gain market share or lose market share, the vital question is, 'How does your company bond with them?' This is the realm of CRM because it requires databases, data mining, customer analytics and campaign management.

Table 7.3 *Some fickle customer segments*

Segment name	Description	Marketing strategy
Strangers	Customers who have no loyalty and bring in no profits	Identify early and do not invest anything
Butterflies	Customers who are profitable but disloyal	Milk them for as much as possible in the short time they are buying from you
True friends	Profitable customers who are likely to be loyal	A softly-softly approach
Barnacles	Highly loyal but not very profitable customers	Find out whether they have the potential to spend more than they currently do

Source: After Reinartz and Kumar (2002).

A second consideration in today's world is that there are no product advantages any more. It is a world of product parity. There is no such thing as a product brand any more; every brand is a service brand. So customer experiences drive success, they drive brand equity, they drive the bottom line. Whether they want it or not, companies have to be customer-centric. What this actually means is that they have to deliver information about customers to everyone who is in touch with the customer, over the net, via the call centre or at the branch office. CRM technologies are needed to provide the information at each touch point, 24 hours a day, 7 days a week. Technology and ideas alone do not move people. The technology is simply the enabler. You still need the carriages to move people from A to B. This is the marketing revolution.

THE R IN CRM: HYPE AND REALITY

Business-to-business relationships and cooperation came to prominence thanks to the excellent work done by the IMP group. Since then many writers have tried to unpick the idea of relationship marketing. They argue that the use of 'hard-sell' tactics is misguided and that customers demand more quality in their relationship with their suppliers.

Relationship marketing is best understood by following a story of what might happen when two businesses start to interact with each other. Imagine an IT executive meeting up with, say, a hotel manager for the first time. The hotel needs a new accounts system put in place and the manager is happy to chat it through. The dialogue begins. They have a series of meetings, phone calls, e-mails. After a while they find they have some personal things in common, both enjoying football. This becomes infused into their business conversations. An agreement is reached about the new system but the IT firm is let down by its suppliers, so the initial promises have to be amended. Throughout this difficult time, the IT exec keeps the hotel manager fully informed and is truthful about the delays. Both agree it is better to be 'honest in business, even if it means losing the sale'. They find they have values in common. The experience builds up trust for both parties and the hotel manager is committed to stay with the IT firm. Their interpersonal relationship improves further at Christmas when the IT firm puts on a party for its customers and the two men get together over a few drinks.

This story illustrates the key elements of relationship marketing: shared ideals, dialogue, trust and mutual respect, based on an actual relationship built up between two people. This is a concept understood intuitively by sales, but difficult to communicate to marketers. If a personal relationship is promised but all customers get is impersonal delivery, then customers will have a hard time feeling human presence in the relationship.

A vast body of writing about the relationship model of business can be summarized by two simple models:

Dialogue + mutual values + mutual interests => trust => commitment => customer retention

This may be contrasted with a typical transaction model:

Communication of benefits => transaction => product satisfaction => trust => brand loyalty

THE CONCERNS: LANGUAGE NOT SUBSTANCE?

The problem remains that a lot of CRM is not always successful. Relationship marketing is often done in a very superficial way. Implementation is often unsuccessful because the firm sees CRM as a strategic option to be tested or as a technology rather than a set of beliefs. An example of this problem can be found with a large retailer in the United States. They were told by Wall Street to implement CRM. The CEO went out and bought an off-the-shelf software package which the IT department implemented. The company continued to do business as usual and sales revenues continued to decline. Fortunately for that particular company, they eventually realized their mistake and are starting all over again by reviewing their business approach first.

At the heart of the confusion endemic in CRM implementation lies the transaction–relationship marketing dialectic. In other words, are we primarily interested in using CRM tools for better targeting, creating propositions, selling directly and avoiding wasting marketing budget? Or do we want to generate a two-way dialogue, give up market power to customers, make and keep long-term commitments and nurture that most precious of all commodities, trust?

Critics of the relationship concept such as Brown (1998) put a cynical case: 'Ponder what customer in their right mind would want to establish a relationship with a marketing organization? Do marketers really believe that today's customers, having been [cheated] for years, have concluded that marketers have turned over a new leaf and really, really care about their customers' welfare?... Something tells me that customers have probably concluded that our sobbing on their shoulders and promises to be a better boy in future are little more than pathetic attempts to elicit sympathy prior to picking their pockets... Marketers would be far better off being open about their commercial intent. We do not love you, we just want your money and lots of it!'

It is probably true that practitioners are, by and large, struggling to get past the first stages of CRM. Some companies have taken a CRM-as-IT approach, and business cases are founded on infrastructure costs savings rather than growth cases. This is no surprise to the marketing director when they fail to provide value. Just aligning the channels properly so that a common view of the customer can be obtained is hard, difficult work. Spotting and coordinating tactical selling initiatives is probably the next stage. As so often, cross-sell dominates the business case for investment. This customer who has just rung in fits the profile for a credit card but does not have one. So offer them a credit card. Nothing wrong with this, but it is as yet a long way from learn and grow together, build trust, nurture relationships. As things stand, customers may be justified in asking, where is the 'R' in CRM? Many companies are probably committing relationship fraud at the moment, or operating a CSUGBR strategy: Cross-Selling Under the Guise of Building Relationships.

HOW DOES CRM MAKE MONEY?

CRM acts for a business in two ways. First, it is a management tool that allows companies to segment, target and predict where to deploy their efforts both in selling and in relationship-based marketing. Accurate cross-selling is potentially hugely profitable: take, for example, financial services. Response rates to direct marketing for cold selling of, say, credit cards will be of the order of 0.2 per cent, yet cross-sold credit cards to current account holders may yield a 2 per cent response. This is a massive difference in profitability.

Second, CRM is there to help the customer make best use of our organization. So our inbound service can be improved. Gartner found that direct mail with cross-sell offers is typically seen as intrusive. If, however, the marketing contact is related to a customer event, such as moving home, customers regard the contact as much more convenient for them. Response rates may rise to 20 per cent. Even better, if the cross-selling effort takes place when the customer rings in to the company on their own initiative, 40 per cent response rates can be achieved. Software vendors such as E.piphany and Siebel have successfully built and marketed rule-based software to specifically assist this process in call centres.

Other priorities lie with enquirers, former customers and recent lapsers who should all be held on the customer database. They have already shown an interest in the company and its products. Indeed former customers and recent lapsers may not, in their minds, have lapsed at all. As Tapp (2004) pointed out, people drift in and out of relationships with companies without seeing this as active switching. They may have a repertoire of brands to provide variety; they may have forgotten to renew their subscription or a dozen other factors may have affected their status. The only instance in which lapsers are not the best prospects is when they have experienced dissatisfaction with your company and this has not been resolved.

CRM CAN BE PROFITABLE

Companies have been successfully implementing CRM strategies for several years and are investing heavily in CRM today. It is no coincidence that these are the same companies that set the standards for levels of customer experience and for speed in responsiveness. The leading exponents of CRM are the companies that are revolutionizing both themselves and the markets within which they operate.

Forward-thinking companies understand that CRM is a core discipline requiring process, organizational and technology revolution across multiple dimensions. It is not a single step, a single phase, or a single programme; on the contrary, it is many capabilities coming together to enable positive, fundamental change in how an enterprise approaches, manages and profits from its key relationship. One 2003 IBM study found that 52 per cent of executives believe that CRM is relevant or highly relevant to improving shareholder value. Nearly 90 per cent recognize CRM's positive impact on driving value in sales, marketing and customer service. Leading enterprises know that customer management can pay. In an increasingly commoditized world, customers' experience of a company can make or break the business.

The IBM/Ogilvy alliance is an organization that measures CRM performance and implementation worldwide. They have found a strong correlation exists between business performance and customer management. Companies can expect to gain between 2 per cent to 50 per cent increases in turnover from improving customer management. A more reliable guide is that companies can also expect a 400 per cent return on investment from well-managed programmes. Customer satisfaction is linked to profit. In their Ogilvy / QCi State of the Nation report of 2003, they reported a close correlation (0.88) between the Dow Jones and the American Customer Satisfaction Index (ACSI) (see Figure 7.4).

Ogilvy also showed strong correlation (0.8) between good customer management performance and business performance. In other words those companies that look after their customers and are truly customer-centric are more likely to return better financial results. In a global study of major corporations, IBM's Institute for Business Value found that across industries, CRM creates the most value by improving the customer experience and expanding the existing customer base. The results are highlighted in Figure 7.5.

Studies like these are showing that CRM is thriving. Companies are pursuing and executing multiple CRM initiatives and they are succeeding. On average, approximately one-third of European companies are gaining benefits from CRM, particularly in the areas of customer service, brand management and loyalty. In customer service and brand management, close to 50 per cent state that they are achieving 'some' or 'full' success.

CRM is creating value, particularly through improving customer experience and underpinning the retention and growth of existing

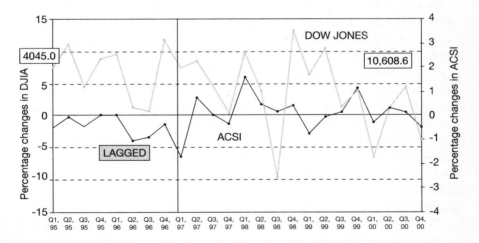

Figure 7.4 _Relationship between customer satisfaction and the Dow Jones index_

159

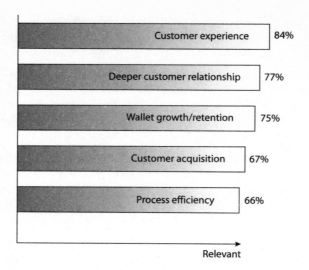

Figure 7.5 *How does CRM create value?*
Source: IBM Institute for Business Value.

customers. The profound and tangible benefits of CRM are recognized. More than three out of four European businesses determine the success of CRM by its proven customer impact, with a further 70 per cent rating it by its contribution to revenue growth. In a world that is refocusing on the top line, CRM has a critical role to play.

Most of the benefits that have been achieved by CRM are in the traditional fields: improving the retention and satisfaction levels of customers, enhancing revenue growth and improving customer insight. Yet there are still benefits which many companies have yet to tap into. Segmentation, for example, which up until now has tended to be based on a batch-based labelling of customers according to needs, is moving in the direction of on-demand segmentation. Companies can now fuse real-time deployment with 'what if?' scenario planning, resource optimization and complex clustering. This is being driven by the complexity of doing business where goals are often in conflict with each other and where constraints can be found at all levels of customer communication across the enterprise. Some leading banks have had to revolutionize their marketing and offer allocation so that it works for several hundred propositions, in real time. Entirely new types of capability are being developed in order to ensure immediate customer relevance and marketing effectiveness. Customer insight is becoming more than simple analysis and reporting. Comprising elements such as data gathering, data warehousing, analysis, data mining and predictive modelling, the results are then being made available at the point of contact with the customer. This means that it can be modified according to what the customer says or does during the transaction.

Such advanced uses of marketing and analytics are reaping rewards for leading-edge organizations. One North American provider of roadside assistance and auto services, seeking to protect market share while growing and improving customer marketing, has seen its campaign revenue increase by 68 per cent and produce an ROI of a staggering 442 per cent.

CRM IS THRIVING

Almost half of the European and Middle East participants in the IBM 2004 global survey were pursuing enterprise-wide CRM efforts. It is a major strategic focus for many companies, so getting it right is crucial. Yet one of the greatest myths of CRM is that 'most initiatives fail'. Nothing could be further from the truth. While different CRM initiatives do have different success rates, the IBM Institute of Business Value Study (2004) shows that there is less than a 7 per cent chance of failure for most initiatives. A focus on failures may not be as instructive as studying the many success stories, especially those 15 per cent of companies who are most successful. These include airlines such as Lufthansa that has implemented a worldwide CRM solution which is reducing costs, streamlining processes and achieving better time-to-market. The German airline is equipping its sales force with consistent, high-quality customer information, opening the door for cross-selling activities as well as enabling a more personalized service. Or take Poland's national telecommunications service supplier, TPS. This company is making progress in productivity, enhancing customer satisfaction and reducing churn rates as the result of its CRM customer-centric service revolution.

CRM increases value for both customers and companies. In a separate IBM study conducted in 2003 among large UK corporations, marketing effectiveness was found to be their biggest business challenge. CRM is at the heart of the marketing agenda. CRM has provided the highest positive impact in the areas of improving the customer experience (88 per cent) and in helping companies to retain and expand their customer base (75 per cent). Those remain the core business value areas. Customer service and after-sales support are the areas that have provided the greatest degree of success. These encompass the provision of standardized levels of customer services; the optimization of customer service programmes, channels and call centres; the use of customer satisfaction tools and complaint resolution processes; and the creation of win-back programmes. This may well be a blind spot in many companies that are often embarrassed to go back to previous customers. Yet such initiatives can have a high return on investment, as competitors frequently provide a worse service. In the IBM study, nearly half of the respondents stated that this had been a complete or partial success.

Companies also believed that CRM had been successful in their strategic brand management, as they seek to develop a consistent brand image built around the goals of the CRM initiative. Just under half described this initiative as a complete or partial success. This convergence of CRM and marketing is the marketing revolution.

It is not just in the fields of customer service and brand management, however, where CRM is creating value: 42 per cent and 40 per cent of respondents respectively said that they had enjoyed success with product optimization, management, loyalty and retention programmes. At the other end of the scale, the success rates of CRM outsourcing were low, 25 per cent, and the failure rate higher than average, 17 per cent, reflecting perhaps the greater complexity and scale of such projects if outsourcing is not well managed. There is some suggestion though that these rates have actually improved since 2000. There is a key lesson to be drawn from the low success rate of CRM outsourcing. CRM is not a process that should be outsourced without a commitment to business revolution.

Case study: HSBC

Banks and financial services companies are now managing more business and customer segments than ever before, juggling an increasing number of customer interaction channels and evaluating an ever-growing cast of business partners. HSBC Bank plc knew that it had good CRM solutions in place but did not have any way to benchmark them externally against other companies. IBM undertook a project to assess the bank's customer management capabilities. The bank was compared against companies within the finance sector, versus institutions in different regions and against firms noted as being 'best in class'. HSBC believes that it now talks to customers when it has identified a real need, when the timing is right and when the bank has something to offer. Products are not pushed at random. As the project progresses, the bank will be reviewing data-mining capabilities and will introduce tools that can be applied across its entire range of branches.

REVOLUTIONIZING THE BUSINESS WITH CRM

To make a success of CRM-based revolution, various steps must be taken. These include buying the right technology, making organizational changes according to the market context, and leading a culture change. This culture change must orientate people towards the outside, so that what is done is driven from the outside in, rather than the other way round. Of these three things, the technology is all too often the one that receives the most attention.

The commonest fault is to buy the technology and then think the job done. Organizational and strategic barriers are more important than technical barriers, but this is still not generally understood. Too many companies have bought the technology but avoided the more difficult organizational and cultural changes needed to make the most of the technology. According to Foss and Stone (2002), people and organizational issues are the greatest contributors, and in many cases the greatest obstacles, to the successful adoption of CRM practices. Too often big firms fragment into departments that exist as separate silos that communicate poorly with one another.

CRM requires an organizational change inside the company, away from products or silos and towards customer service delivery. Organizational changes mean people having to change who they work for and where they work. This in turn means the inevitable political jockeying for position that always happens at senior levels of the firm. Cultural changes are often even more difficult. If you have worked in a large firm you will know how difficult it is to ask someone to change the way they work, the things they do on an everyday basis. Without a shared, culturally bound vision, the implementation of CRM systems might fail because of political infighting over the ownership of systems and data.

Senior managers need to focus on the underpinning strategy behind the CRM decision or its implementation. In over 37 per cent of companies today, senior management is actually impeding the success of CRM projects. In many companies senior managers were not thought to give clear, visible leadership in achieving excellence in customer management. Only 13 per cent of senior management have regular contact with customers. CRM is a leadership issue. Currently senior management takes a pragmatic view on CRM. Nearly 40 per cent of EMEA (Europe, Middle East and Africa) companies viewed it as 'useful, not critical'. Indeed more were likely to see it as a technology function, an IT tool, than as a critical function, 'a way of life'. Such attitudes actually detract from success (see Figure 7.6). This mindset sends a message to employees that the CRM effort is not a company priority.

Senior managers listed a number of obstacles to successful CRM implementation. These included:

- Approaching CRM on a piecemeal basis rather than as a holistic investment.

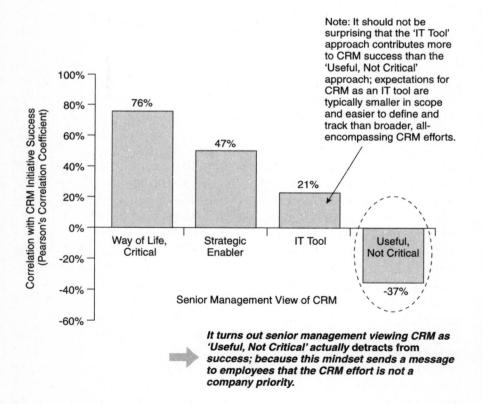

Note: It should not be surprising that the 'IT Tool' approach contributes more to CRM success than the 'Useful, Not Critical' approach; expectations for CRM as an IT tool are typically smaller in scope and easier to define and track than broader, all-encompassing CRM efforts.

It turns out senior management viewing CRM as 'Useful, Not Critical' actually detracts from success; because this mindset sends a message to employees that the CRM effort is not a company priority.

Figure 7.6 *Impact of senior management views on success*
Source: IBM Institute for Business Value.

- Continued emphasis on customer acquisition at the expense of retention. Acquisition has often thoughtlessly achieved dominance because its budgets are controlled by one department – marketing. Acquisition spending is mainly media based which is relatively straightforward to organize. Retention spending on the other hand requires cross-departmental resources in people and processes. It is of a more long-term character. Long-term projects are more difficult for companies to deal with.
- Culture change. Changing the mindset of the organization from being, say, product, production or sales led to being customer (service) led, is a long, hard road that must be driven from the CEO downwards. It is often a battle of transaction versus relationship cultures that most starkly divides companies. Has the firm introduced CRM systems to cut channel costs, increase cross-selling or create relationships? The CEO may say all three, but they are not easy to reconcile. If you are cutting retail service while at the same time preaching relationships, do not be surprised if the troops are cynical.

Perhaps not surprisingly, these symptoms are most visible in the question of ownership of CRM in an organization. Research shows that the ownership of CRM is largely in the wrong place today as the responses to the IBM 2004 survey shown in Figure 7.7 reveal.

When the senior leadership team owns CRM, from the CEO's leadership team downwards, there is a much higher success rate. Unfortunately this is only true in just over a quarter of companies. The research also uncovered a shift over time in attitudes and behaviour from the view of CRM as an IT tool or departmentally focused initiative, to a strategic enabler for the corporation and an enterprise-wide initiative.

Having the buy-in and support of the leadership team is not enough. Employees need to use CRM in their everyday activities too. One reason projected CRM returns are not being fully realized is because three-quarters of US and European companies do not fully use CRM once it is implemented. Companies today are underestimating the importance of employee alignment with a true relationship approach (only 17 per cent aligned), viewing it as a distant second to customer alignment (42 per cent aligned). Employee commitment to CRM has been historically tepid in many organizations. In order for CRM to take root in the hearts and minds of employees, some critical stakeholder issues need to be addressed. A

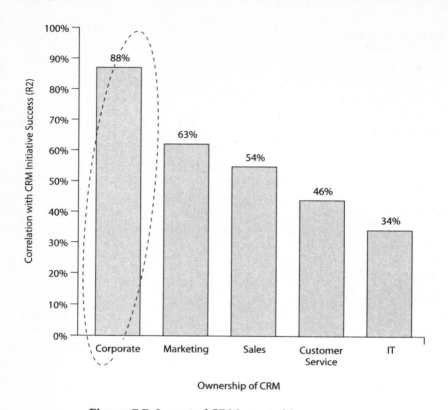

Figure 7.7 *Impact of CRM ownership on success*
Source: IBM Institute for Business Value.

CRM strategy forces an organization to rethink its functions, roles and performance metrics and, most importantly, it emphasizes the inter-dependencies between functions and people. CRM implementation will suffer unless employees are trained and empowered to manage customers within an organizational structure that is customer-focused and flexible. The importance of a strong governance structure cannot be overestimated.

Companies that are aligning CRM goals with the objectives of employees are actually realizing the most success with CRM. It is the alignment of all communities with the relationship philosophy so that each stakeholder community can realize the value that this will add, which critically determines the likelihood of a successful implementation.

Figure 7.8 illustrates what needs to be done in an area such as channel integration and optimization.

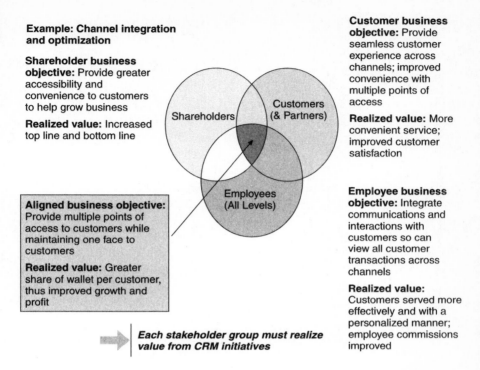

Example: Channel integration and optimization

Shareholder business objective: Provide greater accessibility and convenience to customers to help grow business

Realized value: Increased top line and bottom line

Customer business objective: Provide seamless customer experience across channels; improved convenience with multiple points of access

Realized value: More convenient service; improved customer satisfaction

Shareholders

Customers (& Partners)

Aligned business objective: Provide multiple points of access to customers while maintaining one face to customers

Realized value: Greater share of wallet per customer, thus improved growth and profit

Employees (All Levels)

Employee business objective: Integrate communications and interactions with customers so can view all customer transactions across channels

Realized value: Customers served more effectively and with a personalized manner; employee commissions improved

Each stakeholder group must realize value from CRM initiatives

Figure 7.8 _Aligning stakeholder objectives for each CRM initiative_
Source: IBM Institute for Business Value.

IF CRM IS DONE RIGHT, IT WORKS

Performing the right activities for an initiative can triple the chance of success. There are some basic steps, such as securing buy-in from senior management, analysing customer needs and managing the initiative budget. There are also some enabling steps. It is these that will spell the difference between successful and unsuccessful initiatives. Whilst the enablers are put in place less often, it is the focus and execution of these steps that can triple the chance of success. Research by leading consultancies shows that there are eight critical areas (three broad and five key) where success will stand or fall.

Broadly, there are three types of activities:

- _Foundation-building steps._ These are activities that have to be performed but which do not impact on success.
- _Contributing steps._ Activities that are important and can influence success.

- *Differentiating steps.* Activities that will make the difference in a project between success or failure.

Each of these steps build one on another. They are each equally important. Based on returns from 153 global companies, Figure 7.9 shows in a quantified form the contribution to overall success of each stage. Whilst the foundation steps only explain 6 per cent of successful results, without them (with the first stage of the pyramid as it were) the rest cannot happen.

There are four key activities that distinguished European companies that claimed success with their CRM activities from unsuccessful ones:

- *Capabilities and risk assessment.* Identifying and prioritizing of the necessary capabilities and business requirements for a successful CRM initiative or effort. Identifying and addressing risk factors in order to maximize the likelihood of success and minimize the likelihood of failure.
- *Customer data integration.* Consolidating and aggregating customer, product and partner data, cleaning and updating customer records and addressing the issue of who owns the customer data.
- *Change management.* The development of programmes to ensure employees and management fully adopt CRM and customer focus. The creation and setting of specific CRM related performance measurements, incentives, bonuses and targets. The creation of a plan for communicating CRM strategy and production of an implementation plan for all stakeholders whilst keeping everyone informed by regular progress updates.
- *Programme governance.* The establishment of an ongoing management of CRM initiatives. Organizational alignment, changing the responsibilities and organizational structure of the marketing, sales and service departments to support optimized processes and CRM business objectives.

At its heart, CRM is a change management issue and that is never easy. Over 60 per cent of companies find that change management is either a difficult or a very difficult approach step for CRM. It is the most challenging element. When asked to name the most problematic obstacle to completing CRM initiatives and performing CRM approach steps, an insufficient focus on change management was cited, by some margin, as the most frequently encountered (Rock,

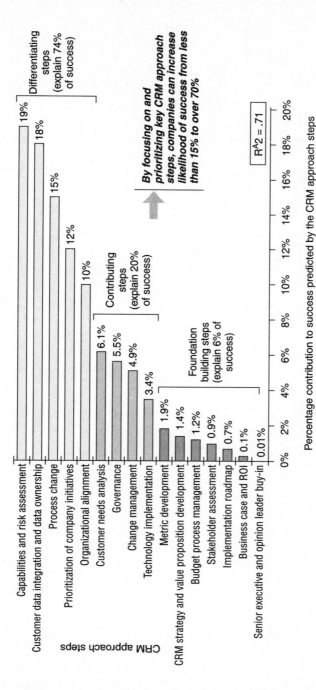

Figure 7.9 *Drivers of CRM success*
Source: IBM Institute for Business Value.

Marsella & Stone, 2004). It will be hard for companies to revolutionize their CRM processes without adequately investing in change management. Nor will simply increasing the number of change management efforts necessarily yield results.

It is a widely held, widely validated view that soft factors are the hardest ones to deal with successfully when it comes to successful CRM implementation. Process change refers to analysing, optimizing and aligning marketing, sales and service business processes to become more customer-focused. It includes aligning existing projects and processes such as marketing campaigns, lead generation, sales pipeline management and customer service with CRM business objectives. They are crucial to successful revolution and we will discuss them in more detail in Chapter 11. Technology is the most visible expenditure of a CRM development, especially since it shows up quite clearly in the company accounts but it is not the most expensive element. These are the human factors. It is interesting to reflect on cultural differences to implementation approaches that tend to highlight this point (illustrated in Figure 7.10). Whilst US and European companies tend to go straight into implementation, in Asia a consensus-based approach is preferred.

PUTTING CRM REVOLUTION INTO PRACTICE

The first message is clear: get the basics right. Recent benchmarking research (Woodcock, Stone and Starkey, 2003) indicated that many companies do not understand their current position in relation to their customers. Nearly two-thirds did not know how many high-value customers they lost. Three out of four did not know the reason why key customers were lost. Only one in ten could measure the cost to serve at a customer level. Although 52 per cent looked at the quantity of customers acquired, only 8 per cent looked at the quality. Hardly any, a meagre 4 per cent, had an enterprise-wide customer information plan. This seems very much like driving with your eyes closed then wondering why you had a crash. The complex process of introducing CRM systems into large firms falls into three major stages.

First, channels such as the web, call centre, e-mail, mail and text all have managers that tend to defend their turf very carefully. Yet all these need to be amalgamated into one integrated customer file for CRM to stand any chance of being effective.

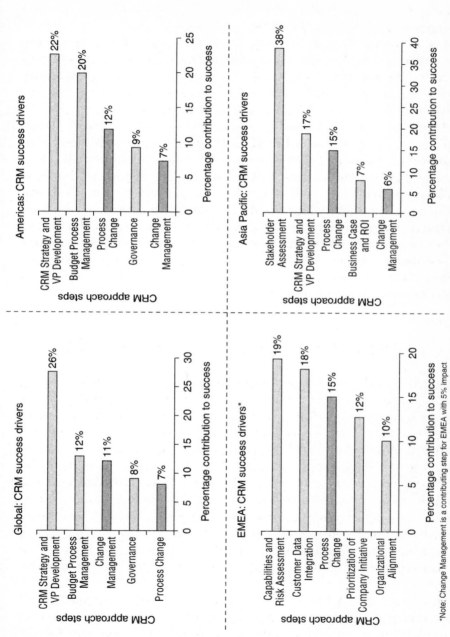

Figure 7.10 _Top five CRM steps in different regions_
Source: IBM Institute for Business Value.

Second, in order to work well CRM systems require access to financial data to give marketers the opportunity to share decision making on high-value customer account enquiries. Linked to this are database marketing systems, inventory systems to ensure that stock is controlled and call centre management systems in order to ensure that customer queries about products, support calls and the like are factored into decision making. Finally, enterprise resource planning software must be integrated into the mix to ensure these systems talk to each other.

The third complex dimension is the different product lines. These need to be similarly amalgamated so that cross-sell opportunities can be identified. However, in many companies each product has its own manager who often competes with other product managers for access to the customer. This is almost certain to happen in sectors where product or brand managers dominate. Internally competitive brands fighting each other's cultures are hugely embedded and hard to shift. If they are not resolved, the resulting nonsense can hugely damage the relationship effort. Anyone for a loan and a savings plan mailer on the same day?

The main steps can therefore be summarized as:

- *Stage 1* – customer data from each channel are grouped into one data record. This is complex and takes time to establish.
- *Stage 2* – database marketing predictive techniques are used to sell to customers efficiently. This is transaction marketing.
- *Stage 3* – introduces IT enabled CRM. Here CRM systems are part of a major, company-wide commitment to creating and maintaining relationships with customers.

If these ideas are thought about from the outset, the chances of success are enhanced. Take, for example, Smile, a UK-based internet banking start-up. This is a classic case of 'small is beautiful'. The most striking thing about Smile is effective cross-functional working. Silo mentalities have not had time to bed in and teamwork is good. Morale is high and the customer comes first.

Strong companies segment their customers by value, by how much they are worth to the firm. They also segment by lifestyle, what the firm can offer to each group. They work to understand customer motives, hence getting into benefit-led marketing. A customer proposition is generated and segmented accordingly. Weaker companies are poorly focused, they organize their data by product not customer, do lots of number-crunching but with few tangible outputs. They present a fixed customer proposition, taking no account of changing circumstance.

Cultural change

The IBM Institute for Business Value CRM study identified that the most important culturally-related changes required are:

- Training employees to use new CRM tools, processes and policies.
- Defining and communicating the CRM initiative as customer- and business-driven.
- Reflecting CRM commitment in employee performance management plans and programmes.
- Engaging change agents to support the continuing changes in CRM process, mindsets and culture.

There is no magic formula for creating culture change. The only way is through sheer hard work and careful planning. On the list of essential items include training employees to use new CRM tools, regularly communicating to target user groups the plan for using CRM, reflecting CRM commitment in employee performance management and engaging change agents to support the ongoing CRM process.

As Gronroos (1996) has pointed out, the key to relationship marketing is a recognition that it is a process, not a strategy. The IBM and Ogilvy/QCi research cited also confirms the need to focus on process. The CRM process design needs to be done with an understanding of each element of the process and how it interlocks with other sub-processes. Someone needs to be assigned to be CRM process change owner, accountable for changes. Approval and sign-off of the CRM process change must be obtained from key board members, otherwise other parts of the company in their functional silos may simply ignore it.

CRM AND CORPORATE REVOLUTION

For companies to realize the full benefits, CRM strategy must be linked closely to corporate strategy. Leading market organizations have already understood this message. Their business performance has improved as customers become more committed because they enjoy dealing with the business. They enjoy dealing with the business because its employees deliver the right customer experience within an organizational framework that is customer-centric.

The principles behind successful CRM implementation also underpin the successful management of companies as a whole. Employed in concert, they significantly increase corporate wealth. Customer management competence is becoming of increasing importance to investors. They want to get behind the headline figures of customer satisfaction, churn rates and customer numbers, all of which can be misleading. They are not looking for a simple growth message but one that communicates a complete revolution, including CRM and generating real returns from it. This is not an issue confined only to companies and their stakeholders. It can be seen just as evidently in the relationship between government and citizen.

CRM has probably been the most important marketing led change to impact on large enterprises since brand management was invented 50 years ago. With service standards falling, CRM initiatives have proved to be an invaluable tool to stop the rot and put in place the first steps for change. CRM turns the logic of reaction, waiting for users to contact us into the logic of pro-action. The firm gradually becomes more proactive and customer orientated. A mindset that places profit per customer at the forefront, changes the way revenue and costs are assessed. It provides for a longer-term view of each customer contact. The concept of customer management is powerful.

For big companies with entrenched processes and discrete channels, implementing CRM has proven to be a major challenge. Only 15 per cent of attempts to put the process in place could be fully described as a success. This is a poor return. The key success factors we have described can increase success rates massively. Buying an off-the-shelf IT 'solution' without regard for these issues is the short road to disaster. Customer insight is vital. So is sensitivity to manager and employee concerns. CRM is a vital part of the revolution programme and will act as the trigger for change.

8

From customer insight to customer action

IS MANAGING CUSTOMERS THROUGH MARKETING GOOD FOR BUSINESS?

Using customer insights to revolutionize the marketing process moves us into the realms of 'customer management', which might be thought to be nothing to do with marketing as such. After all, customer management appears to be a predominantly tactical process at first sight whereas marketing, if properly pursued, is essentially strategic. 'Customer management' and 'marketing' are widely used and often misunderstood terms that are closely related. Both activities are under the business microscope and questions are being asked about their role and function.

Marketing encompasses two main activities:

- *Proposition or offer management* – which defines what is going to be offered to the customer, when and how, under what brand and through which channel.
- *Customer management* – which offers the proposition to customers and manages their use of it.

Enterprises have and need both, but their relative importance depends on which of the four principal value disciplines – product leadership, operational excellence, brand mastery or customer intimacy – the enterprise has chosen for its principal strategic thrust. For example, brand promotion, speaking to the market about the company's brands, is core to brand mastery. Customer management, listening to customers, developing relationships with them and understanding their emotional responses to products or services, is central to customer intimacy.

Customer management might therefore be described as 'the things organizations do to plan, define, target and manage their customers before, during and after the sale, as long as a customer has any dealings with the organization and possibly after they have stopped buying if winning them back is feasible'. So customer management includes sales, customer service, direct and interactive marketing (using media such as direct mail, telephone, e-mail, the web and wireless messaging), distribution channel management and all communications with customers.

Marketing might be described as 'the things organizations do to define which customers they serve and how they serve them so as to meet both customer needs and those of the organization.' So as Figure 8.1 shows, under its traditional '4 Ps', marketing includes most aspects of customer management, as well as all aspects of proposition management. However, in its treatment of areas such as branding, product planning, pricing and distribution channel selection, marketing strikes a balance between the organization's needs such as the need for profits and surviving in the face of competition, and customers' needs, though naturally the latter are always important. The difference is one of emphasis. Customer management tends to focus more on the effect of decisions on customers, while marketing tends also to focus on the effect of decisions on the company.

That does not assume that one or the other focus is right or predominant. They are both important. The main reason for investigating these definitional issues is to help clarify what an organization needs to do and how it should be managed, rather than to achieve perfect definitions. Precise definitions are probably better discussed in the context of individual organizations and the accountability of their senior managers. It is apparent, from what has been written earlier, that there is still a strong commitment to marketing in the majority of major organizations. How this commitment is expressed in terms of, say, how members of the main board might share responsibility for

Figure 8.1 *Customer management and the marketing mix*

different aspects of marketing and customer management, is a case for an industry and an organizational context.

MARKETING AND CUSTOMER MANAGEMENT ARE UNDER THE MICROSCOPE

Marketing is at a kind of crossroads; as a discipline, it seems to have become devalued. Practitioners seem to have lost confidence in their role and their ability to add value to the organization. In terms of competitive positioning, where service might be a key differentiator, there is still a strong belief that brands are important. On the other hand, changing customer demographics and what might be called 'marketing fatigue' have led to a situation where customers see brands as increasingly similar. Customer management and customer intimacy are also seen as important, but disciplines such as customer relationship management (CRM) also appear to have lost their shine. Companies know they should understand and care for customers and they want to develop the data and the processes that will allow them to do so (for a profit) but they also know that most CRM initiatives miss their targets. At the same time, they also know that when they market well, the business does well, but when the finance director or CEO asks them what value they add, marketers find it hard to show why. They find it hard to produce a quantified measure in ROI terms.

In other words, they do not seem able to speak a language that stake-holders such as finance managers, chief operating officers or even customers can understand.

The nature of marketing has changed – more than once. Originally, in the golden age of distribution management, the aim of marketing was to sell what the factory produced. As competition became more sophisticated and more acute, marketing developed a strong focus on brands and brand promotion. In the process, it argued for and acquired some influence over products. More recently marketing has paid more attention to customers. It has developed notions of customer management, merging many of those activities with functions that had a prior claim to them, such as customer service.

Customer management became a strong business focus. Information and communications technology increasingly enabled organizations to do much more in terms of managing individual customers. The hardware and, more important, the software for managing and mining very large databases provided a tool that enabled a big supermarket chain to match and surpass the customer intimacy of the neighbourhood grocery store on the corner of 50 years ago. The consumer movement then put the spotlight on failures by organizations to use these new capabilities properly to satisfy customers. Consultants and researchers rose to the challenge to examine the cause and nature of these problems. Suppliers of systems and software designed to help companies manage their customers created a tidal wave of interest and aspiration, especially in areas like CRM. At first CRM seemed like a good solution; it certainly was a child of its time, positioning the new technologies for a more effective role. However, gradually it emerged that once again the problem at issue was not the deployment of a technology, however well done, but the management of change. Thus the wave of enthusiasm retreated and businesses once again are asking what value they are getting from their new capabilities.

HOW TO VALUE THE MARKETING CONTRIBUTION?

Marketing and customer management are challenged to prove their value. Concern about the 'value' of one business discipline or another is of course far from new. The reason that the British catering company Joe Lyons (now defunct but a great innovator for the first half of the twentieth century) turned aside from the exploitation of its implementation of perhaps the world's first application of a computer for commercial use (the famous LEO – Lyons Electronic Office – Mark 1) was that it did not see a widespread need for them. Indeed even early IBM assessments by people like Thomas Watson came to the conclusion that the world requirement for commercial computers was for around a dozen machines – globally! As their usage became more widespread, debates about the value of IT raged. Even today, questions such as 'How does a company establish an ROI for its investments in technology?' still feature in the management press repeatedly, though many of the views expressed owe more to fashion than to analysis. The value of any business activity is hard to assess because:

- There are many stakeholders for each activity: internal customers, external customers, suppliers and resource providers. Each has particular ideas about value. Actions that add value for some stakeholders may reduce value for others.
- Each activity is closely interlocked with others, so it is hard to isolate the value that each adds. CRM is a good example here. IT is a key enabler but without the right capabilities and processes in finance, operations and logistics, it can achieve nothing.
- Business disciplines, such as process management and customer management, have been hijacked by software suppliers so that the terms have come to refer to the software rather than the management discipline that the software supports. Ironically this has been achieved through clever marketing, encouraging customers to think they are buying 'solutions' when in fact they are often buying much less.

KEYS TO SUCCESS IN USING INSIGHT FOR MANAGING CUSTOMERS

Customer management affects every department of the enterprise. To instil that discipline in a 'traditional' organization, that is, one which regards customers as an undifferentiated mass of walking wallets, requires changes to systems, procedures and, above all, attitudes.

There are five requirements for success:

- set the strategic context;
- define the customers and the relationships;
- create the agenda for change;
- change the organization;
- keep up the pace.

Set the strategic context

An effective customer management initiative involves substantial direct and opportunity costs. Direct costs include customer data acquisition, marketing materials, software, hardware and the costs of change. The opportunity costs relate to the allocation of scarce resources in marketing, product management and systems people as well as in brand management and parts of the business development budget. Given the scale of the costs, the initiative must be part of business strategy. It will not succeed if it has a superficial, 'let's be nice to the customers' feel to it. Orthodox strategic thinking would position customer management as one step in a top-down progression from medium-term objectives to specific actions. Though useful as a reference model, this is rarely the reality. Most enterprises have overt or implied customer strategies, although they are not always well articulated or even coherent, so that customer management must be introduced as a modification to the existing strategy, not something new that is being added. In other words, the specific implications for change must be recognized. A commitment to customer management demands changes in customer service, sales and marketing and product or service management departments. It demands changes in processes, metrics and even bonus systems. It usually falls to the marketing function to make the case for customer management to be part of strategy. Marketing managers must ensure that they get top management commitment to the associated changes, as well as to the customer management initiative itself. Too little opposition is as dangerous as too much because it shows that executives have not understood the scope of what is needed.

Define the customers and the relationships

Once top management has got on board the customer management train, it is time to flesh out the agenda for change. A customer management initiative demands changes in many parts of the business, all driven by a better understanding of customers and the organization's relationships with them. The first step is to identify and characterize customers, including types of customers you want but don't have. The analysis must include customer profitability, as well as revenue. It was observed over 300 years ago that, 'there is nothing new under the sun' (albeit in a different context!) but it is true here that a traditional Pareto curve probably applies to the distribution of customers in many companies. Many organizations find that 20 per cent of the customers generate 80 per cent of the profits. Nothing can be done about this until the nature of this distribution has been recognized. The next step is to decide what kind of relationship the business wants. The range is from intimate through impersonal to anonymous to none. No relationship is a perfectly acceptable business strategy for some types of company (such as charter airlines with their holiday travellers). Almost no business, and certainly no mass-market business, can afford intimate relationships with all its customers. Nor do customers always value intimacy. It must also be said that sometimes a business is better off without certain kinds of customer (notably 'bad' customers such as some kinds of debtors or people who abuse service systems). The watchword here is realism.

Create the agenda for change

Now comes the real work. The business must rethink its governance, processes, metrics and rewards in the light of its decisions on customers and relationships. Most businesses are structured by business function, locality or line of business. If customers are important then customers or customer segments must appear in the structure and not just as sales territories! Then there are the processes, particularly marketing, sales and service processes. These must be defined for each kind of relationship that has to be supported, from intense key account-type relationships with very valuable customers, to near-automated processes for the large number of less valuable but very much wanted customers. The choice of supporting software comes after that. The myth that customer management is synonymous with software deployment is possibly the biggest cause of dissatisfaction with customer management. Software is a good servant but a poor master.

A customer-focused enterprise also needs suitable metrics. The metrics such as sales per customer, rates of customer churn, or customer profitability, may not be new. What is new is to report them by customer segment and to report them individually for major customers, rather than by territory or product line. No business can be said to be managing its customers unless it has meaningful performance measures. The metrics are important. It is all very well for a business to invest heavily in assigning costs and calculating profitability per segment every week. Unless someone is accountable for increasing that profitability in each segment it might as well not bother. So the rewards of the segment managers must depend on these metrics. (See, for example, Stone, Woodcock and Foss, 2002 for further ideas on metrics.)

Change the organization

These changes must be rolled out across the enterprise. People must believe in and buy into the new philosophy. (Well, it is best if they actually believe in it, but failing that, believing that management is determined to do it may serve.) So the change programme must also explain the reasons for the changes and what they involve in detail, in a way that everyone understands. The change programme must be professionally managed. Organizational change is difficult. It demands specialized methods. Communication is essential but both the content and the form need to be matched to the situation.

Keep up the pace

Customer management is not a one-off initiative. On the contrary, it requires continued attention to ensure that it remains aligned with business needs.

THE WAY FORWARD: USING INSIGHT TO ACTION THE MARKETING MIX

Traditional marketing is based on the idea of the marketing mix and takes a predominantly short-term transactional approach, using the concept of exchange. Even by the early 1980s it had become apparent that this paradigm was no longer the best framework for business-to-business marketing or even for services, where long-term relationships with customers is often critical to success. Nevertheless in many companies this perspective still dominates the marketing approach. This leads to a framework, which many researchers have tried to model over the last 25 years or so, where an attempt is made to integrate or balance the marketing posture between the 'four Ps'. Thus, for example, a high price is meant to be related to high product quality. Short distribution channels (place) are meant to be linked to point-of-sale promotion. It is easy to spot flaws with this approach. Not only are there more exceptions than rules, but most significantly it is an essentially static approach. It seeks to generalize a marketing environment in terms of its customers and its competitors. After all, price might not be an important factor at all stages of the purchase decision or for all customers. What is needed are better insights into the drivers of customer behaviour so as to be able to adjust the marketing posture in both the long and short term, more dynamically.

Managing customers through insight is not a quick fix. It can deliver real business benefits, but only when the hard work of process definition, application deployment and cultural change has been done. Customer management is not a package or an off-the-shelf solution. Managing customers through insight is not a marketing project. Marketing must play a leading role in customer management but customer management will not be effective until it changes the ways that customers are treated. Customer management will not succeed if divorced from business strategy or restricted to one function. Many business functions have a role to play and they must work together seamlessly if their goals are to be achieved. More on goals below!

Of course it is good to be nice to people, but customer management is about selectivity, about being nice to people in a way that they will appreciate and which respects them as consumers. It also seeks to distinguish categories of customer. Not all customers are equal and the more valuable the customers, the more they need care and attention. Customer management is managed change. It depends on data and the right metrics.

CUSTOMER INSIGHT DATA AND MARKETING

Earlier, we discussed the gap that seems to have opened up in some companies between chief executive officers (CEOs) and marketing managers. Something appears to be broken and needs fixing. So, what are CEOs concerned about? In 2004, The IBM Global CEO Study found that 83 per cent of CEOs considered revenue growth to be the key factor in strengthening their companies' financial performance over the next three years. Whilst CEOs identify new products and services as the greatest opportunities for growth, they realize that achieving fast, efficient growth requires introducing their existing core products into the right new channels and markets.

The call for rapid growth means that companies have to squeeze more revenue from existing products and increase market share when the opportunity arises. However, knowing what it takes to win more customers with existing products is difficult. Customers have more choices to make, and more variables affect those choices than ever before. Customer experiences touched by a company's marketing, sales, supply chain and operations strategies have an impact on why a customer does or does not buy from a company.

What does it take to increase revenue? Knowing why customers buy or do not buy is vital to addressing the urgent challenge of increasing revenue. Companies therefore need deeper insights than those provided by conventional market research. To be able to prioritize which actions can have a decisive impact on growth, companies must be able to quantify why customers make the decisions they make. Armed with insights that better explain why customers choose certain products, channels and competitors over others, companies can focus on growth by increasing sales volume and market share from their competitors.

Customer decision process modelling

Customer decision process (CDP) modelling is a combination of traditional market research and quantitative modelling which aims to achieve a deeper understanding of why customers do or do not buy. With CDP, companies use detailed customer insights to analyse why customers buy, and turn them into strategies they can use to capture market share and grow incremental revenue. Customer decision process modelling therefore provides deeper insights into customer purchase decisions. It deconstructs customer decision processes into literally thousands of tactical elements that affect decisions: from customer attitudes to competitive prices, from advertising messages to salesperson tactics and from customer emotions to product characteristics. CDP uses data on hundreds of customer decisions to measure how much impact an element has on the final purchase decision. CDP modelling can help to increase and capture a larger market share.

It is not easy to understand the basis of a customer buying decision. Both rational and non-rational behaviours are involved, some overt and easy to observe, some intrinsic and less easily grasped. A regular customer might switch to a competitor product for all sorts of reasons. Maybe he has married and his wife now helps to make decisions on key purchases. Occasionally she changes his mind, which produces a change in the decision-making process. Perhaps the preferred brand wasn't in stock, whereas the competitor's was. This produces a rational decision based on an issue with out-of-stock inventory in the supply chain. It also illustrates that in this case the brand effect was not powerful enough to cause the customer to defer the purchase in search of the brand. Perhaps the sales clerk was more informed about, or had a specific incentive to sell, the competitor's model and therefore made it sound more attractive. This means that there are issues with competitors' strength in the retail channel.

Qualitative interviews will reveal these details but it takes quantitative research to prioritize which of these possible reasons affect enough customers for a response to be required. Is it necessary to address the problem strategically in marketing terms or was it just, perhaps, an unusual situation? Maybe the sales clerk will not be on duty next time or maybe he or she was just an individual with a preference for the competitor's product.

To examine this problem requires a combination of qualitative and quantitative approaches. The initial, qualitative approach will probe the explanations for the change in behaviour. Then quantitative modelling is used to measure how hundreds of minute and exact customer choices impact on the customer decisions of when, what and where to buy. The more complex or more valuable the purchase decision, the more difficult it becomes to pinpoint why customers make their ultimate decision. This is where new marketing approaches have to play their part. For companies to achieve short-term growth a concentrated effort is needed to quantify and prioritize the critical decisions that drive a customer to buy from one company or another.

Customer decision process modelling and traditional market research

CDP applies quantitative analytical techniques to the insights into why customers do or do not buy a product or service. Thus it 'welds' together the data from separate qualitative and quantitative research studies. This is accomplished in five integrated phases as illustrated in Figure 8.2.

Phase 1: One-on-one in-depth interviews

In-depth interviews provide a crucial first understanding of how customers work through their purchase decisions. The interviews allow customers to talk about their total purchase experience in their own words. These interviews differ from traditional qualitative research in that they are entirely 'emergent', or completely open-ended, interviews. As a result, customers have an open forum free

185

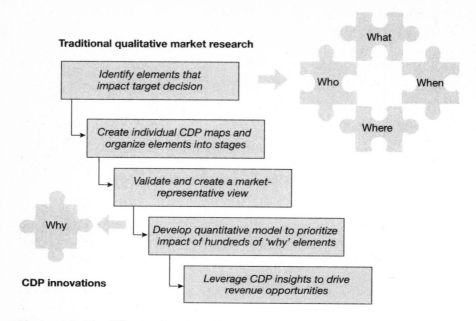

Figure 8.2 *The difference between CDP modelling and traditional market research*
Source: IBM Institute for Business Value.

from possible bias. This avoids the risk of direct questions about what customers did or did not like about a product or service, which might lead their answers in a particular direction. In addition, the one-to-one approach provides customers with an individual forum to talk frankly about their experiences in the most minute detail if they want to, allowing them to reveal the 'hidden' reasons why the customer did or did not buy from a company. Very few limitations are used to pre-qualify customers, in order to select the broadest cross-section possible of a company's target customer base.

Typical 'emergent' interviews address some basic questions. Through the customers' self-exploration of their recent purchases, the interviews identify the many elements that might impact on purchase decisions. Elements include both 'hard' influences (customer wants and needs, customer actions, competitor actions) and 'soft' influences (customer beliefs and emotions). A typical way of facilitating these interviews would be with questions such as: 'Could we go back in time to the first moment you can remember thinking about this product? What started you thinking about and looking into it?'; 'Could you tell me about your shopping experience?'; 'What shopping-related activities did you engage in? '; 'Could you elaborate a little on these things you did?' Table 8.1 describes the kind of factors that are investigated.

Phase 2: Convert these elements from individual customer decision interviews into a process map

These elements are then converted into a process map, like the one illustrated in Figure 8.3. Each map may reflect several steps or actions undertaken by the customer, brought about by the various influences or elements that impact upon the decision process. Often, the number and type of elements that do or do not impact upon the purchase decision can be staggering.

Customer process maps are then drawn together to help organize customer decisions into stages. The customer purchase process is then summarized into stages, which help to organize the elements that affect decision making. Some of the most common stages include:

- *Incubation.* Customers have identified a need and are actively seeking options for a purchase but for various reasons are not ready to buy or are delaying the purchase. The incubation stage for complex purchases can last for a number of years. Typically this might be the case for expensive products such as a boat or a house, but it may also be for less expensive products or services that would infer a lifestyle change such as a new style of clothing or a different haircut. This is a window of opportunity that

Table 8.1 _Elements that might have an impact on purchase decisions_

	Elements	Examples
Tangible influences	Consumer wants and needs	• Preferred product features
		• Preferred sources of information
	Customer actions	• Making the best choices from the evoked set: the 'evoked set' describes those purchase actions and outcomes that have been successful in the past
		• Seeking new opportunities and ideas
	Competitor actions	• Reposition pricing for products and services
		• Launch a new marketing campaign as a counter strike
Intangible factors	Customer beliefs and emotions	• The perceived reputation of the brand and attitudes to that reputation
		• Emotional drivers for the purchase (is it a gift, a utilitarian purchase, an impulse buy etc?)

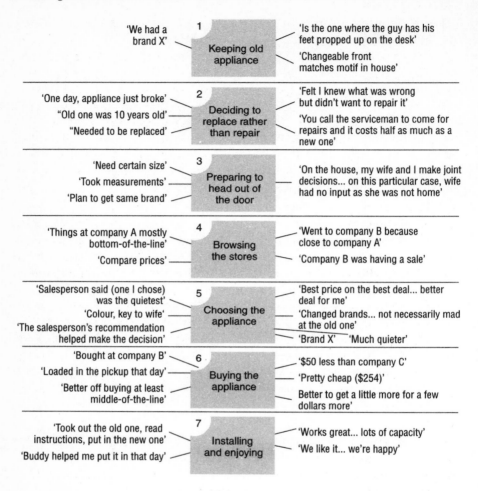

Figure 8.3 *A customer process map showing the factors impacting upon the decision process*
Source: IBM Business Consulting Services.

companies focused on a quick sale could be neglecting. For example, in Figure 8.3, (1) 'Keeping old appliance' would fall into the incubation stage.

- *Trigger.* Any number of events, including the breakdown or poor performance of a product, obtaining a new line of credit, a windfall from a raise or bonus at work, the birth of a child or even a forthcoming social event, might trigger entrance into the purchase mode. The customer is still seeking information, taking measurements and weighing product features and other variables, such as the immediacy of their need or their ability to delay gratification, even as they leave the house. For example, in Figure 8.3, (2) 'Deciding to replace rather than repair' and (3) 'Preparing to head out of the door' would be categorized in the trigger stage.

- *Shopping and purchase.* Customers shop with an intent to buy, choose and purchase a product. Customers make the crucial price-to-value trade-offs during final product selection and only shop, and ultimately purchase, at those companies that were considered positive influences during the incubation stage. For example, in Figure 8.3, (4) 'Browsing the stores', (5) 'Choosing the appliance' and (6) 'Buying the appliance' would fall in the shopping and purchase stage.

- *Post-purchase expectations.* Customers evaluate expectations of after-sales issues such as product performance and installation, repair or warranty services even before making the final purchase decision. Failure to adequately position a company's ability to deliver after-sales service can cause the loss of current as well as future sales. During actual post-purchase, which could last for several years, the customer assesses their overall satisfaction with the product. This affects future evoked sets and may change repeat purchase patterns. Thus these post-purchase assessments are an important feedback mechanism into the series of 'incubating' purchases that are to follow. For example, in Figure 8.3, (7) 'Installing and enjoying' would be categorized in the post-purchase expectations stage.

This brings us back to the problem with customer satisfaction surveys in the previous chapter. A customer might buy a competitor's product, even though content when completing a satisfaction survey, because it did not measure up to long-term wear and tear as well as hoped. Or perhaps Company A did not recognize the customer's interest in the product at the incubation stage and failed to provide the contact, advice and information needed in the months before a purchase. These issues can be explored well using CDP.

Phase 3: Validate findings of individual customer decisions by the use of a quantitative market survey

The volume of respondents participating in the quantitative surveys, from a few hundred to perhaps a couple of thousand, are used to validate which actions and influences have the broadest effects on the marketplace. They provide the depth of information necessary to identify patterns and trends in customer decision processes. The survey is structured around the stages and covers areas such as:

- *Incubation stage.* When did you first start thinking about buying a new product/service? What actions did you take during the period of time before you decided to purchase the new product/service?
- *Trigger stage.* Thinking about your purchase, what best describes why you chose to buy the new product/service at this time?
- *Shopping and purchase stage.* Which product features were in your decision to select your new product/service? Which attributes of different retailers affected your decision to shop at specific retailers for your new product/service?
- *Post-purchase expectations stage.* What best describes how you installed your new product/service? How satisfied were you with the retailers' after-sales service?

Survey questions are then built directly from elements defined in the qualitative research process (see Figure 8.4). The market survey assesses the proportion of customers whose decision processes were affected by each element. This validates how customers make decisions so that a market-representative view of the customer decision process can be created.

Phase 4: Develop a quantitative model

The survey responses are then used to map how the product selection and decision stages affect the 'target' customer decision most important to the company. For example, was it the channel where the item was purchased (such as a retail store, website or catalogue), the retailer where they purchased, the product features selected and/or the service level chosen? Next, the elements that affect the product selection, at each decision stage from incubation to post-purchase, and the target decision are mapped. This is shown in Figure 8.5.

Then CDP modelling uses sophisticated modelling techniques to identify objectively which elements exert the most influence over the purchase decision. Each element is then scored in terms of their level of impact on the purchase decision from critical to negligible. Techniques include:

- *Structural equation modelling* (SEM). A technique based on multiple regression analysis, an advanced form of linear regression or 'best-fit' models that are sometimes used to

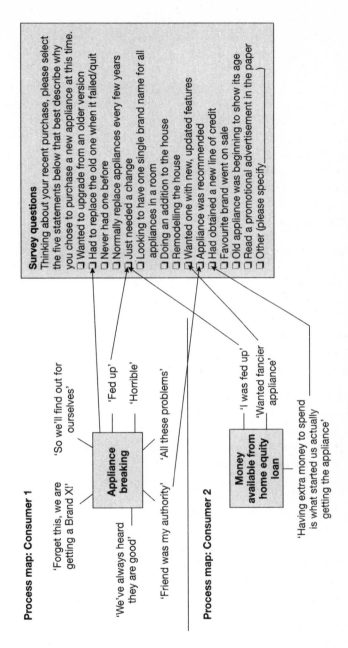

Figure 8.4 *Developing a survey based on customer process maps*
Source: IBM Business Consulting Services.

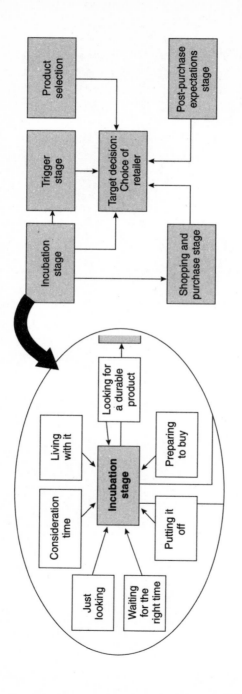

Figure 8.5 *Mapping elements that impact upon each decision stage*
Source: IBM Institute for Business Value.

determine statistical relationships between data sets. Data from SEM are used to produce the scores and convert the CDP maps into a quantitative model based on how many customers take an action compared to how many buy from a particular company.

- *Path regressions.* Tests thousands of relationships between elements and decisions. They then use cross-validation testing to find the model that has the 'best fit' for explaining why customers make specific decisions.
- *Impact scores.* Uses a standardized scale based on the SEM's coefficients to prioritize the relative 'impact' of an element on the final purchase decision.
- *Score mapping.* Assigns an 'impact' to every element-to-stage and stage-to-decision link in the CDP maps to identify which linkages ultimately impact the final decision. Figure 8.6 illustrates how this might be applied.

Comparisons can then be made across purchase decision stages to see when a specific element, such as price, brand influence or quality, most affects a customer decision. Elements often have different importance at different times in the decision process. For example, in car purchases, customers may use price during the incubation stage to set a budget expectation, then at the time of purchase, use price to

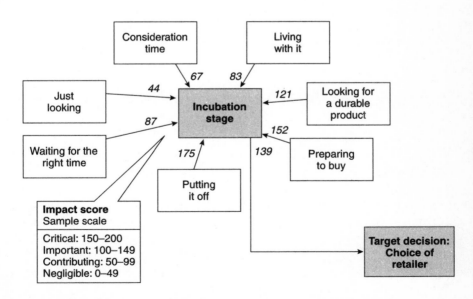

Figure 8.6 *Impact of elements and stages on the customer decision*
Source: IBM Institute for Business Value.

193

make feature and value trade-offs. They may not pay much attention to price at any other time in the decision process.

Phase 5: Leverage the CDP insights to drive revenue opportunities

A full CDP model creates a quantitatively, or objectively, derived process map of all the factors that influence customers' purchase decisions, along with their relative importance. A CDP diagram is too complex to reproduce here as it would show all the elements, linkages and importance (impact scores) affecting a choice.

Starting with a foundation of the overall market CDP model, different versions of this CDP model are then built to make the comparisons necessary to facilitate strategic decision making. If the focus is on determining why customers buy at one company and not another, then separate CDP versions are built for customers of each target competitor. Analysing the differences between the CDP version for one target company and its key competitors identifies the significant differences in why customers buy from one company versus another. An understanding of these differences is combined with other competitive intelligence to pinpoint where companies can be more effective. It also highlights opportunities where market share might be gained from competitors. Similarly, differences identified by CDP models can be combined with measurements of customer brand perceptions to identify areas where intangible perceptions, as opposed to tangible product or service differences, might drive decisions.

HOW TO TURN CUSTOMER INSIGHTS INTO ACTION

Which brings us back to the basic question: how does a company seeking to increase market share and increase sustainable revenue turn insights into action? Companies can use insights gained from CDP throughout the organization in areas such as corporate strategy, sales and marketing, information technology, supply chain management and human resources to enhance their position in the marketplace. The example in Figure 8.7 also illustrates how the 'boundaries' of marketing become diffused throughout an organization. Insights obtained from CDP modelling help to focus the entire company on revenue-building elements it can actually control to help increase sales

CDP insights

Consumers believe that the quality of installation differs between companies

Consumers want Company A's associates to be informed salespeople before purchase and then provide professional installation services after purchase

Consumers want product information in the incubation stage and the best price in the shopping and purchase stage

Consumers are most influenced by a product's style and brand and have been attracted to Company B's brand rather than Company A's brand

Consumers are looking to buy the product online

Consumers expect certain products to be in stock and other products to be customizable

Consumers are looking for assistance rather than a hard sell

Company actions

Corporate strategy
- Act on the most critical competitive gaps

Sales
- Tailor sales messages for consumer needs that differ throughout the decision process

Marketing communications
- Design communications to target consumers by stage in the decision process

Branding
- Revise advertising and branding strategies to address perceptual gaps in company performance versus competitors at the most critical 'turning points' in the decision process

Information technology
- Change areas of IT incapable of supporting consumers' most preferred buying environments

Supply chain
- Change merchandizing mix and in-stock inventory
- Align supply chain to provide customization

Organization and human resources
- Update training and identify employee skills that support assisting consumers

Figure 8.7 *Using customer insights to drive growth*
Source: IBM Institute for Business Value.

volume, drive intimacy with existing customers and increase market share over the competition by closing competitive gaps or answering unmet market needs.

Case study: a major US retail company

With hundreds of stores and billions in revenue, a leading retailer was quickly expanding across the US and could foresee issues with growing market share once store expansion finally reached saturation. The retailer was also exploring the re-prioritization of store operations, merchandising and human resource policies to keep up with a rapidly growing employee base. Although the company already used transactional data mining, attitudinal segmentation and tracking surveys for customer insights, it needed a deeper understanding of its customers to plan future incremental share growth strategies. Specifically, the company wanted to understand why customers purchased at specific retailers within four high-potential merchandise categories and help plan proactive steps for achieving share growth before expansion slowed.

Gaining market share in a saturated environment required repositioning the retailer to better compete with smaller-scale, specialty retailers in each of the four high-potential categories. CDP insights yielded two targeted repositioning strategies. The first was better customer education. In each category, significant market share (from 30 per cent to 70 per cent) was going to specialty retailers that focused on people-driven assistance and high levels of customer education early in the process – where customers have identified a need but are not ready to buy. The second strategy focused on enhancing post-purchase service messages. CDP modelling found that, for the purchase of big-ticket items, customers were strongly factoring in post-purchase expectations (eg installation, warranty) and the associated strong post-purchase reputation of specialty stores was putting the retailer at a disadvantage. From an operational perspective, CDP insights found that the role of in-stock inventory for big-ticket items differed significantly by merchandise category. CDP modelling enabled the retailer to identify required inventory changes to capture additional share. For one category, taking home the purchase the same day was absolutely necessary and more than 60 per cent of customers would switch to another retailer if take-home inventory was not available; focusing on inventory availability of this merchandise became an imperative for the retailer. For another category, having the product to take home on the same day was not required, but CDP modelling found that having sample inventory displayed for visual comparison would make or break the sale with 80 per cent of customers. Therefore improving product layout and enhancing in-store display capabilities became an important initiative for the retailer in this merchandise category.

Within weeks of using CDP, the retailer implemented customer-facing changes throughout the organization to improve win rates. In the supply chain, it made a strategic decision to maintain and increase inventory in two growing merchandise categories. In sales and marketing, it invested in a nationwide advertising campaign and test marketing in an otherwise stagnant merchandise category to highlight and improve its post-purchase installation service reputation. It also reviewed store operations and training programmes, enabling store staff to use an assistance-driven approach with customers, rather than the hard-sell approach typical to the market. It expects the combined impact of these inventory and sales strategy changes, as well as an ongoing price leadership position and related execution improvements, to capture over US$1 billion dollars in incremental revenues, most of which is based on an increased market share from 8 per cent to 9.5 per cent.

(Source: IBM Research)

MARKETING REVOLUTION: PRODUCING NUMBERS THAT FINANCE CAN ACCEPT

Earlier in the book we raised the question as to why marketing seemed to have lost its way. The answer to this was couched in terms of changes in society (new demographics, different social patterns, different life experiences) and an increased inability to demonstrate a real return from the money invested in marketing efforts. The old joke about, 'half of all advertising expenditure is wasted – problem is, we don't know which half', is coming home to roost.

CDP is not easy to deploy. It requires significant investment, large amounts of carefully collected data and a great deal of work for the analysts. However, we need to address some 'soft' questions such as:

- Why do we win the business of certain customers and lose others?
- Are we getting the right products in the right places for our customers?
- Who will be the highest-value customers in the future? Are we capable of adapting to their needs?
- Are our employees focused on the right value propositions for our customers? What needs to change in the future?
- How will we improve the customer experience?
- Do we have the necessary operational or technology infrastructure to make these changes?
- What are the turning points in customers' purchase decisions? Are our competitors doing a better job of managing these turning points?

It also helps to focus marketing decision making in areas that will strengthen the company's competitive position. To achieve these benefits, CDP starts with strategic issues such as market share growth or competitive gaps, and selects those customer decisions that provide the best information for that issue, for example, why customers choose a particular channel or retailer. It then offers ways of leveraging the answers so that changes, based on insights uncovered, can be implemented.

Of course at the end of the day, in a complex environment, it will still be difficult to draw a one-to-one line between an analysis, the interpretation of the analysis, a chosen response and a result. However, that argument remains true for all strategic and many tactical decisions, even in areas like finance and operations. It also depends on a shared commitment to implementing the solution and making it work. Thus a company-wide understanding of what has been discovered and a shared belief in the response are essential.

The road to successful revenue growth is challenging but CDP can help to manage the different elements of the marketing mix more precisely. It does this by helping the company to focus on what it takes to win the next customer's purchase in a given market. The key to success in revenue growth is knowing what will or will not sway the customer decision in your favour. However, when it comes to why customers make specific purchasing decisions, the sheer volume of data can be daunting. Literally thousands of elements can affect a single purchase. New data collection and modelling techniques capable of assimilating and analysing large amounts of data can help to transform individual insights into a real basis for managing the marketing mix. CDP modelling is a revolutionary marketing tool that blends qualitative research and quantitative modelling, and goes some way to providing a real handle on how to integrate the marketing mix.

9

Creating the capability for operational analytics

THE ROUTE TO BUSINESS SOLUTIONS THAT ADD CUSTOMER VALUE

Why do we win some customers and lose others? How can we grow revenue? These are the two vital questions that are drawing the attention of CEOs and marketing managers, like rabbits caught in headlights. With the certainty of the observer watching such an unfortunate creature, the fate that will befall them if they get the answer wrong is about the same. They will get squashed. The problem is that whilst some companies may choose not to undertake the task of obtaining and then, more importantly using, more precise customer insights, others will. Those that use techniques like customer decision process modelling (CDP), described in the previous chapter, will then offer better value to their customers because their basic marketing proposition will be more relevant. In turn, customers will choose to invest their time and effort building relationships with those suppliers that are capable of creating and delivering exceptional value. Referring back for a moment to some of the changes that have taken place in the socio-demographic composition of markets, most companies can mark some important changes in the nature of their customer base:

- *Customers are more knowledgeable.* Customers are more knowledgeable than they used to be. The media are flooded with articles and programmes about how to get the best value for money. It is also important not to forget internet sites like www.moneysavingexpert.com, www.thisismoney.com or www.uswitch.com in the UK which will provide customers with advice on how to take control of their relationship with companies, how to obtain services most cheaply and, not least, how to get the best returns on their money. Many customers are therefore constantly seeking new ways to work with suppliers to create value.

- *Customers are more selective.* Not all suppliers are equal. Many customers treat suppliers according to the value they provide. They are willing to invest time and other resources with the most competent suppliers to improve mutual understanding. Companies unable to create exceptional value are excluded.

- *The customer wants to be in the driving seat.* It was right back in 1960 when marketing managers first recognized that more or less everybody was in the service business. Signs of the emergence of customer-led consumerism, which first found expression with activists like Ralph Nader in the 1960s, have been around for many years. Of course it is still possible to find rogue traders and shoddy products but today's consumer laws and consumer watchdogs mean that any company of repute is going to offer a reliable product or service. Indeed in some cases the standards are so much higher that customers are even unimpressed by exceptional performance. You happen to have left your car in the drive for three months whilst you are working overseas. When you return, you expect to get in, start it up (first time) and drive away. If that happens, nobody thinks about the engineering that underlies such a product. It is accepted as routine. If it does not happen you tell all your friends. So exceptional performance from many products is the norm. Today it is truer than ever that service is the key differentiator. Marketers must plan from the customer backward rather than from production forward. In most markets the customer, not the product or service, is the scarce resource. Companies are therefore forced to create greater value for a smaller number of customers. From a company's perspective, becoming customer-led requires radical business revolution.

During the era of product-led consumerism, business designs were created to maximize operating efficiencies. Management resources were focused on production. Today those resources are focused on distribution. To become customer-led, companies must revolutionize their businesses. Nowhere is the need for revolution more evident than in the sales and distribution functions, although ultimately change must occur throughout the business. From the company's perspective, sales and distribution are the functions closest to the customer and, in many companies, they have remained unchanged for decades.

- _Customers expect what they find from the best._ The service standard set for a company is not necessarily benchmarked against that of a named competitor. It may not even be benchmarked by a company in the same business. Customers set their standards by the best service level they might have encountered and expect other businesses to be able to match it. If an airline can design a catering system that will provide catering to hundreds of people on a relatively short flight, why can't a train company? If a supermarket can target customers individually with a customer base of millions, why can't my health service provider?

DELIVERING VALUE THROUGH MASS-CUSTOMIZED MARKETING

The challenge for marketing managers is therefore to 'mass-customize' their marketing activities, as they are experienced by the customer through services. Services do not create exceptional customer value, they deliver it. Services create exceptional value when they are customized to satisfy a customer's needs. Exceptional value is created for a customer when a company combines services and products in ways that address relevant customer conditions. Solutions create and deliver customer value and solutions are services-led.

According to Michael Hammer (2002:38), 'In the customer economy... you must go beyond merely giving them [customers] your products and services; you need to help them solve the problems that motivated them to ask for your products and services in the first place... It goes beyond simplifying your customers' interactions with you to delivering solutions to your customers' problems, of which your products and services in their native forms are but small pieces.'

He goes on to explain: 'When products are well-differentiated, customers may be willing to pick and choose from among the best ones and endure the trouble of integrating them. But in a world of commoditized products and powerful customers, the key to success lies in turning your focus away from yourself and your products and toward your customers and the solutions they seek.'

CUSTOMER SOLUTIONS[1]

For a customer solution, the specifications of the product or service are less important than the process. Value lies in the process and is defined in terms of how the product is used, not so much in its feature and functions (what it does). Of course, it has to 'do what it says on the tin'; it has to meet customer expectations, but the key differentiator is often in terms of the context or conditions of the marketing contact. Thus, using techniques like CDP, companies need to understand the bigger picture of systems, processes and activities in which the product or service is used. Rackham (1998:17) described these kinds of people as extrinsic value customers: 'These customers focus largely or exclusively on the benefits or extrinsic elements of the value equation. For them, value is not intrinsic to the product itself but lies in how the product is used. Extrinsic value customers are interested in solutions and applications... They put a premium on advice and help. They expect sales people to give them new understanding of needs and options. They will willingly invest time, effort and cost in working with sales people to create customized solutions.'

Solution creation and delivery

Solution creation and delivery aims to create exceptional customer value and is best provided on a foundation of mutual trust and understanding between the customer and their supplier. Solution creation and delivery is different from product marketing, selling and distribution. Solutions are created and delivered by teams of people who come together often for short periods of time. Solution sales people help customers understand their issues and opportunities, and assess the options for addressing them. They can then work with customers to create and deliver unique solutions. Solution salespeople focus primarily on customer value creation, the product often being of secondary concern. By contrast, product salespeople tend to push products and focus on communicating their value. These traditional approaches tend to push products into the market. That may have worked well when demand was high, but is often less effective now the customer is a scarce resource. Solutions business models are emerging. Solutions are built on capabilities and enablers as illustrated in Figure 9.1.

Marketing cannot provide solutions in isolation. A cross-company, cross-functional commitment is required to create and deliver solutions. Solution marketers must focus less on product value and more on value delivered through the most effective integration of customer needs (in context) met by a service solution delivered at the right time and place. The solution sales effort must get to know customers at least as well as their customers know themselves. Often opportunities to create value must be discovered and made explicit; they are not always obvious. Solution salespeople help the customer to understand and evaluate the options available, even if that means choosing to work in partnerships or using competing products. Solution salespeople and consultants must also become adept at helping the customer's understanding of how the service adds value and, even more difficult, understanding where they, the customer,

Figure 9.1 _The solutions marketing hierarchy_
Source: Cerasale and Stone (2004).

might need to change to take best advantage of the service being provided. In conventional marketing terms that is heresy. A lot of companies have gone broke trying to educate or change their customers, but in a more complex and competitive market environment, customers sometimes have difficulty understanding where best value might lie. Take, for example, telephony. When buying a phone, the customer has to make choices about the handset (from a range of hundreds), the service provider (from a choice of maybe half a dozen, and the calling package (from a range of dozens). In the UK alone, one website will help customers through the resulting 20,000 options to select the instrument, service provider and package that might best meet their (current) needs. More difficult still, this solution is only contextual. If the customer's calling pattern changes for whatever reason, the first selected package may no longer be optimal. The problem is, how to identify that alteration and communicate the need for change.

Thus the nature of service delivery is changing. There are some very real differences between products and services. Despite this, some services are defined, packaged, sold and delivered as if they were durable goods. New processes, management techniques, tools and pricing models allow many services to be delivered in the form of long-term relationships. If a long-term relationship is to be established, marketers must remain focused on creating further customer value if the relationship is to endure.

Solutions are not for everyone

The opportunities to create solutions may be extensive in many industries, but solutions are not for everyone. McKinsey strikes a note of caution, suggesting that too many companies may enter the solutions market and fail. They offer three possible reasons:

- Some companies imagine they are selling solutions when they are just bundling products that create little value when offered as a set. They then find it hard to recover the extra costs of providing the products as solutions.
- Companies may underestimate the difficulty of selling solutions. They cost more to develop, have longer sales cycles, and require a deeper knowledge of customers.
- The solutions are sold just like products. The company does not understand the need to rethink the sales approach.

The key to success with solutions is an understanding of customer needs , today and tomorrow. Strategy and execution are required in equal amounts. Introducing solutions (or transforming entirely into a solutions enterprise) is a long and challenging journey, but for many it is a journey well worth making. According to Johansson _et al_ (2003), 'When a company offers true solutions, its investment can pay off in several ways. Besides generating higher margins for itself and additional value for customers, it might find that it can build longer-lasting and more profitable relationships with them. Sometimes solutions open doors to new markets and even reduce or eliminate competition, in effect de-commoditising sales.'

Low-cost business models

While some customers value solutions, others value lower costs. Customers demanding value through lower costs might choose and buy without a great deal of expert advice and guidance. They consider themselves to be knowledgeable enough to do the research themselves, to compare their options and shop around for the best deal. The cost of marketing approaches is recognized (even implicitly) and rejected as an unnecessary overhead. Cost is the key factor in determining which suppliers they choose. They tend to buy widely available products and services which are undifferentiated and often perceived as commodities.

Customers who seek value through low costs want the lowest total cost of ownership. Total cost of ownership might be defined as the total cost of search, acquisition, usage and disposal. They focus on cutting the cost of acquisition through low prices but they also want cost savings from the procurement process and to cut the cost of maintaining the product or receiving the service over time. They look for opportunities to the most cost-effective distribution channel (often the internet) and look for innovations in low-cost product support and service delivery.

Some suppliers, such as PC manufacturers, grocery retailers and even airlines are revolutionizing their companies and their industries to satisfy the needs of customers who value lower costs. Low-cost business models are emerging in many industries. Thus the service element becomes commoditized.

Nevertheless the two approaches are not necessarily mutually exclusive. A number of companies are revolutionizing themselves to satisfy the needs of both emerging customer types, by lowering costs and by introducing solutions. In either case, customers who are more powerful, knowledgeable and selective will choose to work with companies that can create exceptional customer value. Some customers want exceptional value in the form of lower costs, others want solutions. This is why a new business model is emerging and why many companies, in manufacturing and service industries, are attempting to revolutionize their companies and their industries with a solutions strategy. Some companies are cautious or unable to change quickly. They plan to introduce solutions over time with an evolutionary approach. Other companies plan to reinvent themselves through more ambitious transformation, more akin to revolution.

IMPLEMENTING SOLUTIONS THROUGH OPERATIONAL ANALYTICS

The basic challenge for marketing has not changed. First, the aim is to create a sustainable point of differentiation, that is valuable to the company and the customer, that results in more sales and higher profits per sale. Perhaps the key word in the last sentence is 'sustainable'. The implication of sustainability is that the procedures, processes and underlying sense of shared values across the enterprise must enable the company to maintain its point of differentiation flexibly in a changing marketing environment. This introduces a second challenge. Marketing must help to ensure that the organization has the competence to consistently deliver on the customer expectation and the brand promise (the offer).

In Chapter 8, we referred to the results of the IBM Global CEO Study in 2004. This is a comprehensive assessment of the CEO's agenda for the next 2–3 years. It was aimed at the CEOs and leaders of large business units and regional organizations. Over 450 CEOs were surveyed globally. The study was supported by the Economist Intelligence Unit (EIU) and Nikkei Research who carried out more than 150 personal interviews. The principal finding to emerge from this study is that CEOs, more or less across the world, see their main challenge as driving revenue growth in an increasingly competitive and globalized business environment. Whilst we have referred earlier to the fracturing of priorities between CEOs and marketing, it is evident that some of the key difficulties underlying the challenge for revenue growth lie in the marketing arena. These include:

- The problem of a lack of differentiation in products, channels, value propositions. As far as many customers can tell, at the product level one superstore is the same as another, one airline the same as another. Since the point of differentiation has become service, this difference can only be considered experientially. Service has to be delivered at the point of contact. It cannot be 'seen' objectively.
- There are diminishing returns for traditional marketing spend. One chief executive in the financial services observed that in developed economies, typically a consumer might be exposed to over 700 brand messages per day.
- Traditional marketing methods often neglect the dimensions of time, significance, relevance. A campaign is meticulously planned, launched and evaluated regardless of current events in the outside world and, more particularly, regardless of events taking place in the lives of individual customers.
- There is increased pressure on margins.
- For some products, customers are involved in frequent buying events. Grocery shopping or restaurant services might be examples. However, for many others the number of 'buying episodes' is relatively small. How often would a customer buy insurance, for example, or even furniture? Worse, whilst the retail industry has recognized that shopping can be transformed into a social experience, this is harder to do for some other products. Thus some of these buying episodes have more the character of chores than social experiences. How much fun can you have buying life insurance, for example?
- There is a mixed share of wallet. Your customers are their customers. Customers are rarely exclusively loyal to one company or brand, for all sorts of reasons, some good, some not so good. This presents an opportunity and a threat.
- Organizations have struggled to create a proposition that includes service as a part of selling and dialogue versus an offer push.

The problems of establishing service as a point of differentiation and dialogue versus push are perhaps best illustrated in the area of customer relationship management (CRM). In many companies operational CRM, particularly that associated with an enterprise-wide CRM revolution, failed to deliver the expected benefits. This was largely associated with the sheer difficulty of establishing an enterprise-wide

CRM culture. It cannot be stressed too highly that new marketing approaches which depend on an integrated and coordinated, cross-company commitment must pay critical attention to the introduction and management of change.

Enterprises that want to build effective customer relationships need to think about the roles they play in the lives of their customers. The planning process seeks to understand events that have a particular influence – positive or negative – on the customer relationship. Once these events have been identified, the enterprise is in a position to start planning how to detect when this event has occurred and how to determine the enterprise's response to this event once it has been detected.

Whilst many companies are collecting life-stage and demographic data, which can serve as the basis for understanding what is happening in the life of the customer, most companies are also building the links between different operational systems to develop a holistic view of the customer relationship, which is necessary to understand the implications of a change in customer behaviour toward the enterprise. Yet relatively few enterprises are effectively integrating the understanding of external events that impact upon the relationship with their customers. Unfortunately these events could be those that have the most profound impact on the customer relationship. A simple example is illustrated in Table 9.1.

An example of how an organization monitors external events and provides customer care to its best customers is US Airways. It monitors weather reports at important hub airports around the United States. When a storm looks likely to close an airport, it identifies all affected platinum-status frequent flyers (the top level of its loyalty scheme) and books them overnight hotel rooms, rebooks their flights, and tries to ensure they experience minimum inconvenience.

The aim is therefore to identify the most significant external issues that impact upon the customer, and then ensure that processes are in place to respond to these events. Shortening the time it takes to detect a customer event will be the single largest challenge for enterprises moving to event-driven customer relationships. Monitoring initiatives are changing as the approaches to them become more diverse. Traditionally, enterprises would run standard campaign segmentation schemes (typically overnight) to identify customers with profiles that had changed to match those of predefined segments. The company's reaction would then be based on the pre-defined treatment of that customer segment. Note that the customer is still dealt with at the segment level under this approach and this proved to

Table 9.1 _Some customer events that trigger event marketing_

Event	Detection	Reaction
Event in customer's life		
Moving house	Change of address	Sell relocation services
Birth of child	Spend pattern	Send link to child site
Retirement	Age/income trigger	Offer 'last chance' deals
Changing relationship		
First time purchase	Warranty card	Send accessories brochure
Request for service	Integrate with call centre	Satisfaction survey follow up
Declining spend	Integrate with billing	Refine service proposition
Changing environment		
Market deregulation	User entry	New competition
Falling stock market	Web monitoring	Automatic notification
Fulfilment problems	Integrate supply chain	Offer alternative service

be too broad and generalized in scope. As a result, many of these companies invested heavily in analytical CRM.

Enterprises now had an alternative strategy available that enabled the continuous monitoring of all inbound data flows so that each element can be compared to a predefined norm for the customer. Where behaviour indicates a deviation from the norm, the exception can be detected in real time and a response can be generated more quickly. This approach allows more flexibility in responding to customer events, although it sacrifices the leverage that an enterprise can gain from reusing past customer segmentations from traditional campaigns.

The approach is illustrated in Figure 9.2. This illustrates the pattern that the software might detect for a customer who has been made redundant and received a pay-off from their former employer.

Event-based marketing of this sort was operationalized in a detection, planning and response cycle as shown in Figure 9.3. This example is taken from the Union Bank of Norway, one of Norway's largest financial services providers with about 1 million customers and \$265 billion in assets in the mid-1990s. Union Bank was concerned about increases in customer dissatisfaction, so in 1996 it launched a 'Total Customer' programme which aimed to provide a higher level of service based on customer opt-in to more detailed data collection.

Although initially it was a great success, Union Bank felt that the initiative was beginning to slow as the number of Total Customers began to plateau. As traditional approaches were failing to bring in

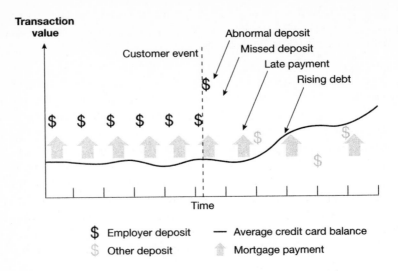

Figure 9.2 *A customer life event is detected by CRM software*

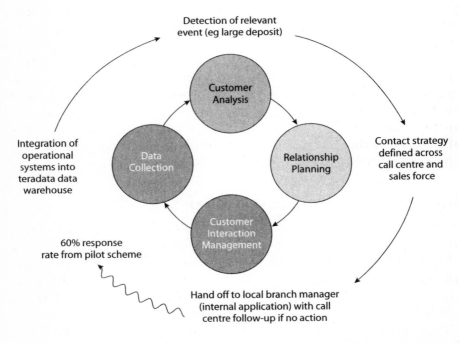

Figure 9.3 *Event-based marketing is operationalized*
Source: Union Bank of Norway.

new members, Union Bank decided to target customers at particular moments when they would be most receptive to offers. Some analysis was done using data about which events seemed to indicate a higher level of responsiveness and these events (eg a large deposit) were included as triggers for the campaign. In keeping with the objective of the project, the local branch was selected to carry out the contact, with the central call centre acting as a reserve to deal with overflow or missed contacts.

Event-based marketing recognizes that life stage, product, service and behavioural changes can signify when a company could be of service to a customer. The analytical software detects and interprets changes (events), and seeks to establish their relationship to predicting future behaviour, their relationship to each other and their significance to each customer. This enables the company to prioritize contacts and channels so that it can engage the customer in a dialogue at the first opportunity, possibly within 24 hours of the identified event occurrence. Alternatively it allows a company to capture, interpret and respond to customer needs which are identified during the customer interaction.

This approach was a big advance on traditional approaches, but even so a large percentage of companies failed to see the expected benefits materialize. Some companies find it hard to accept that communicating less frequently can be more valuable. It also requires a fundamental shift in the traditional marketing approach. Rather than developing segmented products, then looking for a group of people (a segment) to which it can be offered, the approach requires beginning with some sort of customer insight. The insight is based on recognizing a new customer need, based on a change in behaviour, and then trawling through the offers that the company can produce to find the one that might best fit this person's needs.

What was the problem with analytical CRM?

The majority of companies that used traditional CRM approaches treated the customer as a commodity. Customer contact was driven by what the organization thought the customer would be interested in, and not by changes in individual customer behaviour which indicated a real change in customer needs. As a result most companies experienced very low campaign response rates, often in the range of 1 per cent to 3 per cent. Many customers felt they were being bombarded with irrelevant marketing messages 'pushing' product at them.

The traditional campaign management or marketing approach might be summarized as being in two stages. First, discover what the company believes the customer might want based largely on products they already have (or do not have) and on the segment they 'belong' to. Second, make 'unsolicited' offers for the 'next-best product' to customers en mass or to those that have been scored with a high propensity to accept the offer. Too often the goal was to increase the frequency and volume of campaigns to customers in an effort to achieve conversion or revenue targets. What needs to be recognized is that the idea of 'more is better' is not necessarily true. The new approach must recognize that:

- Speed is certainly important. In a crowded marketplace with many similar products, one way to create a competitive advantage is to respond rapidly to changing requirements but in a more precise, customer-relevant manner.
- The renewed effort to capture and make sense of all the available data, especially that which surrounds the customer, to gain the insights required to offer new products and services that are customized to specific customer needs, demonstrates that rapid access to information is becoming critical.
- The world market is becoming more integrated but customer needs are becoming more segmented (not necessarily along traditional lines).
- Companies must become more information and analysis capable in order to compete in this environment. They must expand on their current systems base (such as those used for event marketing) to obtain better customer insight.
- The quality of customer knowledge must be improved. Companies can achieve this improvement and appear to be listening to their customers, hearing what they are telling them, by the use of better modelling techniques to segment customers more precisely.
- In addition, competitive intelligence capability must be developed so that the organization can react quickly to changes in the external marketing environment.

Thus the move is from a traditional marketing approach to the operational analytics approach. This is illustrated in Figure 9.4. In the traditional approach, an analysis and modelling phase is followed by campaign planning. The campaign is then developed in four phases, the customer strategy (stage 1) presents acquisition, sales, retention and service propositions (2) to the customer (3) who makes a response which is measured (4) and used to feedback into stage 1 to adjust future strategies. The campaign is executed and its effectiveness is reported and tracked by the customer database. Again there is a feedback loop to analysis and modelling, ready for the next campaign. Using operational analytics, additional modelling and analysis is used. The analysis and modelling of the customer database is continued, this time to establish norms and patterns in customer behaviour. This is then linked to an event detection routine. Marketing resources in terms of an appropriate offer (what is the best offer for this customer?) are then linked into appropriate campaign development.

However, the campaign is not launched automatically. There is a further intervention which takes into account customer fatigue and optimization. Too frequent a marketing impact on the same customer can cause 'fatigue' in the sense that customers simply get tired of what they regard as pointless messages. Choosing an appropriate contact frequency is something of a black art that needs careful modelling. Too frequent a contact causes fatigue or even resistance, too infrequent a loss of interest. The 'best' frequency will depend on the product, the company and the customer's personal situation. For example, when a customer is moving house, then they might be more interested in loan offers. At other times, these offers may not be of special interest. Leads are then generated over a number of channels. This is a multichannel approach, rather than the one or two channels of a conventional campaign. This is not a 'passive' process as in a conventional campaign. Response rates to each channel are tracked and the campaign is modified dynamically, over a number of channels to monitor effectiveness.

There are many studies to show how substantial returns can be obtained from these improved marketing and customer analytics. For example, Table 9.2 describes the results of a study by the Rotterdam School of Management with Erasmus Graduate Business School over the period 1999 to 2001.

Further positive results were reported by major consulting firms such as Forrester and the Gartner Group. Thus Forrester, in its _'Trends in CRM 2005'_ (26 October 2004), claims that event detection to make CRM more proactive in retail banking and credit card leaders has demonstrated the value of just-in-time decision-making, changing the customer conversation from 'how may I help you?' to offers based on life events. Gartner Group's _Marketing Strategies in Financial Services Go From Push to Pull_ (2002) states that event-based marketing will

213

The standard 'closed loop' marketing process

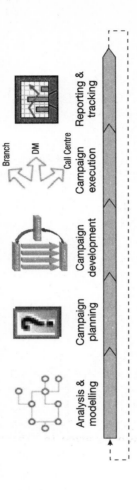

Analysis & modelling | Campaign planning | Campaign development | Campaign execution | Reporting & tracking

Branch
DM
Call Centre

Operational analytics marketing process

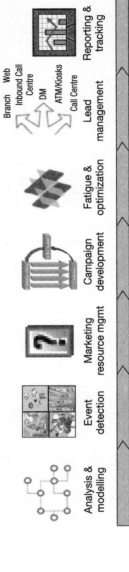

Analysis & modelling | Event detection | Marketing resource mgmt | Campaign development | Fatigue & optimization | Lead management | Reporting & tracking

Branch   Web
Inbound Call
Centre
DM
ATM/Kiosks
Call Centre

Figure 9.4 *The operational analytics approach*

Table 9.2 *The benefits of integrated multichannel marketing*

	Sales conversion rate (%)
Mass marketing	0.2–3.1
Target marketing	2.0–4.9
Event-driven marketing	8.0–34.0
Integrated multichannel / multistep-driven marketing (combined campaign and event-driven)	21.0–62.0

Converted response rates (n = 247, Western Europe, 1999–2001)

Source: Erasmus University / Rotterdam School of Mgt. Research (1999–2001).

become a competitive requirement. Differentiation will come from the events chosen to be monitored.

The benefits for the customer lie in the improved quality of the relationship. The marketing contacts received by individuals are relevant, timely and tailored to their current circumstances rather than being the generic, 'buy something now', type of messaging. The relationship also improves because service (which we have noted as an increasingly important differentiator) is a large element of operational analytics. Not every communication is a sales communication. Many contacts are service calls. Finally, the models incorporate comprehensive communication rules to support the event campaigns. This ensures that the company does not over-contact customers with multiple, conflicting messages. At its most extreme (and absurd) this avoids situations (which have been known to arise) where one division of a company writes to a customer who is in dispute with another part of the company over a previous sale. In a worst case this has even been known to arise in situations where finance concerned over non-payment, perhaps because of a disputed invoice, sends a letter to curtail services on the same day that another division of the company sends a promotional message trying to sell more product!

Differences between traditional and operational analytics campaign execution

The key differences and characteristics between traditional and operational analytic campaigns are summarized in Table 9.3. Figures 9.5 and 9.6 illustrate how these differences might look in practice.

Table 9.3 *Key characteristics of operational analytics*

Characteristics of a traditional marketing campaign	Characteristics of an operational analytics campaign
Small number of large-volume product-push campaigns	Large volume (perhaps as many as 200+) of small campaigns, running every day
Customer contact when it suits the institution ('we have something to sell')	Communication based on changes in individual customer behaviour
Extended campaign and model development times	Campaign execution fully automated
Limited automation of analytics	Proactive servicing campaigns alongside sales and retention

The tools for operational analytics

A number of vendors now offer event detection engines. An event detection engine is essentially a large computer program that trawls through the customer database to identify certain incidents. It is a rule-based application which monitors daily transactional behaviour and looks for transactional patterns which have been specified by the business as being 'significant'. These include:

- *Who?* An event engine continuously trawls the daily transactions and interactions data for significant changes in individual customer behaviour. Thus the software looks for product events, lifestyle events, behavioural events or external changes that may warrant a response.
- *What?* This is the analysis and modelling stage. Automated data-mining models and business rules are used to determine the likely customer need. They then propose the most relevant offer for this individual based upon the customer profile and recent event history.
- *When?* This is the element that deals with fatigue and optimization (managing the frequency of contacts, in the context of the customer's life events). The optimization engine ensures that the limited channel capacity is used only for the best leads. Fatigue rules are also applied to ensure that the company is not over-communicating with individual customers.
- *How?* Finally, there is campaign management. Multi-stage dialogues are managed across multiple channels driven by the responses received from individual customers at each stage.

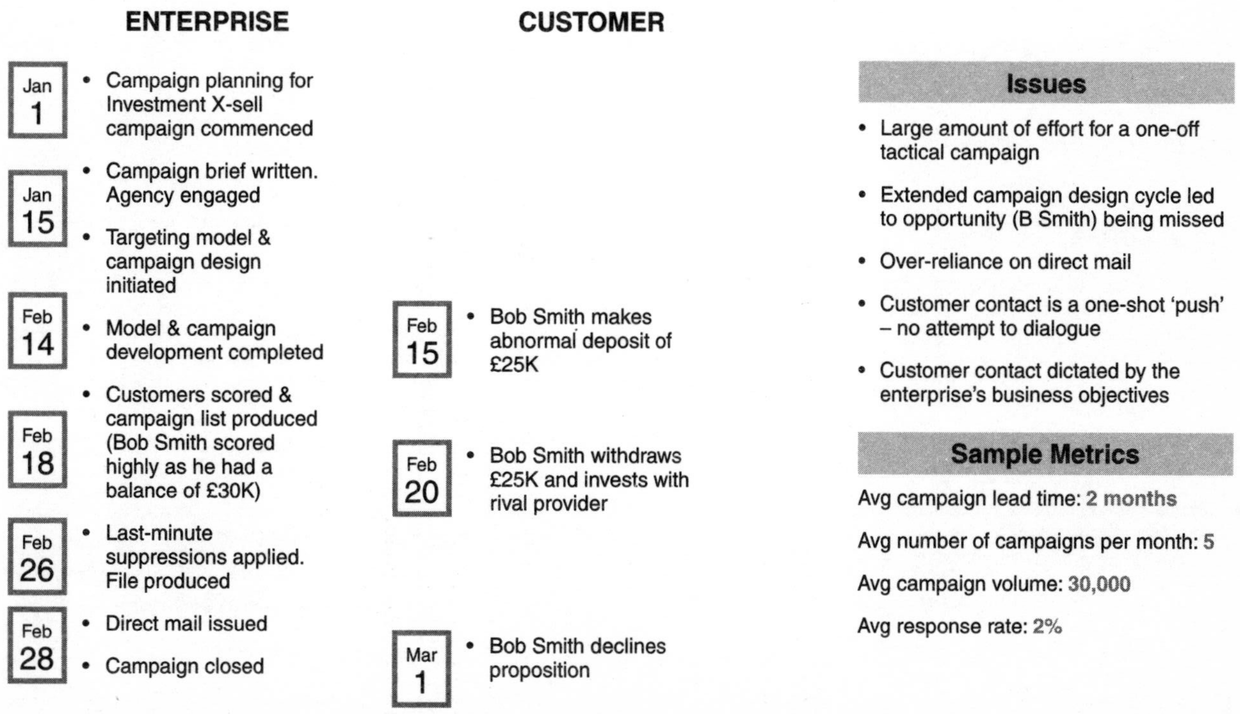

ENTERPRISE

CUSTOMER

Jan 1	Campaign planning for Investment X-sell campaign commenced
Jan 15	Campaign brief written. Agency engaged
	Targeting model & campaign design initiated
Feb 14	Model & campaign development completed
Feb 18	Customers scored & campaign list produced (Bob Smith scored highly as he had a balance of £30K)
Feb 26	Last-minute suppressions applied. File produced
Feb 28	Direct mail issued
	Campaign closed

Feb 15	Bob Smith makes abnormal deposit of £25K
Feb 20	Bob Smith withdraws £25K and invests with rival provider
Mar 1	Bob Smith declines proposition

Issues

- Large amount of effort for a one-off tactical campaign

- Extended campaign design cycle led to opportunity (B Smith) being missed

- Over-reliance on direct mail

- Customer contact is a one-shot 'push' – no attempt to dialogue

- Customer contact dictated by the enterprise's business objectives

Sample Metrics

Avg campaign lead time: 2 months

Avg number of campaigns per month: 5

Avg campaign volume: 30,000

Avg response rate: 2%

Figure 9.5 *Scenario 1: a traditional tactical campaign*

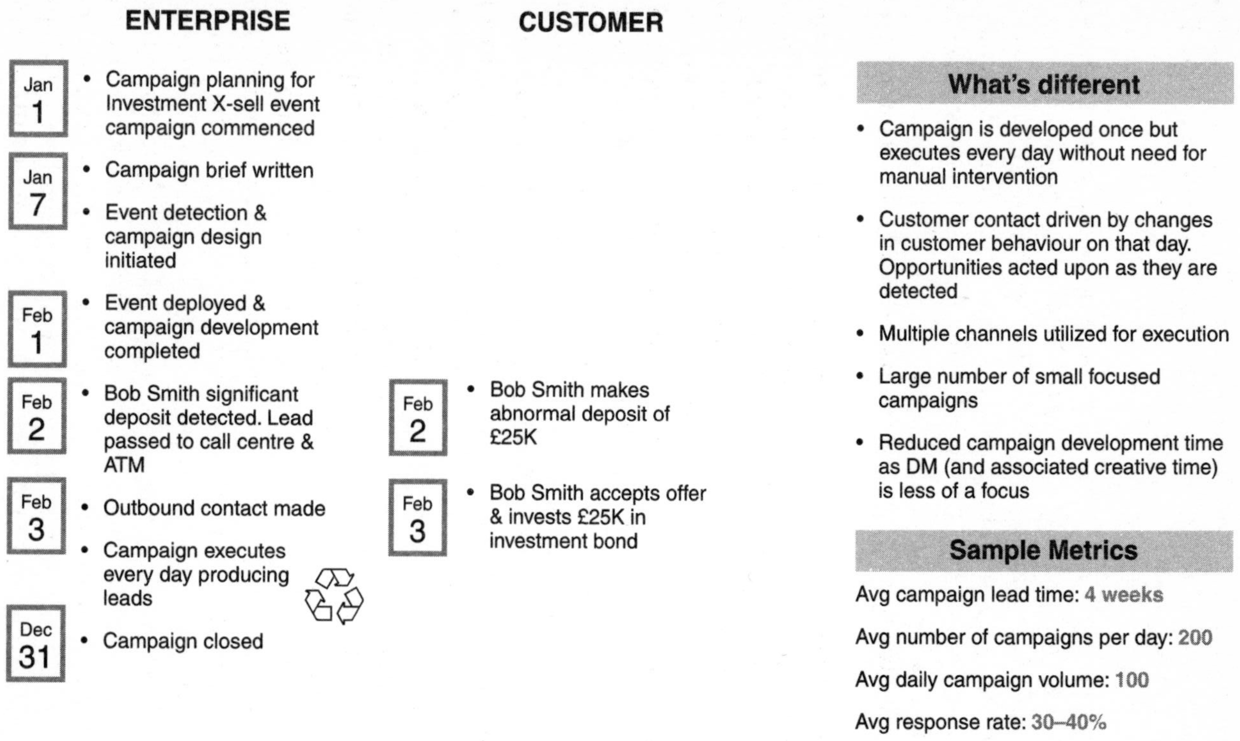

ENTERPRISE

Jan 1 • Campaign planning for Investment X-sell event campaign commenced

Jan 7 • Campaign brief written

Feb 1 • Event detection & campaign design initiated
• Event deployed & campaign development completed

Feb 2 • Bob Smith significant deposit detected. Lead passed to call centre & ATM

Feb 3 • Outbound contact made
• Campaign executes every day producing leads

Dec 31 • Campaign closed

CUSTOMER

Feb 2 • Bob Smith makes abnormal deposit of £25K

Feb 3 • Bob Smith accepts offer & invests £25K in investment bond

What's different

• Campaign is developed once but executes every day without need for manual intervention

• Customer contact driven by changes in customer behaviour on that day. Opportunities acted upon as they are detected

• Multiple channels utilized for execution

• Large number of small focused campaigns

• Reduced campaign development time as DM (and associated creative time) is less of a focus

Sample Metrics

Avg campaign lead time: 4 weeks

Avg number of campaigns per day: 200

Avg daily campaign volume: 100

Avg response rate: 30–40%

Figure 9.6 Scenario 2: operational analytics campaign

Specialist event-detection software empowers business analysts to develop the event rules and offers improvements in speed and performance over conventional SQL. SQL stands for Structured Query Language, which is the software used most commonly to interrogate large databases. The software:

- Supports the rapid test of new events. Trigger events are constantly refined via GUI (graphical user interfaces).
- Executes more daily events than SQL so that the demands on the computer system supporting the main customer database are lessened by reducing the time required for the nightly processing window issue.
- Increases the speed to market, thus reducing management costs.

Events are classified at three levels. The most basic are simple trigger events, such as that given in the examples above. They are associated with simplistic transactional changes involving the update of a single field in the database such as a large deposit. Secondary events are based on triggers linked to additional rules which aim to attach significance to the event to that individual customer. So, for example, the deposit might be identified as three times the normal level, clearly something outside what might be expected in the normal pattern. These secondary events are then used to inform the pattern-building software. These patterns are combinations of multiple triggers and secondary events occurring in a sequence over a period of time. Thus we might imagine a change in employment associated with a redundancy payment (the large deposit). Salary payments are stopped and then new, regular payments are received a few weeks later from a new employer. A more sophisticated example is shown in Figure 9.7.

Rules are not generated in an entirely automated fashion. Segment managers participate in the population of the 'event library'. Whilst events are detected for all customers every night, the resulting campaign activity varies for each segment and is driven by the current business objectives for each of the segments and their related value proposition. There is therefore the possibility of daily communications for each segment (subject to moderation by the fatigue and optimization routines) whether for possible sales, retention activities or offering proactive customer service. These communications can be fully automated.

Thus the behaviour of the system varies contextually by customers. Let us take two examples. Customer A is living slightly beyond their

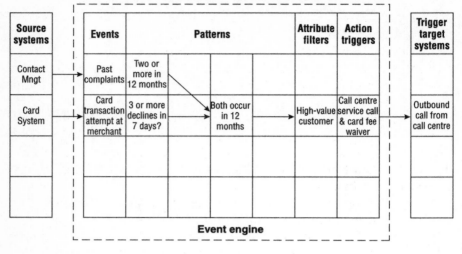

Figure 9.7 *Bringing the pattern concept to life in the form of service*

means. They are struggling to make ends meet. However, they still require access to lifestyle credit but find it difficult to provide a credit track record. The operational analytics will monitor their customer record for early signs of financial distress in order to limit bad debt exposure. Proactive service responses will aim to minimize the costs of service. Thus it might take the form of consolidating customer debts, a simple personal budget and establishing regular payments to reduce indebtedness. Customer B is self-directed and financially sophisticated. Such self-directed investors hold significant investments and have excess monthly capital. In this case, the operational analytics will look for early signs of customer dissatisfaction and potential threats in terms of customer churn. They will aim to identify cross- and up-selling opportunities and seek to develop insights as to where key elements of the value proposition might lie. It might be, for example, that the customer would especially value a mobile phone-based alerting system for price changes on their key investments. This can be offered as an enhancement to the service package. Competitors without access to similar customer data may find it harder to identify such a feature and might therefore have fewer chances to direct their own promotional attacks in the best way.

CUSTOMER EQUITY AND LIFETIME MANAGEMENT (CELM) TECHNIQUES

CELM techniques use advanced data-mining, machine-learning and stochastic optimization techniques to better understand and predict customer dynamics. They aim to drive growth within the existing customer base by optimizing sequential marketing campaigns, by leveraging the knowledge obtained, by simulating future customer transaction behaviour. They increase customer equity and lifetime value through better understanding and predicting customer behaviour. They also increase value by optimizing marketing policies through the continuous monitoring and analysis of customer dynamics (their transactional behaviour). In other words, they help to develop better insights.

At the data-gathering stage, they resegment the customer base. Thus the output here is a value-based, resegmented customer base which forms the basis of new data sets for the exploration of customer dynamics. At the customer dynamics exploration stage they identify typical sequences (such as a value state, an action, a response) for specific customer behaviour by each value segment. Finally, they assist with marketing policy optimization by producing a sequential action plan to trigger required customer behaviours.

Managing customer fatigue

Customer fatigue and optimization rules prevent the campaign managers from over-communicating with customers. This is managed by checking every planned communication against that individual's contact history to ensure that the communication is valid. Thousands of possible offers, multiplied by dozens of channels multiplied by perhaps millions of customers, produces a massive number of permutations. Optimization is therefore used to apply the customer fatigue rules and ensure best use of limited channel capacity. Having hundreds of campaigns executing every night leads to a massive permutation of potential offer and channel combinations for each customer. The optimization routines take into account product targets and budgets, the capacity of the various channels and any constraints on their usage (such as minimum mail volumes for a bulk mailing), and model that against customer preferences and fatigue rules. The optimization mathematically determines the best offer and best channel to maximize the ROI of all campaigns based on individual customer response models.

221

Effective leads management of this sort is vital as the lead response rates drop dramatically as they age. Lead management capabilities include:

- *Lead cascading* – leads are moved to an alternative channel when the primary channel has insufficient capacity or has failed to action the leads within a specific timeframe.
- *Lead ageing and decay* – unactioned leads are reprioritized by the optimization engine every day against the 'fresh' leads with a decay factor applied to reflect the decline in timeliness.
- *Lead rerouting* – leads are routed to the same individual in the contact centre for all phases of multi-stage campaigns to ensure consistency and to maximize ownership.
- *Secondary messaging* – reinforcing messages are delivered to alternative channels such as the internet. Yet further channels such as sales kiosks might also be contacted at the same time as the campaign is deployed in retail outlets to reinforce the campaign message.
- *Active stepping* – campaign responses are retrieved within the same day and the customer dialogue is moved to the next stage automatically by the campaign management system.

SUMMARY

Customers will continue to become increasingly sophisticated. They will increasingly be seeking not just products and service but also solutions to their life-event problems. Traditional marketing campaign response rates show no signs of addressing the issues of a better-informed, more 'promotion-savvy' market. Response rates to traditional campaigns will remain static unless marketers adopt new approaches that are based upon individual customer behaviour and needs rather than a desire to 'push product'. There are diminishing returns on traditional marketing approaches and even if individual companies moderate their communications to customers to take account of fatigue effects, today's customers are often exposed to hundreds of promotional messages daily. Propositions need to become more relevant and timely. They also need to create a sense that service is part of selling. Rapid responsiveness to changes in customer behaviour which produce customized communications, relevant to the customer's life events, can be a crucial differentiator and basis for competitive advantage. Operational analytics addresses these issues. In the next chapter we will illustrate the use of some of these techniques with case examples.

NOTE

1. This section, to p206, is based on Cerasale and Stone (2004).

10

From revolutionary thinking and planning to action

FUTURE MARKETING TECHNOLOGIES

Information technology has undoubtedly supported enormous productivity gains in many areas, from business applications through to robotics and telecommuting, by establishing better and faster communications channels. Countless business hours have been saved by video calls, texting, instant e-mail messaging and videoconferencing rather than by travelling to face-to-face meetings. This does not take away the need to meet in person, but it does cut down on the frequency of such meetings. Businesses have to be agile, flexible and responsive to market demands. In order for this to happen, the correct technical infrastructure has to be in place with applications that will allow change to occur, otherwise constraints will creep in resulting in a loss of competitive edge. It is no good offering yesterday's proposition to today's customers. A company bound by the use of a proprietary system or one that does not meet common industry standards is often faced with a lack of integration between data sources. It also tends to have problems of communication with other systems, both in-house and along the supply chain. At best, the level of complexity created can cause expensive inefficiencies. Standards are becoming more and more important as the level of electronic communication rises.

As IT systems become more complex, the issues of integration have become even more of a challenge than mere application portability. Connectivity and communications are critical today with voice, data and even video linkages becoming important, not only across mobile phone devices but for other client devices too. Video phones are a technology whose time has come. Already in common usage by broadcasting media, they are increasingly useful to the corporate world. Perhaps this is a technology in search of a problem, for example those of copyright issues or illicit photography. It could also turn out to be one of the next disruptive technologies that everyone will take for granted in the next five years. After all, the transition from using a phone to link to a place, to a phone to link to a person, took 15 years or so. As the pace of change increases exponentially, the ability to send video images across the internet could be an important messaging medium for marketers in the next few years.

Another important emerging messaging tool is instant messaging across mobile phones from marketers. This is both push and pull marketing. Push, because the message is originated by the marketer. Pull, because the customer grants permission to be a recipient. Stock market prices, results of sporting contests, a notification of an e-mail response or the need to bid on e-Bay are useful instant alerting mechanisms. Often they are value-added service additions such as messages from airlines to passengers to inform them of flight delays or changes in flight times. The speed of this messaging service can be used to improve corporate response times and lead to increased customer satisfaction, a precursor to loyalty and higher repurchase levels. Communications within an organization are just as important as those outside. Already the intranet is a vital backbone for companies, effectively making knowledge and expertise readily available to the majority of employees. Marketing staff that focus on internal communication have an important role to play ensuring that each employee understands the company objectives, products, competitors and customer sets in a way that is relevant to them.

The fast pace of change means that it is often difficult to foresee how business will look in a few years' time. For instance, how will we use the internet? Will we even know that we are using it? This technology is already being embedded in many devices such as cameras and phones and it is certainly here to stay. Despite the problems of the early dotcom era there are many internet companies in the business-to-consumer (B2C) sector that have been extremely successful. Amazon and eBay are two examples although, strictly speaking, eBay is customer-to-customer (C2C), but there are many others in areas such as real estate, pharmaceuticals, health, legal services, financial services and of course travel and transportation. In the B2B arena the internet acts as a communications and information channel for the majority of firms, lowering costs and increasing responsiveness. It has dramatically revolutionized the way that businesses operate both internally and externally. The internet is an integration enabler, lowering transaction costs and making all areas more efficient and effective. In a world where time lines are important, the increased speed with which businesses can respond to customers is changing the rules and the rate of responsiveness is increasing.

This major change has had an enormous effect on marketing. Not only is the internet a new medium for advertising but it is also a new outlet channel, information provider and communication method (both overt and covert). It has changed the way that marketers think about their marketing strategies as well as being used merely for communication. The world has opened up since the internet came of age. Huge amounts of information are at everyone's fingertips including those of the competitors. Many big retailers now routinely monitor and even publicize their competitors' prices. Customers routinely use the internet as a form of efficient comparison shopping before making a decision to buy. Companies now have to be extra vigilant with regard to public domain information as anything on the web is only a click away. Security is therefore an issue for many companies and vast amounts of research is going into this area. This includes not just firewalls, encryption algorithms and smarter credit card protection, but also into better ways of identifying customers themselves. Biometric applications are starting to appear in areas such as banks, airports and identification cards. Many airlines now take digital photographs of passengers as they go into the departure lounge and these are picked up at every other point of control until they are on the plane. These security challenges are something that marketers must now take into account when planning how they interact with customers and prospects.

It is interesting to consider what marketers call disruptive technologies. These are advancements that are so new, innovative and different that they completely change the current business landscape.

Such technologies have included in the past silicon chips, the PC, mobile phones and the internet. Each has made a significant difference to how business has progressed over the past few decades. Companies that quickly realized how a new technology might be used to change the face of business and exploit it in their business are the winners. The problem is, you can kiss an awful lot of frogs before you find a handsome prince. Sometimes the changes needed in customer behaviour require too great a change before the technology can take effect. For example, companies which make a living by selling surplus inventory depend on both companies and customers turning to the technology for last-minute solutions. In practice, however, few people use a search engine on their mobile phone before picking an impulse-buy restaurant for their evening meal. Not least of all, few restaurants have the procedures in place to notify a central provider of their current demand pattern.

Being quick to recognize that an emergent technology will be a disruptive one and implementing it with the least risk to current business is, however, one way to succeed in this environment. The dotcom failures were often companies that did not have a solid business plan and took too many risks. Technology is simply an enabler to business even if it has far-reaching effects. Discarding the foundations of good business practice in order to embrace a new technology can be extremely risky and often disastrous.

Today's emergent technologies that are likely to have a large effect on business in the future include digital currency or smart cards, intelligent application software and accepted interoperability standards. There are also enhancements to innovative new technologies like videophones that will undoubtedly revolutionize the future. These include bioinformatics, text-to-speech, on-demand and autonomic computing. The latter refers to the progression of computing to a systemic network based on biological systems. It is intended to alleviate the complexity of IT infrastructure that we see today. There will be many benefits from autonomics but the most immediate will be that of reduced costs and higher stability of IT systems due to automation. Business benefits include better management and faster reactions to market changes, enabling improved and timely business decisions.

It is also expected that autonomics can make up for skill shortages or cost inefficiencies in the area of data analysis and exchange. Information can be gathered remotely by automated agents and the text mined, to increase knowledge for marketers and other business users. On-demand analytics carried out by autonomic agents is part of the on-demand services world envisioned for the future. It is expected that many future technologies will be services rather than hardware or software. These might include new internet services and even applications such as salesforce.com. Services are a growth area in the digital economy and we can expect to see this highly competitive sector shake out even more in the near future. This will leave just the major players along with a few smaller niche companies to meet market needs and take this industry forward, as has happened previously with the IT industry. Of course, as new types of services are identified, the first movers will benefit and new players will emerge to take up the ensuing business opportunities. The results can shake even the biggest companies. In the space of less than five years, Disney saw its dominance as the major producer of animated films first shaken and then displaced by the more effective use of technology by Pixar and Dreamworks.

Technology is converging and pervasive. We are seeing this technology convergence from the '4C' point of view – customer, content, communications and computing. Companies need to partner more and more, in order to deliver the wider solutions expected today, whilst keeping to their core competencies in order to deliver a high-quality service. For example, in 'pay as you drive' insurance, an insurance company partners with a mobile phone company to allow reporting of the mileage of a car and the conditions under which it is driven.

Other areas of technologies are coming together between industries, for example within the biotechnology and IT industries. Pharmaceuticals are a key area for the 'on-demand' computing vision of the future, where a grid of computers (as in electricity grids) provides the computing power to advanced simulation and modelling. This reduces the time taken to identify and launch a new drug by less than half, saving millions of dollars in trials and product development.

IBM's vision of the on-demand era is that of customers' servers, all constantly connected, which shift workloads from machines short of resource to those with capacity to spare. This allows 'server farms' to be run much closer to capacity. Excess workloads can even be moved seamlessly to IBM's own servers for processing if needed. However, this development is not just about on-demand technology. It is also about knowledge. IBM services personnel share their industrial expertise across the globe as required. This vision requires total focus by the company on new versions of software, hardware and processes, starting with IBM itself which will become the pilot for the on-demand strategy.

For all of this to happen it is critical that all of the components, people, processes, software and hardware integrate well at every level. It is not simply a matter of ensuring that the hardware and software communicate, but also of making certain that every piece of software can run optimally on all the hardware in the server farms. Processes, data and business logic must all be able to fit within a computing and business grid that is on-demand. Never before has standardization been so important. The so-called open systems of the past are not rigorous enough for the future, and battles taking place between the major suppliers of operating systems intensify as a recognition emerges that whoever wins will set the standards for years to come. The winner must be able to run on all types of server regardless of scale. It must be robust and secure, easy to manage and well supported by the vendor. The question is, how well are companies positioned to take advantage of these changes?

SHIFTING REQUIREMENTS

So far we have emphasized a shift from product or proposition optimizers to customer optimizers if marketing revolution is to be achieved. The former use, own and market data on price, promotion, inventory levels and shipments to determine a marketing and distribution policy. Their data are organized by product and the main analysis task is to make sense of possibly millions of daily transactions in which their products are involved. Leading grocery retailers would be a good example of product optimizers. On the other hand, companies which can manage their customers as individuals need to become expert in analysing customer data. The data analysed include in-depth customer insights in addition to objectively monitored data, combined with transaction and promotional response data.

The analysis required by product optimizers and customer optimizers is different, but many suppliers now realize that they have to do both. Companies will normally need to consolidate and synthesize data from different sources – internal and external, primary and secondary – and from different functions, not only marketing but sales, finance, customer service and operations. A successful approach to analysis requires the company to define the key dimensions in some detail and then to ensure focus on a few areas which can be backed by management action. The needs of different users vary; each will require different tools to support their management actions. This must not lead to a dispersal of data so that the capability for coordinated analysis is lost. Central consolidation of data facilitates reporting to all parts of the organization is essential. To do this effectively, data and analysis requirements must be defined integrally as part of the wider business system. They will not work well as an afterthought or an add-on.

Let us consider how customer optimizers in a revolutionized marketing organization would put in place the capabilities needed to operationalize customer insights.

Advanced data analysis

Improving marketing results, and achieving a more measurable, increased ROI on investment in marketing, can be achieved by enhancing existing customer management systems with a new approach to customer insight. This can increase customer satisfaction, stimulate purchases, increase loyalty, retain valued customers, all while controlling costs. According to Stone, Bond and Foss (2004), this requires combining analytical techniques and computing technologies to enable the business to communicate with individual customers in a relevant way, regardless of contact channel. In this case relevance refers to offering service and purchase suggestions that reflect precise buying habits, needs and desires, preferably in real time. Customer insight is the key, but the ability to use it profitably is rare. As Hirschowitz (2001) points out, 'no matter how sophisticated a company's ability to generate customer insight, it delivers little value without the processes in place to exploit the understanding to build stronger customer relationships'.

Suspect, prospect or asset?

In many companies, customers are not viewed as longer-term valuable assets but merely as prospects for the next contact list for the next possible sale. Only when a company starts to think of customers as valuable assets can it justify investing in individual customers so as to get the best from them and, equally important, offer the best to them. 'Businesses fail when management focuses too much attention on today's immediate needs, such as quarterly profits, at the expense of solving tomorrow's problem, such as discovering and satisfying customers' emerging requirements' (English, 1999).

Many marketing systems use a point-in-time (ie a campaign-by-campaign) logic to make marketing investment decisions. However, customer-focused analytic software allows companies to take into account the cascade effect of one campaign to optimize management of marketing resources and minimize fatigue effects. If customer insight data are managed properly, a marketing plan can be developed almost for each individual customer. The plan is continually re-evaluated so as to feed campaign management with a set of offers that maximize the return on investment for each customer. This provides for managing customers to a budget. Where most event-based marketing triggers an action whenever an event is flagged, this approach first evaluates whether this is the best use of the marketing budget for each individual.

'Sorry, you'll have to talk to our X department'

Customers should believe they are dealing with one integrated firm, rather than a disjointed set of business units who only take ownership of a customer for those interactions relating to their particular part of the business. Data integration through the central coordination of data enables this via a real-time data management system. A data store incorporating analysis models is used to generate propensity scores and a customer behaviour profile which can be employed at all customer touch points. When customers interact with a company their behaviour profile evolves. Hard data (eg what was spent or invested) are combined with soft data (eg attitudes to risk or price sensitivity) and used to generate personalized messages for each individual customer. 'You really understand me', is the impression the company wants to create. Such a system permits customers to acknowledge that the firm understands them and meets their needs. It increases the propensity to continue to do business with that company. What is important here is that the organization not only shows it understands its customers, but it really does understand them. This understanding is demonstrated by the appropriate use of insights. For customer insight to be deployed like this, it must be supported by the right systems. It is therefore important to determine how the insight will be deployed in practice.

Case study: the Australian Bank

The bank's retail business incorporates checking and savings accounts, credit cards and loans. It has a customer base of several million. A team of analysts built customer models to analyse and predict customer behaviour. This initiative, part of a commitment to customer relationship management (CRM), was the largest customer-focused project ever undertaken by the bank's analysts. Phase one involved the identification and preparation of thousands of possible characteristics and the development of tens of behavioural models. Around 70 per cent of the time spent here was dedicated to defining and preparing the characteristics. The behavioural models produced were each able to predict the likelihood of a given behaviour in areas such as marketing, retention and credit decision initiatives. Thus the basic analysis aimed to understand what drives customer behaviour. Once this was done the models were built. Prediction of customers' behaviour is possible from previous experiences. However, the models also identify unusual or unexpected behaviours which can then be used as a marketing opportunity. The bank runs its standard set of models regularly and automatically. The information provided by the models is used by the bank's decision makers for marketing purposes such as direct mail, as well as for collection strategies and cost–risk estimations.

For phase two, the team was able to develop a streamlined approach that made it possible to refine and automate the data preparation process, exploit the data sources and drastically reduce the number of variables to hundreds from thousands, once it was understood which were most predictive and valuable. The bank also created one-off models for specific campaigns, giving even better results and potentially doubling the effectiveness of the campaign. For example, an early model-based credit card campaign resulted in a 67 per cent increase over earlier campaigns. Now that the bank can develop its models in-house, the cost of the exercise is minimal and the return on investment runs to thousands of per cent.

Source (Stone, Bond and Foss, 2004)

DEVELOPING OR ENHANCING THE TECHNICAL INFRASTRUCTURE

Real-time decision making requires new capabilities. After collecting data and transforming it into insight, your storage and retrieval approach must turn the data into a useful corporate asset. In many companies some form of data warehouse already exists. Certain data types require focus to ensure sound corporate decision making. Examples include campaign information, campaign responses both positive and negative, customer characteristics, channels preferred and used and cross-product behaviour, as well as more obvious customer details such as name and address. Where web marketing is used, more dimensions are necessary such as traffic sources, online behaviour segments and content or image categories. This record of historical behaviour provides a vital piece of information for generating analytical models to predict customers' propensity to respond to a marketing event. This generates a view of the customer before a significant event, such as a web page or kiosk screen presentation, or a direct-mail offering. These events stimulate customer behaviour and provide important ingredients for predicting the future behaviour of customers before, and analysing customers after, the next event. With this evidence, a prior view and a response to a stimulus, sophisticated data-mining algorithms can be used to generate models that predict the customer behaviour. The heuristics from this prediction can then be applied to other customers within the population.

Data mining

A simple definition of data mining in marketing is: 'The extraction of previously unknown, comprehensible and actionable information from large repositories of data so as to use it for making crucial business decisions. The information provided must also support the implementation process, including formulating tactical and strategic marketing initiatives and measuring their success.'

Thus the aim of data mining is to obtain a sufficient understanding of a pattern of market behaviour so as to allow quantifiable benefits to be derived from changes in behaviour suggested by the analysis.

Data mining starts with the idea that companies hold a lot of data about their businesses but do not have full understanding of what is happening in detail. By 'digging' into the data it is possible to 'mine' the nuggets of buried information by establishing and interpreting patterns. This approach is mainly relevant for companies that have large amounts of readily available data but have not analysed it much. In these cases almost anything discovered will be interesting but more importantly it may also be of use to the organization. Apparently small insights from the analysis can yield big long-term gains, particularly when repeated over a long period. For example, in one company, increasing cross-sell rates by 2 per cent yielded 22 per cent more profit and 8 per cent better retention. However, data mining is more than simple data analysis. It is machine-aided consultancy that requires:

- Understanding of industry conditions.
- Appreciation of specific factors that apply to an individual company.
- Familiarity with a wide range of analytical tools.
- The ability to present extracted information in ways that managers can understand and interpret.

As we have pointed out elsewhere, revolutionizing the marketing function by informing it in this way is primarily an exercise in change. Managers may be able to respond to new information sources intuitively, but it is fairly unlikely. The data-mining activity must therefore be supported with training, possibly consultancy advice and a significant period of testing (simulating decisions and their likely results) before managers will be confident in using the new approach.

The exploration characteristic of data-mining software is made possible by advances in computing, in particular the ability to compare very large numbers of attributes of cases (a case refers to an individual data record) to see which cases are similar. It helps marketing managers in a number of ways. First, they can better understand and predict customer behaviour (Selby, 2003). Take, for example, the phenomenon of the frequent flyer. Here there are many variables requiring analysis, such as where and how far in advance the ticket was purchased, how often the flyer has not shown up despite buying a ticket, what class they are flying, how complex their total itinerary is and so on. Second, to discover customer groupings that would be hard to uncover using theory-based hypotheses. For example, a life insurance company discovered a low-risk group of smokers within the high-risk group of all smokers. These were customers who were prudent in every other way, except that they smoked. These customers could be profitably retained by a slightly lower insurance premium.

Data-mining activity in marketing

It is useful to look at some applied examples to give a better idea of where data mining can help revolutionize marketing:

- *Customer gain and loss analysis (churn).* Understanding why customers are gained or lost is useful though surprisingly few companies search out the data and, more important, use them systematically. Variations in behaviour may be random, or may correlate with business trends, economic or social factors, or competitors' activity.

- *Customer migration.* Why do customers switch products and services? Buying patterns may show that they buy one particular product followed by another. So after buying a dress the customer buys a matching hat in the spring in 70 per cent of cases. The link between product types and the susceptibility of a customer to follow a sequence could determine how items should be placed in a store and how they should be merchandized or promoted at certain times in the year.
- *Customer solicitation.* How effective are marketing campaigns in reaching the right customers? Increasing campaign yield, for example the number of positive responses, or decreasing the cost of finding new customers, can produce big savings. The propensity of customers to buy certain products can be used to predict future behaviour for new products.
- *Customer response analysis.* What causes customers to respond – or not – to a campaign? Which respond most often, to which offers?
- *Promotion analysis.* What are the results of a marketing promotion? Which customers bought particular products and why? The key task is to explain observed behaviour in terms of a mix of customer and product types. This can be achieved by comparing the segmentation of customers before and after the promotion in question.
- *Purchase analysis.* What types of products and services are individual customers buying?
- *Seasonality analysis.* How does the buying profile change during the year? Seasonal patterns in products and in the strength of links between products can be studied.
- *Priority analysis.* In which sequence do customers prefer to buy products? How does this vary by customer type?
- *Customer loyalty.* Which factors cause a customer to remain loyal to a company or product? Customer loyalty and lapsing are two sides of the same coin.
- *Cross-selling.* What additional products could be offered to existing customers? The propensity of customers to buy a product can be used to infer how they will respond to new cross-selling opportunities.
- *Niche market determination and target marketing.* What segments exist or have specific buying patterns that have not been identified before? The existence of many, often small, previously unidentified and possibly high-value segments may suggest new products or service. For example, finding a small group of older drivers who had very few accidents despite owning fast cars that were costly to repair led to a special insurance offering for vintage sports car enthusiasts.

- *Channel of communication and media analysis.* Which channels do particular types of customer prefer to use? Do their preferences vary for inbound and outbound communications?
- *Channel of distribution analysis.* Which channels are different types of customers using, when and for what products? Which would be most suitable, given customers' geographic location? What is the optimum number of branches needed to cover the market?
- *Basket analysis.* What associations are there between products, within the shopping basket, between products bought in the same week, month or year? This is the classic application of product link analysis to determine dependencies between otherwise apparently unrelated activities.

Case study: mobile telephones

The telecommunications industry in Europe is very competitive. Preventing customer attrition is a key focus since churn in the industry can reach 30 per cent per year. That is a lot of customers to replace. A European cellular phone operator therefore sought to develop a churn model that would indicate clearly which customers were most likely to leave, to enable them to take action before 'good' customers were lost. The company also sought to discover cross-selling and up-selling opportunities. The company asked IBM to research and implement a data-mining based churn model, with clustering, classification and predictive algorithms. With IBM's scalable data-mining algorithms, the company developed models using all its customer data, not just a sample. The output from the models provides a list that assigns a probable attrition value to each customer. This business intelligence approach brings together both transactional and customer base data and helps the company understand the various segments of its customer groups. It provides the company with crucial insight into the characteristics of different customer groups and their churn probability. The probability scores it generates give the company a better understanding of the customer base, which allows it to devise different marketing strategies for different groups.

Case study: banking

A North American bank aimed to be the only bank its customers needed. To get to know customers on an individual basis and treat them personally, it needed a systematic approach to anticipating and meeting client needs. In order to improve productivity and build market share, it needed to:

- Establish a central repository for customer information.
- Unite customer information that had become fragmented within product-centric legacy systems.
- Rely on a comprehensive, long-range predictive customer segmentation model rather than using ad hoc methods that required expert statisticians to spend lots of time sourcing and extracting relevant data.

It realized that its segmentation was too product-centric, focused on finding the right customer for the product rather than vice versa. So it sought a solution to help it segment customers and create a framework for a systematic approach to managing customers. If the bank knew its customers better it would be able to assure consistent treatment across channels. It now scores all its nearly 10 million customers monthly through data-mining tools. Scored profiles are made available to branches, contact centres and support employees. Advanced campaign management software uses these new profiles to select customers for targeting. The bank has developed and deployed various models. Now, in each segment, the group has a model-based approach to determining how to engage with each customer. With relevant information tailored to each customer's financial needs, the bank's employees can treat customers consistently whichever channel they use to interface with the bank. The bank now sends each customer three tailored offers monthly. Through relevant bundling of products and services based on individual needs, the financial group is better positioned to retain customer loyalty and expand its market reach. Using additional credit analytics and event triggers prompted by various segmentation-driven initiatives, it handles overdrafts more efficiently. Now, the group automatically extends overdraft protection to help retain customer loyalty and reduce handling costs. Delivery speed for products and services has also increased through event triggers for next-business-day leads. The bank's decision implementation time has improved as well because:

- It can now identify which individuals constitute a household, and the portfolio of products held by the household.
- Customer matching is performed monthly rather than quarterly.
- More than 40 models are run against the full customer base in a two-day period, improving efficiency and significantly reducing the cost of segmentation analytics.
- The new campaign management system allows better marketing techniques to be used more quickly.

Case study: ING Direct in the United States

As the leader in direct banking, ING Direct is committed to finding new and innovative ways to provide the right products and outstanding service to its customers. By enhancing its systems with E.piphany Interaction Advisor,[1] it has created more intelligent interactions with its customers and offers them products and services tuned to their specific needs and wants when they are relevant. The company has deployed E.piphany Interaction Advisor to 500 agents in its contact centres, and on many pages throughout its website. E.piphany Interaction Advisor uses a combination of rules and real-time analytics to deliver the most relevant offer to customers, when appropriate, during an inbound interaction. An average of 2.4 million online visitors and 100,000 callers per month receive personalized offers via the analytic solution. E.piphany Interaction Advisor provides a number of benefits to ING Direct including direct and indirect revenue generation, cost savings, and improved marketing efficiency. Using E.piphany Interaction Advisor, ING Direct has been able to generate excellent response rates to offers delivered on its website and through its contact centres:

- Contact centre offer response rates as high as 42 per cent.
- Average contact centre offer acceptance of 9.23 per cent – 25 per cent higher than the channel average of 7.44 per cent.
- Web click-through rates as high as 28 per cent.
- Average web offer acceptance rate of 3.86 per cent – more than 17 times the channel average of 0.23 per cent for non-rich media advertisements.
- 39 per cent of click-throughs on ING Direct product offers delivered by E.piphany Interaction Advisor resulted in an opened account.

Strategic benefits

The following is an overview of the strategic benefits achieved by the Interaction Advisor solution:

- *Increased cross-sell revenue*. Customers are presented compelling offers to open additional accounts or utilize other services provided by ING Direct, while promotion of other products and services within the ING family (ie ING America's Retirement website) help to increase company-wide cross-sell revenue.
- *Increased up-sell revenue*. Customers are encouraged to make incremental investments or increase their credit for their existing ING Direct accounts.
- *Retention*. Customers who have accounts that may be coming up for expiration are encouraged to retain their balances in existing ING Direct accounts. Customers are only presented with relevant information or offers increasing customer satisfaction and retention.
- *Acquisition*. New ING Direct customers are acquired through the promotion of the 'Refer a Friend' programme. Satisfied customers tell their friends and family about ING Direct.
- *Cost savings*. Targeted offers ensure customers' time as well as ING Direct's time is not wasted, while optimal timing of offers ensures that unnecessary cross-sell attempts are not made. Operational efficiencies are gained through the collection of missing or incorrect account information while the customer is interacting with ING Direct.

(Source: E.piphany)

DATA-MINING METHODOLOGY

The basic steps of a data-mining analysis are:

- data collection and cleaning;
- data analysis; and
- presentation of the results.

The data to be mined should be those which are likely to be relevant to the business problem and may give business insights if analysed effectively. Most of these data are transactional and collected at the time of sale. Often only a part of the available data are captured and retained at that time. These data are primarily product, not customer data. Response data may also be available. Negative responses are often not collected, yet these are equally important. The full data set includes campaign responses, survey or research data and complaint data. Data on customers, how to access them, their profile and so on may be collected during transactions or by a special collection effort. Combining one or more product sources may also provide more insights into customer behaviour and the relationship between customer and company and on past customers. Data may also be sourced externally. The steps typically involved in data mining are:

1. Understanding the business issue and the factors which affect it.
2. Data collection and warehousing (extraction, transport and loading).
3. Data cleaning, merging and purging, grouping (including house-holding).
4. Variable redefinition and transformation using mathematical techniques.
5. New data collection – typically items revealed as missing.
6. Data mining – often in several steps as 'internal clients' learn about the type of results that can be achieved.
7. Data visualization.
8. New requests for analysis, additional information to be collected and analysed.
9. Assimilation, extrapolation and scoring.
10. Planning – including action and monitoring and deciding whether to do it online rather than offline.

Traditional market segmentation approaches tend to be weak when it comes to understanding how customer behaviour varies over time and location. This is partly because adding these dimensions makes data analysis much more complex. Increased availability of geographical data and an ability to map it means that marketing managers are becoming more demanding when it comes to understanding spatial dimensions. Where time is concerned, time series analyses often led to simplification of the specification of the problem because of the difficulty of handling complex sequences of behaviour. The difficulty in both these areas was not that the statistical techniques could not handle them in theory, but that their introduction multiplied the complexity of the problem and made it hard to implement hypothesis-led approaches.

Too often, companies lose historical data. For example, a customer's new address overwrites the old one. As prediction usually involves analysing current and past relationships, companies should consider keeping past versions of the database for analysis. The simplest example of problems caused by failure to retain historical data would be if a retailer tried to understand why a customer bought at a number of different branches without knowing that the customer had lived at three different addresses!

Basic approaches of data mining

Discovery-led

This is the usual start point for new data-mining users, as they are interested in how existing data can be better used to help solve business problems. The aim is to use self-organizing methods to determine the nature of variation (correlations) within the data, without preconceived ideas as to how the data might be organized. Thus a company might believe it has three customer types: average customers, ordinary buyers of the service or product; very good high-value customers; and bad customers (such as debtors or defaulters). A marketing campaign might aim to reduce defaulters while increasing cross-selling to high-flyers. A discovery-led analysis of the data might show that there are several types of high-flyers with different needs. Alternatively it might show that defaulting is related to particular factors, to which some parts of the 'good' group may also be susceptible.

Hypothesis-led (also known as verification-led)

This is the conventional approach of standard querying, reporting, statistical and neural network or 'mathematical' techniques. Neural networks are particularly appropriate in noisy or dirty data where statistical techniques fail to predict customer behaviour well enough. A hypothesis is formed as to which types of customer have certain characteristics (eg those who might be good prospects or those vulnerable to the competition). A test is then performed to see if this view has significant support from the data. While this approach is still valid, it has the drawback that the hypothesis must be invented before it can be tested. A hypothesis-led approach may lead to critical issues being missed. The hypothesis may be confirmed, but it may not be in the best form or as complete in coverage as it could be. However, later on hypotheses come into their own as discovery techniques start to suggest new areas for hypothesis formation. It may be better to use discovery-led procedures to identify possible hypotheses and then focus on particular factors for testing. For example, a general segmentation of customers into retail buying groups could suggest that there exists a large group of elderly couples on low incomes. The hypothesis that this group also correlates with those who take up low premium insurance policies could then be tested.

Data-mining operations: for hypothesis- or discovery-led work

Data-mining operations can be classified broadly into three types as defined below. The division between these three is not fixed – there is overlap between them. Within each type there are many variations of methodology and application. Note too that each method can be used as part of a discovery approach or a hypothesis approach. It is often the sheer volume of data that pushes companies towards discovery-led approaches because of the difficulty of determining which factors to hypothesize about!

Correlation (or association, or sequencing – if over time)

Correlation seeks to examine how one factor or group of factors relates to another. Simple correlations (whether linear, algebraic or rank) between two factors, usually with an associated confidence factor, are the easiest to understand for managers. Thus income may correlate with the propensity to buy retailer own-brands. Whether a higher income causes this behaviour is a different question, not answered by that analysis but suggested by it. The hypothesis that higher income causes more buying of own-brands may depend on a psychological argument about a diminishing need for the reassurance provided by a manufacturer's brand.

In retailing, correlation analysis is known as 'basket analysis', for obvious reasons. For example, correlation analysis might show that there is a group of customers who buy bacon with eggs and ketchup. The store might then want to place bacon, eggs and ketchup close together for customer convenience. It might also want to place them far apart to ensure that the customers see other products that they might be tempted to buy. Customers found to buy gin and tonic might be offered coupons for a different gin type when they buy a tonic. Actioning the data is a primary management decision. Sequencing refers to an association over time and is a key area for applying data mining. If buying or response behaviour is very frequent, as in, say, grocery retailing or frequent flying, then data mining is needed to explore possible sequencing patterns.

Segmentation (or clustering or classification)

Segmentation involves defining classes and assigning individuals to a particular class based on one or more criteria. For example, a set of customers can be classified according to age, or according to home location. Typically this reveals little about the members of the resulting groups, as there is still high variability in each group. Multi-dependency classifications can be created by techniques such as neural networks which learn to discriminate between individuals based on a composite view of their behaviour. For example, a neural network trained on product-buying activity could learn the past behaviour of customers and be used to predict if new customers would or would not buy the product.

Cluster analysis, or clustering, is a term for grouping similar items together using some numeric criterion of proximity or similarity. The groups are chosen such that they maximize the differences between the groups, while minimizing the differences within each group. There is no prior decision on which groups might exist, or which factors may be important. Relational analysis is used to associate similar customers and put them in the same group. The characteristics of each group can then be examined. For example, a segmentation of bank customers might show that older, retired couples in the UK have smaller mortgages than middle-aged couples with children. Very often the segments do not correspond with exact definitions. They do, however, show tendencies that all the members in a group follow to some degree.

'Segmentation' is a much-abused term and carries with it the dangerous implication that, once grouped, all customers within the group behave in the same way. In some companies the term implies the use of certain determining variables such as geo-demographic or industry sector, even though these may not be the most important dimensions by which customer behaviour differs. Segmentation is the process of separating out groups of customers who are similar but not the same. Segmentation methods vary. They may presuppose that the number of groups is known and try to find them, assume that only large groups are important, require an estimate of the typical members of the group and attempt to find all non-members, or even try to find typical members at the cost of including some who are not typical.

There is no mathematical proof for segmentation. Many outcomes are possible. A good answer is one that is actionable by the business and the best answer is the one that produces the best commercial results. Note too that data-based segmentation is normally validated by market research techniques. This can create confidence as to the validity of the approach.

Text and web mining

Text mining is the mining of words, showing how they are associated. For example, complaints e-mails can be mined to find out what kinds of complaints people have. Many companies mine data about how customers interact with their websites (in particular web logs), to find out which types of customers are interested in particular products, offers and communications. The most advanced form of text mining is IBM's WebFountain project. This uses a massive storage facility to keep an up-to-date copy of the worldwide web. The copy is used for data-mining purposes, via various text-mining applications.

Here are two examples of its application to customer insight:

- *Reputation tracking*. In every enterprise, a healthy reputation is the foundation of the business. Web mining develops an early warning system that can monitor and identify issues as they emerge online. It can identify and track global issues that could affect a company's reputation, spot new and emerging issues and provide a 360° view of how the company is perceived by customers and others. This is useful in industries where public perceptions heavily influence a company's operations such as those concerning sustainable development, the environment, or health risks, such as petroleum/ energy, customer packaged goods, retail, automotive, financial/ investing, health and pharmaceuticals.
- *Buzz tracking*. This enables monitoring of the 'buzz' or 'customer chatter' about a company or its products. It is used to develop or adjust marketing strategies. Even simple buzz measures can

provide useful insights. For example, 'active buzz' is a leading indicator for CDs and DVD sales for pop chart movement.

Example of data-mining techniques in action

At first sight, data-mining applications appear to be horrendously expensive and time-consuming. Of course, the word 'expensive' is relative. Since, as Peter Drucker famously remarked in the 1950s, survival is not compulsory, companies need to spend money in order to survive and be profitable. One also needs to consider ROI. If the margins are higher and the gains outweigh the investment then it is worth pursuing, especially when there is the right time window and this will provide the company with a competitive edge. Industries that have already started to develop very large additional data sets such as utilities or retail cards, or industries that have been gathering these data sets for some time, are now in the situation where better analysis is more important. Increased competitive pressure or the realization that the data holds clues to competitive advantage such as in frequent-flyer programmes or retail product data also lend themselves to this technique. Major user industries therefore include financial services, retail and distribution, especially those using direct mail, telecommunications and utilities and travel and transportation. Many such companies now treat data mining as a normal part of their activities. In fact the software they use to analyse data, in particular for clustering, may incorporate data-mining approaches of which users are unaware, so routine has data mining become.

The benefits are substantial. The first is a reduction in marketing waste, because the increased response and conversion rates means marketing resources can be saved. The second, equally important, is sustaining reputation and brand, as customers start to rate companies more highly for their attempts to listen and respond relevantly. Let us follow through an example for the deployment of data mining in sense and respond marketing. Sense and respond is based mainly on what companies do already in terms of systems and processes but with a much enhanced data set, working at much greater depth, faster, more comprehensively and with better integration. This is illustrated in Table 10.1.

Propensity scoring and targeting

The example in Table 10.1 shows that the company identified the customer in some way from amongst perhaps millions of records in a

Table 10.1 *Example of data mining in practice*

Customer view	Company view
The customer receives a message, asking whether they would like to provide some information about what they are planning to do in the next year or so. The questions are initially closed-ended, referring to the main life-cycle and product-cycle events that produce value for the company and its customers' events such as change of job, move of house, marriage, divorce, have a baby, pay off a loan, buy a car. The customer does not have to complete every question. Once a question is answered positively, the customer receives a few additional questions relating to it, how much they will spend, when, and possibly why. There is also an unstructured field for any further information that the customer wishes to give. This field will be analysed by text mining.	The company profiles the customer within its customer database. This triggers a lead that this is a customer with whom the company would like to do more business and with whom the company would like a peer-to-peer, adult dialogue. In particular, the company decides it would like to know more about the events likely to happen in the customer's life where the company would be able to help the customer and give good value. So the website prompts the customer with a series of questions about what is coming up in the customer's life, their preferences etc. It also asks the customer what they would like to know about what the company is (a) thinking in terms of meeting the customers' needs, and (b) planning in terms of changing its products, services and channels to meet the needs of customers like this one.
The customer is then asked whether they would like the information they have given to lead to a response by the company and in which channel or combinations of channels (eg letter, telephone call, e-mail, invitation to visit the branch). They are also asked when they would like the response.	The customer's newly given data are analysed along with existing data to work out what kinds of things the company could do for the customer. Suggestions are made to the customer about what these should be.
Information on the desired response is stored, and made available to replay to the customer whenever they log on (or perhaps in any channel).	Responses from the customer are analysed, and where the customer has asked for a positive sales or marketing response the action is triggered but in the same adult-to-adult style.
The information is acted on and the customer either buys or changes a product, or registers satisfaction with information received.	The information is acted on and sales are closed.

large data set. This type of analysis is an extension of correlation or segmentation. It is based on the question, 'What is the propensity of x to be associated with y?' A critical question might be, what are the characteristics of a customer who is likely to stop buying our product? Special techniques exist to do this type of study and there are applications in diverse areas such as basket analysis and customer loyalty. Identifying the factors which predispose a customer to an action, such that a numerical score or probability can be assigned, is typically done by fitting an optimization function on multidimensional data and measuring the difference between a given individual or group from the general behaviour of all the groups. For example, a predictive model fitted to the lapsing behaviour of an insurance company's customers can assign a probability to the likelihood that some groups of customers might lapse. The size of the group can be used to calculate the risk to the company and the profile of the group's members can be used to create a marketing plan aimed at retaining those customers.

In many cases, companies want to apply these ideas at the point of contact with the customer so that appropriate offerings can be made. Data collected in customer dialogues can now be utilized by such predictive scoring models almost in real time. Thus scripting which prompts the staff member in their dealings with the customer can now be more dynamic and responsive to what is being exchanged. Following prediction should come testing. This is usually a sample-based marketing activity to validate the prediction or discover where it does not work. Data-mining techniques can be easily adapted to this process. An analysis of several segments of high-value customers can be used to build a model to predict future high value customers. This is then tested for accuracy when applied to new customer data sets. Figure 10.1 illustrates the overall cycle of events between customer dialogues and the use of data-mining techniques. It shows how the enabling infrastructure is used to build business capabilities that respond to customer insights.

FROM BELL CURVES TO WELL CURVES

In today's evolving marketplace, companies are facing extremes characterized by unprecedented complexity, intense competition and market polarization. Customers are increasingly demanding relevant value propositions that meet their individual needs and preferences. They will seek out those companies able to provide them. This new environment requires a shift in thinking from a traditional distri-

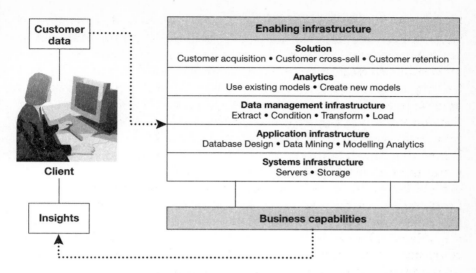

Figure 10.1 _Building capabilities that respond to customer insights_

bution of volumes and value, from bell curves to what might be called 'well curves'. Well curves are based on an idea put forward by Pink (2003) and describe the situation where growth and perceived customer value migrate to opposite ends of the competitive spectrum.

To compete, companies need to become truly customer-centric in strategy and execution to avoid being overtaken by more sophisticated competitors. Customer-centricity starts through a deeper understanding of the multiple dimensions and drivers of target customers' buying decisions. By developing proprietary customer insights developed through data mining, companies can create a more tailored and relevant customer service. Data mining to support marketing based on operational analytics helps companies to deal with some of the marketing revolutions that we have looked at so far:

- _Customer value drivers are fragmenting._ Micro-market segments are resulting from pronounced shifts in demographics (the 50+ market), changes in attitudes (the marketing-savvy customer) and in patterns of behaviour. Customers are trading up to premium brands whilst simultaneously trading down to low-cost providers.
- _Gatekeepers are becoming more guarded._ Overwhelmed and time-strapped customers are exerting greater control over their interactions with businesses. Empowered by new technology and regulation, customers will protect their identities and personal data more aggressively from 'me-too' marketing tactics.

- *Information exposes all.* Customer choices are being shaped through unparalleled access to information, virtually wherever, whenever and however they want it. There are many internet-based sources for comparison shopping, investment advice and consumer reports.
- *The Super Corporation has arrived.* The world's top companies are rapidly expanding across geographies, formats, and product and service categories, blurring market segments and devouring market share. Financial services, retail banking, utilities, retailers, transport and telecommunications have an increasingly transnational character as corporations expand their reach internationally.
- *Partnering has become pervasive.* Leading companies are creating flexible value networks based on strong integration and collaboration with alliance partners. Competitors will be challenged to match the responsiveness and agility of these connected market leaders.

These major trends are driving industry to a world of extremes where customer diversity and individualism are pervasive, and traditional segmentation is rendered inadequate. Customers demand low prices for basic goods but pay premiums for products that matter more to them personally. Consequently, those best positioned to grow and succeed will be huge transnational corporations at one end of the spectrum, and targeted retailers at the other. Meanwhile undifferentiated companies, lost in the middle, risk fading into irrelevance.

A marketing revolution is therefore needed to respond to the changes implied by a switch from bell curves, where firms try to serve a generic mass market but do not meet anyone's needs particularly effectively, to what Pink called well curves, where companies drive growth by applying distinct models in each part of their business to deliver the greatest value to explicitly defined groups of customers. The well curve idea is illustrated in Figure 10.2.

Deeper insight fosters innovation and a competitive edge. Customer value drivers are inherently multidimensional and getting more complex all the time. Traditional classifications and segmentation (largely based on demographic characteristics) are increasingly inadequate to predict accurately whether and to what degree new initiatives (for example in marketing, merchandising and services) will succeed in generating the desired customer response. Companies need to develop deeper customer insights through more sophisticated approaches to segmentation and innovative analytical models.

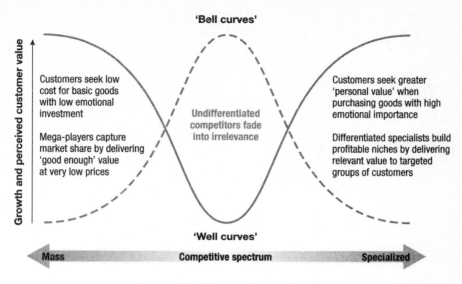

Figure 10.2 _The 'well curve' concept_

DEALING WITH COMPLEXITY: MARKETING RESOURCE MANAGEMENT

So far we have argued that the marketing revolution requires a different role for marketing and a different, more customer-centric posture for the company. Using customer insights derived from data mining, companies will seek to find patterns in their customer database, to model the behaviour of customers within those segments and develop perhaps hundreds of mini marketing campaigns that respond fluidly and dynamically to changing customer needs. So far so good? Clearly, this new marketing environment is much more complex. Table 10.2 summarizes the significant challenge that this presents to marketers.

Marketing resource management (MRM) is a set of processes and capabilities that aim to enhance a company's ability to coordinate and optimize the use of internal and external marketing resources. MRM applications facilitate planning and budgeting, they coordinate execution and measure the impact of marketing efforts. The five key functionality components of MRM are shown in Figure 10.3.

Imagine a large retailer which currently runs perhaps 20 or 30 annual marketing campaigns for its 5 million customers. It now plans to change its approach, running maybe 200 or 300 campaigns for an

Table 10.2 *The challenge of increased marketing complexity*

Marketing complexity arises from...	Evidenced by...
Increased volume of promotional campaigns	Campaign volumes have decreased as targeting has improved but the overall frequency of campaign activity – the number of campaigns – has increased.
Availability of more communication channels	More channels and the integration often needed in multichannel campaigns means campaign planning, prioritization and execution is far more complicated.
Increased legislation	Compliance processes are more convoluted and involve more people than ever. This can be an administrative nightmare, especially if combined with increased campaign velocity.
Move to real-time communications	The move to real-time marketing with databases that are refreshed in real or near real time means that the planning cycle has been reduced.
Industry consolidation	Growth of enterprise marketing functions that have to support multiple brands and/or business units; further complications for campaign planning and execution.
Lack of process support in marketing automation solutions	Limited or no support for project/supplier management, planning, competitive analysis and product management in existing marketing toolsets.

increased customer base of 8 to 10 million. To manage that, it needs to streamline its creative development process, improve its ability to manage the approvals needed internally at each stage of the campaign, control brand guidelines and control versioning (different versions) of each stage of the creative process. The company needs better visibility and accountability in its marketing operations as a whole, tracking the status of all initiatives, including budgets, expenses, impact on revenue and other key metrics. Not surprisingly therefore, according to Forrester Research (2005), MRM strikes a chord with very large firms: 'Close to half the companies contacted with turnovers greater than $5 billion indicated that they will adopt the process that allows them to manage the marketing process and resources such as people, creative assets and money.' The aim of this is to reduce the time to market of new campaigns by up to 40 per cent and to achieve cost savings of as much as 10 per cent. If this provides the competitive advantage to be expected then a trickle down effect will occur, as happened with other technology-based approaches such as CRM, enterprise resource planning (ERP) or even direct marketing.

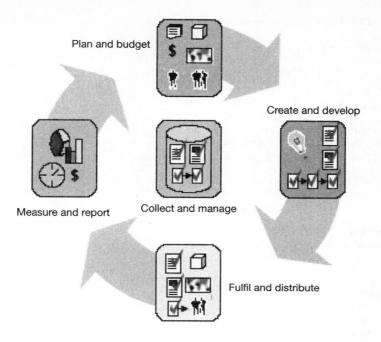

Figure 10.3 *The components of MRM*
Source: Gartner (2004).

New technologies are hardly well known for their modest announcements and many new approaches suffer from the disadvantages of overhyping in the early days, promising significant and substantial savings and benefits in the short term. In reality of course, what is being offered is a road to a new way of doing things based on a major change effort. The bigger, the more substantial the investment, the more painful and fundamental the corporate changes necessary to exploit it to the full. Nevertheless early signs are promising. According to one study of 164 companies carried out by Gartner in 2004, most (MRM) applications already provided basic measurement and reporting capabilities that enhanced the visibility of marketing plans, activities and budgets (including actual and committed spending to date). These basic measurement and reporting capabilities often provided the first real overview of marketing programmes for most marketers, who have traditionally lacked such data. In the study 40 per cent of companies cited the deployment of such measurement and reporting capabilities.

MRM functionality is typically flexible enough to support tying marketing programmes to marketing departments, investment accounts, geographies or regions, audiences or segments, brands and products which enable marketers (and financial managers) to data-mine all of the marketing activities to get a clear view of what is happening by department, budget, geographic region, industry, brand, product or customer segment. Work remains to be done in areas such as measurement relative to market performance of marketing activities. The effective deployment of such capabilities often requires integration with a variety of custom-built or prepackaged marketing-point solutions, as well as customer relationship management (CRM), ERP and financial management applications. The panacea of true enterprise-wide marketing resource optimization is still rather futuristic for the time being. In many companies, however, the vision has begun to get closer to reality. Figures 10.4 and 10.5 illustrate how efficiencies promised by MRM can be delivered.

MRM enables integration of the various stages of the marketing approach more seamlessly at each point. One of the key capabilities of measurement and reporting is the ability to track forecast, committed and actual costs and results in more detail and more frequently than is typically done for marketing initiatives. This capability allows decisions to be taken that avoid overspending in a timely fashion. It also enables better post-event analysis to refine and plan future marketing strategies. Knowing exactly how decisions might affect the

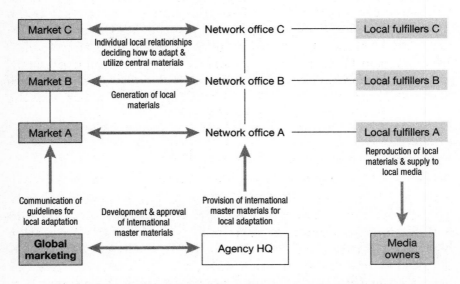

Figure 10.4 *Traditional marketing processes can be very inefficient*
Source: Adgistics Corporation.

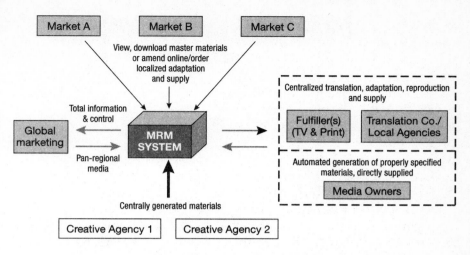

Figure 10.5 _Efficiencies produced by marketing automation_
Source: Adgistics Corporation.

performance of the brand and the achievement of marketing objectives is critical to the success of any 'joined-up' business process. Revenue, spending, profit, return on investment, earnings before income tax, cycle time, project management and more can only be driven by better understanding how decisions affect the outcome of these behaviours and activities. MRM capabilities provide a user-friendly opportunity to track all information and plans compared to actual results at the product or customer level, and identify and share best practice across the enterprise. By providing regular updates of critical performance information, users can respond more quickly and accurately to variances in a plan. Opportunities are more readily exploited and problems are resolved more quickly at less expense. Table 10.3 summarizes these benefits. Figure 10.6 shows how MRM can deliver benefits in the approvals process for a new advertising campaign.

Contributions and benefits of MRM

Many software vendors are now offering an MRM capability, including Oracle PeopleSoft and SAP. Probably the leading company in this area in 2005 is Aprimo, closely followed by Unica and SmartPath. These vendors all support data-mining analysis campaign results or marketing metrics, by providing the ability to look at results by business unit, brand, product, customer segments, sales channel, media or vendor. Industries primarily interested in these capabilities include brand and consumer product goods, media and retail

Table 10.3 *The challenges faced by MRM*

Marketing function	The challenges
Goals and strategy	• Collaboration • Share best practices • Knowledge sharing
Content creation	• Poor visibility internally • Access and availability • Versioning and adaptation expenses
Creative execution	• Long cycle times • Duplication of effort • Cost replication
Localization	• Adaptation costs (customizing campaigns by country or region) • Reliance on third parties (local agents) • Maintaining brand consistency
Fulfilment	• Wastage • Inventory management • Forecasting
Contact management	• Effectiveness • Response tracking • Developing customer insights and the application of learning

companies. Several decision points within the business process require more sophisticated analytics than just measurement and reporting. Areas such as financial and volume forecasting, financial return on investment, marketing mix allocations, scenario planning and simulation need to be supported. MRM packages thus provide a platform whereby companies can incorporate internal or external statistical models and intellectual property content into decision processes. These might include predictions on tactical behaviour, for example, customer response and conversion rates by value. Such capabilities help drive better marketing efficiency by analysing the data as to how consumers will respond to brand promotions, product introductions, loyalty programmes and direct marketing campaigns.

Optimization and simulation are advanced analytical MRM capabilities. Marketing function optimization analyses various marketing programmes and their associated activities. With it, marketing managers can choose what portion of their marketing resources to align with specific promotions, direct outbound marketing campaigns and event-triggered retention and cross-sell campaigns. It can also help determine trade-offs in value between more centralized marketing campaigns driven to direct channels, and local field marketing initiatives within those channels. Marketing mix optimization is the decision process in which the user determines how to

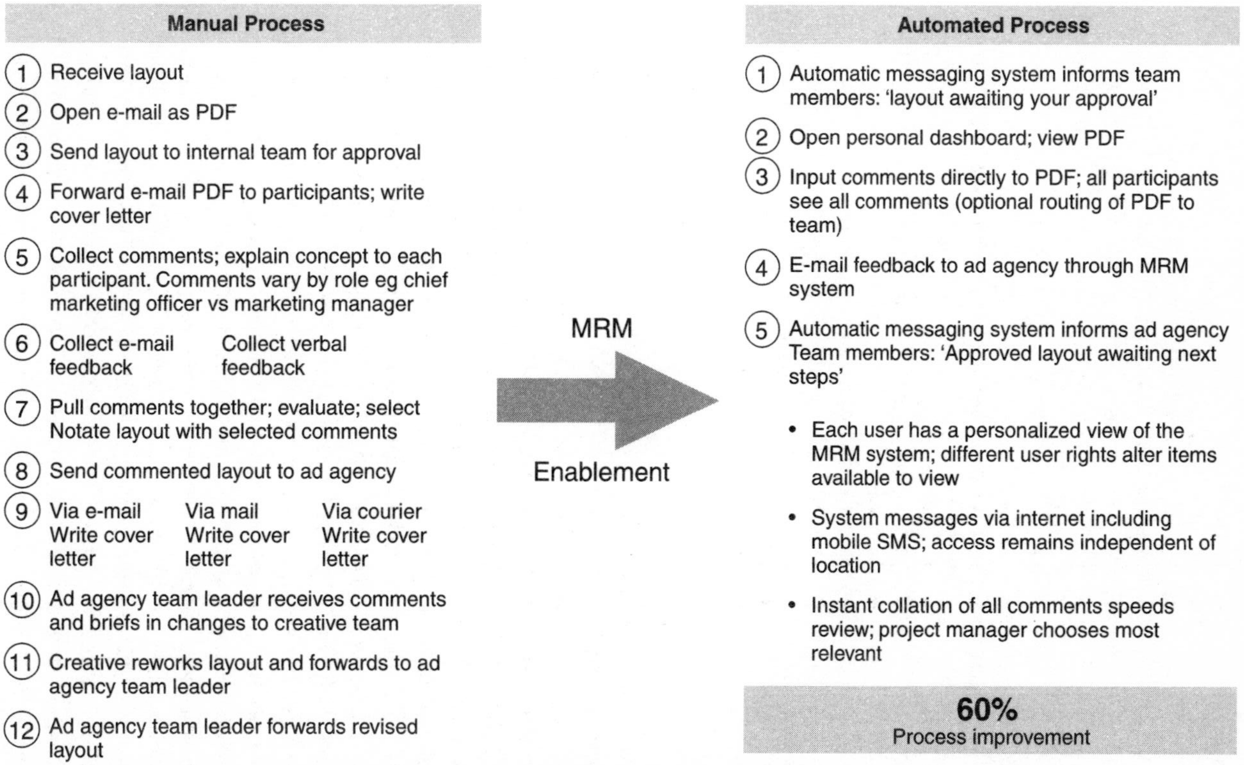

Manual Process

1. Receive layout

2. Open e-mail as PDF

3. Send layout to internal team for approval

4. Forward e-mail PDF to participants; write cover letter

5. Collect comments; explain concept to each participant. Comments vary by role eg chief marketing officer vs marketing manager

6. Collect e-mail feedback   Collect verbal feedback

7. Pull comments together; evaluate; select Notate layout with selected comments

8. Send commented layout to ad agency

9. Via e-mail   Via mail   Via courier
Write cover letter   Write cover letter   Write cover letter

10. Ad agency team leader receives comments and briefs in changes to creative team

11. Creative reworks layout and forwards to ad agency team leader

12. Ad agency team leader forwards revised layout

Automated Process

1. Automatic messaging system informs team members: 'layout awaiting your approval'

2. Open personal dashboard; view PDF

3. Input comments directly to PDF; all participants see all comments (optional routing of PDF to team)

4. E-mail feedback to ad agency through MRM system

5. Automatic messaging system informs ad agency Team members: 'Approved layout awaiting next steps'

- Each user has a personalized view of the MRM system; different user rights alter items available to view

- System messages via internet including mobile SMS; access remains independent of location

- Instant collation of all comments speeds review; project manager chooses most relevant

MRM

Enablement

60%
Process improvement

Figure 10.6 *How MRM achieves efficiencies: approval of a new advertising campaign*
Source: Adgistics Corporation.

allocate the annual marketing budget across and within all the components of the marketing mix: media, advertising, consumer promotion, public relations, and trade spending and programmes. Product portfolio optimization allows the marketer to determine the best mix and pricing of products and services in an individual customer's or customer segment's entire portfolio, based on customer value. Simulation and scenario-planning capabilities for product portfolios include the ability to identify the next-best products to offer to increase the value of the product portfolio, using 'what if' modelling.

As with new forecasting techniques, where the standard approach is to forecast the past so that the performance of the forecast can be compared with known outcomes, before forecasting the future, the recommended approach to introducing MRM is to first use optimization and simulation on established data sets. Once confidence has been developed in the results, the techniques can be applied to new products, brands, channels and customer segments to enable more efficient planning and budgeting for product development or better execution of new product campaign launches.

SUMMARY

The benefits of MRM are not open to all companies. Primarily, companies with international scope, deploying large marketing budgets, using a predominantly traditional marketing production process and where complexity is high due to the need to comply with legislation or the constraints of the brand, will benefit most. In these circumstances, MRM will establish the capability for a company to exploit the improved insights that its data-mining and modelling processes will provide in a number of ways. These might include:

- reducing the overall cost of marketing products and services;
- improving, formalizing and standardizing the marketing production and approval processes to a more consistent standard;
- developing the capability to plan and execute promotions in shorter cycle times to improve 'speed to market';
- establishing the ability to ramp up/down or modify marketing message content according to the consumer demand over time;
- helping get products and services to market more quickly and consistently;

- increasing the productiveness of the marketing department(s) so that they focus less on administrative tasks and more on demand-generation activities;
- providing a holistic view of all promotional programmes and campaigns both in calendar form and from a financial perspective.

Case study: Peugeot

The French company Peugeot is the sixth-largest car manufacturer in the world. It was concerned about wasted costs and delivery delays in development of 300+ brochures to promote its cars across the globe. It was also worried about the inefficient collaboration across multiple global teams. All its marketing campaigns had to meet the appropriate ISO (International Standards Office) certifications which complicated the approvals process. The approach it adopted was to create a centralized, global platform for digital marketing assets, task management and process measurement. The marketing production and digital asset management tool that it deployed, managed the design and fulfilment processes for more than 70 people across extended teams, located worldwide. The benefits achieved were in three main areas. Reduced cycle times to launch were obtained by the use of process workflow templates and the sharing of best practices by catalogue type. Improved accuracy and visibility of marketing activities was established by means of the centralized repository of assets, details and notes coupled with automated, real-time reporting against process time lines and the delivery of outputs. Costs were reduced by shortening learning curves for new team members, by improved internal communications and by better relationships with suppliers.

(See Aprimo, 2003.)

NOTE

1. E.piphany Interaction Advisor is a registered brand of E.piphany.

11

Revolution through people

ARE MARKETERS SMARTER THAN FROGS?

To succeed in the revolution of the marketing function is to succeed in introducing a major organizational change. Whilst this book is not the place for a major discussion of approaches to change management (see, for example, Burnes, 2000 for a full discussion) it is worth reviewing a few of the key principles and offering a framework to increase the chances of success. If existing studies on the implementation of marketing change, such as the introduction of a customer relationship management approach, or a radical change in business model are considered, it will be seen that the biggest barrier to successful change is deployment of change management techniques. When companies do deploy them, the change is much more likely to be successful and profitable, but such success is rare. Putting it another way, marketers are not very good at managing change, but when they do it well, it works.

Why should this be so? The 'obvious' answer is that people do not like change. It threatens the existing state of affairs and introduces many unknowns. Therefore they resist it and maybe attack the change agents. Conversely, a lack of resistance is clearly not a good sign; it probably means that people are either frightened or simply do not care. So, some resistance is to be expected and this can be unpleasant for all involved.

Which brings us to the first, important question we need to address. Are marketers smarter than frogs? Sadly, the answer is often 'no'. Frogs are very good at spotting radical external changes to their environment. If you drop a frog onto a saucer of very hot water, the amphibian will sense the sudden change in its external environment, understand that it cannot adjust its body temperature that fast, and hop away without suffering any great harm. Most managers can do that too. Present them with a sudden, radical change and they can understand the need to take action. However, if you take the same frog and place it gently in a saucer of water at room temperature, it will be perfectly happy. Heat the water gently and the frog will adjust, little by little, to the change in temperature. Sadly, at around 50° the frog will pass into a coma and around 80° it will cook and die. The point being of course that anyone can spot sudden change, but recognizing gradual, incremental change is much harder – and a failure to do so can be fatal.

Marketing training rarely focuses on change management. Further, marketers are rarely exposed to good change management practice and even more rarely rewarded for achieving high-quality change. Their rewards are more related to how well they deploy their existing marketing mix. This is fine in companies in which the way marketing is done does not change much; but where changes in regulation, technology or market forces constantly change how marketers need to work, it is very dangerous. For a marketing director, the implications are clear. Examine your own change management record, consider the scale of the task you are undertaking and make sure you plan for change. This may mean going back to school to train yourself up, or hiring in consultants as change agents to assist the process.

If the nature of the marketing revolution is considered, the frog can also provide us with another example. Frogs do not walk, they hop. They can hop in any direction and may do so in an unexpected direction. Thus the marketing revolution requires moving to a future that is not related to the past. This is not a linear change, it is a case of looking around and jumping to a new point. The guideline here is based on the 'four Is':

- _Imagine_ – what can be done. An innovative company responds to and anticipates new kinds of customer services, new kinds of relationship, new kinds of marketing campaigns. This is the realm of inspiration. A 'me-too' approach is probably too slow. Scenario planning and brainstorming might be used here to identify what kind of PANS (pretty amazing new stuff) will be in action in three (or five) years' time.

- *Ignition* – always put the customer first, be innovative and creative. Better customer insights are needed, new technologies must be deployed to develop these insights, but once the insights are achieved they must be actioned.
- *Inspire* – the team. What would be true if the marketing director were able to bring about this change? What kinds of values would be important to the marketing team? How will this be achieved? There will be a need to change cultural values.
- *Implement* – and measure. This means measuring not only current marketing performance and customer relationships, but also morale and values within the marketing team. It is these movements of morale and values that are probably the leading indicators as to whether the change is likely to be successful.

Writing in the middle of the last century, famous social scientist Kurt Lewin, noted for his work on field theory and organizational dynamics, observed, 'There is nothing so practical as a good theory'. If a marketing revolution is to be achieved, marketing managers need a good working model for introducing the change. The process is illustrated in Figure 11.1.

THE PRESSURE TO CHANGE

Three dimensions of change need to be considered: the marketing environment, the enterprise itself and people as individuals. We will be concentrating on changes as they affect members of the enterprise in this chapter, but it is worth remembering that customers might need careful change management too.

Organizations and individuals have different drivers for wanting change. Both are driven by the external environment. The external environment drives both individuals and the enterprise to change how they work and build relationships. Whilst technologies like data mining have changed many of the characteristics of work, the technology itself drives neither the CEO nor the post boy. They are both driven by what technology has done to invent competitiveness on a global scale, to integrate incompatible industries, to compete in allied market sectors, to work within integrated value chains, to adapt to

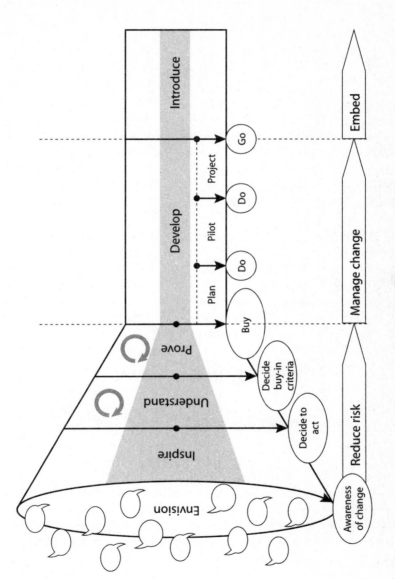

Figure 11.1 *Managing the marketing revolution*

changing customer attitudes. Along the way this has altered working practices, allowed the enforcement of more complex regulation, permitted customers to insist on an ethical stance on environmental issues and to make processing power a commodity.

For the enterprise, the change is driven by the need to develop a more customer-centric, responsive and fluid organization. The company must invest in becoming more responsive in its approach to market forces. In the medium term, it must build profitability whilst avoiding a tightening spiral of efficiency initiatives that first strangle employees and then customers. At the same time, the company must hold onto the loyalty of its shareholders and maintain the confidence of the capital markets so as to be able to raise capital to enhance its competitiveness in new markets and new countries. Above all, the change must focus on being viable (being profitable and competitive and with a cost-effective infrastructure) in the long term. In other words, the change is seen as both strategic and tactical.

All this could create concern at the individual level. Individuals fret over their lack of security, even in the short term, questioning their job satisfaction. Driven by company initiatives to cut corners, they live with the threat of redundancy, whatever the quality of their work. Recognition and rewards are difficult to achieve in a cost-cutting atmosphere; financial gain is beyond imagining. Individuals are now driven to look out for themselves, to plan for several careers, retraining opportunities and step changes in title, seniority and salary. Advancement may be slow, while even in the medium term there may be little security.

TOOLS AND TECHNIQUES

Marketing managers rarely have a second chance to achieve change efficiently and effectively. The choice of tools and techniques is critical to the change process. Using them systematically and correctly will make the difference between success and failure.

Figure 11.2 illustrates the criteria to be considered when looking at how to introduce change. The degree of change experienced depends partly on the approach taken to building the organization needed for the solutions enterprise. The renewal or 'Big Bang' approach means big changes, creating a new organization from scratch very quickly, with some completely new business processes and IT systems. New employees may need to be recruited to bring their experience of change or of the new marketing solution from other companies. Companies may even be acquired or new subsidiaries be set up to handle the change. The alternative is an evolutionary approach. This involves developing the organization over time, building on existing structure and resources. Each approach has advantages and disadvantages. The revolutionary approach enables a company to move quickly and get the benefits of its strategy early. However, this approach often involves more disruption. Mergers and acquisitions, for example, must be managed carefully. The evolutionary approach is often easier to execute. It can allow fewer issues to be dealt with at a time. However, if the change process is too slow, fewer benefits may be realized. This may be a bigger problem in highly competitive markets, where first-mover advantages can be great.

It is in everyone's interest for the change to be managed for the greater good of all those who are involved in it. When changes are being made to a way of working it is important to understand how to manage the change for the benefit of oneself, the team or the group. A repertoire of techniques can be envisaged which in turn give an indication of the type of approach to which the change management process lends itself. Table 11.1 suggests the scope of the change and the likely complexity of the associated change intervention.

The five levels described are chosen to differentiate sufficiently the various uses for tools and techniques. The passive role has little complexity for the change manager, though it thoroughly frustrates the change process. The fire-fighting role is acceptable, in that a reaction has been generated, possibly by provocative statements or actions. The reactive role has more complexity than passivity because the reaction may not be wholly supportive of the change process. The change agent may be the individual or team that has created the reaction. Acting as a catalyst, the team will interact in many different

Degree of change

	Incremental	Radical
Participative	Evolutionary	Renewal
Autocratic	Conventional	Survival

Style of change

Figure 11.2 *Degree of change*

Table 11.1 *Choosing a change role*

Role	Complexity (on a scale of 1 to 10)
Passive (do nothing)	1 (low)
Reactive (fire-fighting)	3
Change agent (catalyst for change)	5
Proactive (shaping the team)	7
Leadership	10 (high)

ways with all levels of the organization, deploying tools and techniques in many different situations. Complexity is higher in reactive roles, though provided the catalysts themselves do not change, their complexity rating will remain in the middle range. The proactive shapers are those who are ready to change and be changed, with less predictable outcomes. They require strong leadership to ensure that the change process remains on track. A brainstorm with many proactive members can be quickly derailed if all the basic corporate values are dismissed one by one and the group devise a highly original, wholly unworkable outcome! The final leadership role is the most complex. A great deal of power is placed in the hands of one person or a small team, who can be inspired or who can become a cabal or clique. The leadership role can bring resounding success or abject failure to the change process. Generally the nature of the marketing revolution that we are advocating is going to demand a position at the upper end of the scale, where the change manager takes a proactive or leadership role.

Change must be planned and managed. Otherwise there is risk of failure. LaClair and Rao (2002), in a recent study of change programmes in 40 organizations, found that 58 per cent failed to meet their targets. The remaining 42 per cent of companies that reached or exceeded their expected returns had strong change management capabilities and a change management infrastructure in place. Indeed the US Department of Labor has estimated that organizational productivity can drop by as much as 45 per cent whilst major change is taking place, as employees focus on coping with and internalizing the changes. Figure 11.3 illustrates the effect of the socialization processes which are essential to absorb the change.

Managing the change transition helps to reduce the dip in performance and maximize the return on the (often large) investment required by the company to revolutionize its marketing processes. A leadership role for the management of the change may:

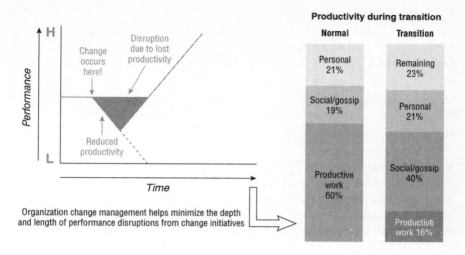

Figure 11.3 *Effect of change on productivity*
Source: Abbot, J (2004) in Cerasale and Stone.

- Help allay any personal fears employees have about what is expected of them.
- Focus on creating the right organizational environment for people who need to change, by helping them to thrive and the company to succeed.
- Explain and set expectations about the changes that are needed, a prerequisite for the development of new capabilities.
- Foster commitment from those parts of the organization which may not undergo deep change themselves but which must provide vital support, such as finance and logistics.

This should help marketers understand the challenges and opportunities involved in moving to a new approach. It should ensure objectives are set, measures of success established and that there is a plan for delivery during the transition.

DIAGNOSING THE ORGANIZATION: A STRUCTURAL ANALYSIS

It is almost a truism to say that unless the people who are to effect and be affected by the change are fully considered, the chances of success are small. A useful first step is therefore to look at the organization in which the change is to be introduced. Based on an instrument devised by Carnall (1990), the questionnaire shown in Table 11.2 can be used to diagnose the status of the existing systems and processes, along with their effectiveness. The questionnaire which we have used to evaluate the approach to change needed to implement customer relationship management more effectively, is designed to look at how the organization works now in eight important areas. These are: the key tasks of the company, the organization structure, people relationships, motivation, support roles, management and leadership, attitudes towards change and performance. Members are asked to complete the questionnaire independently, responding to each of the questions on a seven-point scale, from Agree Strongly (1), Agree, Agree Slightly, Neutral, Disagree Slightly, Disagree, to Disagree Strongly (7). Individual scores are then entered on a score sheet (see Table 11.3) and aggregated.

Table 11.2 *Diagnosing the marketing organization*

No.	Statement	
1	I understand the marketing objectives of this enterprise	—
2	The organization of work here is effective	—
3	Managers will always listen to ideas for better customer focus	—
4	I am encouraged to develop my full potential	—
5	My immediate boss has ideas that are helpful to me and my work group	—
6	My immediate boss is supportive and helps me in my work	—
7	This enterprise keeps its marketing policies and procedures relevant and up to date	—
8	We regularly achieve our marketing objectives	—
9	The goals and objectives of this enterprise are clearly stated in marketing terms	—
10	Jobs and lines of authority are flexible	—
11	I can always talk to someone at work if I have a work-related problem	—
12	The salary I receive is commensurate with the job that I do	—
13	I have all the information and resources I need to do a good job	—
14	The management style of my enterprise is helpful and effective	—
15	We constantly review our customer focus and introduce improvements	—
16	Results are attained because people are committed to them	—
17	I feel motivated by the work I do	—
18	The way in which tasks are divided is sensible and clear	—
19	My personal relationships with fellow workers, customers and suppliers is good	—
20	There are opportunities for promotion and increased responsibility in this organization	—

21 My enterprise sets realistic plans —

22 My performance is regularly reviewed and I get feedback about my relationship management skills —

23 There are occasions when I would like to be freer to make changes in my job —

24 Everyone at work is very cost-conscious and seeks to make the best use of resources —

25 The priorities of this enterprise are thoroughly understood by all employees who are highly committed to them —

26 There is a constant search for improving the way we work —

27 There is a good cooperative atmosphere to get the work done, we all own customer problems —

28 Encouragement and recognition is given for all tasks in the enterprise —

29 Departments work well together to achieve customer goals. There are no functional silos in my enterprise —

30 It is generally recognized that the management team provides inspiring and effective leadership —

31 This enterprise has the capacity to change —

32 The work we do is always necessary and effective. We get things done! —

33 In my own area of work, objectives are clearly set in relation to customer management and each person's role is absolutely defined in those terms —

34 The way that work is structured within the enterprise produces a good, general level of satisfaction —

35 Conflicts of opinion and views are resolved by customer-orientated solutions which are generally understood and accepted —

36 All individual work performance is reviewed against agreed standards —

37 I always know that I can call on other departments or parts of the supply chain to help if I have a problem —

38 My boss's management style helps me in the performance of my own work

39 Creativity and initiative are encouraged. Staff don't have to refer up the line for trivial decisions —

40 Everyone is always concerned to do a good job —

Table 11.3 _Score sheet for organizational diagnosis_

Key tasks	Strctr.	Rltns.	Motiv.	Support	Mngmnt. & leadshp.	Attitudes to change	Perfmnce.
1	2	3	4	5	6	7	8
9	10	11	12	13	14	15	16
17	18	19	20	21	22	23	24
25	26	27	28	29	30	31	32
33	34	35	36	37	38	39	40
Total							
Average							

The diagnosis will not reveal how to introduce the required changes into a particular company or enterprise. However, it will help to show areas of strengths and weakness that may require special attention in the change process. For example, if management performance is seen as ineffective with weak leadership, this might be particularly frustrating to members of the marketing team who will be looking for a strong leadership role to effect change. Conversely, high levels of motivation and a positive attitude to change can be used as important building blocks. These results can be especially useful to highlight differences between departments or divisions of the company. A small, key group of change leaders can use the results of the diagnosis to plan their change strategies more effectively.

The exercise has another, more profound application. In the history of competitive enterprise, from war through to games, it has been shown that good morale can do a great deal to overcome deficiencies in material. Examples abound of various Davids overcoming their respective Goliaths. Morale is important and self-belief by both managers and staff are crucial to successful change. If managers have low expectations of their people or lack confidence in their abilities then they are setting out on a difficult venture in a negative frame of mind. The response they are likely to elicit will probably be adverse. The diagnostic tool will show all those involved that managers recognize the scale of the change they are about to introduce, are interested in the concerns of their staff and are prepared to address those aspects of organization culture that may hinder a response. Wrong assumptions about culture and morale can lead to poor decision making. The diagnostic tool forces managers to put the change effort into a formal context, to recognize better where training might be needed and to understand more fully the nature of the concerns that people have about their new future.

LEADING REVOLUTIONARY CHANGE: EIGHT KEY STEPS

Many organizations attempt to revolutionize their operations to fit changing business conditions. Over the last 20 years or so, change efforts have also been made to respond to new managerial panaceas ranging from management by walking about (MBWA), just-in-time (JIT) inventory control, total quality management (TQM), business process re-engineering (BPR) and many others. The evidence suggests that the majority of companies fail to reshape their activities to the desirable degree. Since firms often have little experience of the renewal process, they tend to make errors which inhibit the achievement of radical change.

In a seminal article in 1995, John Kotter drew on his experience of over 100 enterprises which have undertaken transformation initiatives and identified eight key errors which must be eliminated if proper restructuring is to be accomplished.

The objective is to provide a vision of the change effort necessary to increase the opportunities of revolution for success and to minimize the chances of failure. Understanding of these eight key change phases helps to provide a framework for change and ensure that not only is a new reality created, but that the revolution is embedded in the enterprise. In other words, once all the excitement is over, people do not simply return to the old way of doing things.

Step 1: create a sense of urgency

The creation of a sense of urgency has many possible sources. One good reason for using consultants is that, as change agents, they can address problems in the enterprise more dispassionately and therefore tend to be more credible as they are not seen as trying to make political points. Sometimes change has to be initiated by hiring a new director of marketing to shake things up. The newer the leader, the greater the chance of a frank discussion about unpleasant events taking place.

Alternatively, if there is no new face available, then individuals or groups committed to change may bring in outsiders to deliver the message. Financial analysts, consultants or even customers are appropriate. Sometimes financial performance gives impetus to urgency. The trouble is that, although bad figures catch the attention, they also imply less room for manoeuvre. Perhaps when the ratios are satisfactory, this represents the optimum time for change. The problem here is that in this case the need for change is less apparently urgent, and those who suggest it may be considered mad.

Leadership is vital. Company leaders need to inject personal energy to secure the revolution. The idea for the transformation often comes from one visionary leader or group, with a strong view that radical change is needed and that old ways must be abandoned. This individual or group must be supported by leaders and others who can help to lead the transition. Sometimes there is no single individual change leader but just many people in different roles, who support the change in business direction.

Leadership from the very top, at CEO level, must be sustained. The idea that organizations can be revolutionized from beneath or within is often sadly mistaken. It may be salutary to remember that the penalty for mutiny is usually death, and this applies in the corporate world too. The marketing revolution agenda is going to be cross-enterprise, affecting the whole business, and will be wider than the core project team. Leaders may need support from other groups from inside and perhaps outside the organization, particularly from other important external stakeholders such as customers, shareholders, unions and possibly external regulators.

Most companies create a business case for change:

- It gives management a quantitative and qualitative assessment of whether the introduction of a solutions approach is sensible and should be prioritized ahead of other initiatives.
- The business case can be used to support communications throughout the revolution programme, reminding people why the change is taking place and providing hard underpinning to the reasons why it should be made.

At this point, the change leader literally needs to create a sense of crisis and urgency. The business case therefore needs to be expressed in strong terms. It might include:

- need for revenue growth;
- need to shift the balance of companies revenues from over dependence on one sector or activity;
- changes (declines) in market share;
- the need for better product and service profitability;
- wider adoption of common management processes;
- greater skills and improvement in morale of the marketing team;
- new markets and opportunities developed.

Error number 1: failure to create a sense of urgency

The transformation effort can be shot down almost from its inception if the sense of urgency for change is lacking. Urgency is a motivational factor which provides the cooperation vital for change. It has been estimated that at least a 75 per cent conviction rate amongst staff and line management is needed, or serious problems arise later. There are four common reasons for failure at this point.

The first is underestimation of the comfort zone. In 1994, Hamel and Prahalad posed the question, 'Why do great companies fail?' They came up with two main answers. First, they become mesmerized by their own success. There is therefore no gap between performance and expectations. Thus they eschew change. They substitute resources for creativity simply because they have lots of them. Failure follows an absence of adaptation. Second, they lack the ability to invent the future. They have optimized their business systems and are unable to invent new rules when some force for change (like technology) requires different ways of doing business. There is a leadership failure because they mistake the momentum of success for progress.

The second is overestimation of the panic factor. The answer would be to create a sense of panic. Unless we act now, catastrophe will follow. However, if (as is usually the case) catastrophe does not ensue (the lingering death of some large corporations can last several years) credibility is destroyed and commitment to the change effort is withdrawn.

The third is lack of patience – moving too soon. This is not a case for 'just do it'. Employees may be uncomfortable with the change for a number of reasons. Some may have seen similar initiatives come and go without achieving anything (a fact of life in some large organizations) and will want to see good evidence that this change is for the better. Equally they may lack the personal ability to make the changes demanded of them, and may need reassurance that support will be provided.

The fourth is paralysis by downside possibilities. This results from a fear of revolution. The symptoms of paralysis are easy to recognize. Senior executives, faced with suggestions that urgency is the order of the day, often become defensive. They react to transformation initiatives, typically, by pointing to the potential hazards. 'Events will become uncontrollable', 'morale will drop', 'financial performance will deteriorate' are common responses. The problem is that all these arguments are potentially true. These are often justifiable fears and must be treated logically if a proper degree of urgency is to be developed. That is the immediate problem and it is much easier to overcome if the transformation team has its crisis projections at the ready. The consequences of failing to make the transformation attempt must be perceived as more damaging than doing nothing. Typically a failure at this point is common in companies that are overmanaged but under-led.

Step 2: creation of a powerful guiding coalition

Managers with different agendas and perspectives often oppose a change if they fear loss of power or influence, and externals can help by introducing an independent perspective. External help should be chosen with care. Teams that already exist within the company are essential to the creation of the new enterprise (although they may require expert external support). When given opportunities to apply their specialist knowledge, teams often create practical and effective approaches that take into account the unique aspects of the organization. Buy-in can be improved by involving many teams from across the business.

In successful revolutions the guiding coalition is powerful enough to ensure that the anticipated opposition to change remains fragmented. In small to medium-sized firms the coalition may consist of three to five managers, whereas in larger enterprises the desirable size is between 20 and 50 executives. Job titles, personal reputation, experience, information and above all networked relationships are key attributes for members of the guiding coalition.

Although the impetus for coalition formation may start from the perception of a need for urgency by a very small portion of the company, it must grow rapidly to achieve the initial mass necessary for change.

There are three critical features that a powerful coalition needs for a successful revolution:

- The team must work outside the normal corporate hierarchy. It is a cross-section of senior managers from different functions and different divisions of the company. It reports directly to the CEO.
- Line management must be a part of the team, rather than confining its membership to staff functionaries from human resources, quality or strategic planning. Line management authority is essential for credibility.
- Offsite retreats are usually helpful to develop the necessary shared perceptions of problems and opportunities. Trust and communication are also enhanced by this requirement.

Error number 2: letting an opposition form

If the guiding coalition lacks power, then opposition to the corporate hijack will develop a countervailing critical mass and prevent change, or limit it. Not all senior managers will buy into the change. The less the power of the participants, the more likely it is the number of refusals will escalate and deflate the exercise. Furthermore, if the coalition operates within 'normal' channels then intra-firm politics will take over and quash the initiative. This would be especially so if line management are excluded. There are many opportunities for using the formal organization to defeat change. The larger the company, the greater the opportunities for using the formal structure to resist change. Existing protocols, boundaries between functions, defined roles and responsibilities are all devices which can be used to limit and inhibit action. Experience of unsuccessful revolutions shows that, equipped with these tools, even coalitions of managers relatively low in the corporate hierarchy coalitions are sufficient to stop the transformation at an early stage of the eight-phase process.

Step 3: drafting the vision statement

Successful transformation teams invariably develop a vision of the future which is easy to communicate to the organization's stake-holders: customers, employees, suppliers and the capital markets, and employees. In fact, the first duty of the guiding coalition will be to draft the new mission blueprint, and clarify the future direction of the enterprise. The process of drafting is usually the mechanism by which the small change team magnetizes support. Completion must occur within 3 to 12 months depending on the complexity of the organization. Clearly a process of refinement will have to be accepted. The first shot will be urgency to hit the target. Strategy gets added to vision subsequently. Testing is vital. If the guiding coalition is unable to produce a vision which is communicable within five minutes and gets a positive reaction, then this stage of the transformation process is incomplete. An interesting exercise in any corporation as a 'back of envelope' test of internal integrity is to ask people to explain what they think the current vision for the enterprise is at the moment. There is clearly a problem if the answers are not reasonably consistent. The new vision must have its own strap lines and, whilst not being glib, must be easy to explain so as to achieve rapid buy-in from across the company.

Error number 3: underdeveloped or over-complex vision

Transformation efforts which lack an encompassing vision often dissolve into a set of confusing and incompatible projects which are easy to resist because of their piecemeal character. Even if partially accepted, the organization proceeds either in the wrong direction or nowhere at all. A typical transformation or change error is to present people with a whole set of detailed corporate plans involving, for example, a new information architecture for accounts, a radical and complex human resources appraisal system, a checklist of over 100 points for total quality in manufacturing or, perhaps in this context, a cultural refurbishment strategy for the sales force. Without the unification provided by vision, these do not add up and often confuse or alienate the employees. More often than not they inhibit change rather than stimulate it.

It is also important to test strategic integrity at the top. Ask each senior manager to answer the question, 'How will the future of our industry be different?' Do not define 'future' and do not define 'industry'. Give them a week or so and then compare the answers. Are they thinking next year or next decade? Are they seeing extensions of current markets, products or services, or are they seeing something totally new? How competitively unique are their answers? Do your eyes open in surprise or close in boredom?

The point is that organizations which concentrate on strategic fit are guaranteed to atrophy and stagnate. Too cosy a fit, too tight a fit, means that the organization is perfectly equipped for exactly what it does now. Perfect if the world does not change, but of course the world is changing all the time. Thus some sort of bridge is needed between strategy as a grand design and strategy as a repositioning exercise which copes with a whole new agenda. Wal-Mart was successful because it changed the rules of the game. The competition had an investment in assets that was more or less unassailable. So Wal-Mart did not assail it. It decided that it was not in the retail business, but in the logistics and distribution business. It did not compete on the basis of retail space but on the basis of very fast, competitive responses to consumer demand, and it used IT to do it. Strategy as stretch recognizes the paradox that while leadership cannot be planned for entirely, neither does it happen in the absence of clearly articulated and shared vision. IBM is a good example of a corporation that was revolutionized by strategic stretch. Over the decade after 1992, it transformed itself from a computer company to a consultancy service, undergoing a couple of medium-term revolutions on the way. In marketing terms, it abandoned its apparent dominance of a manufacturing base and sought closer partnership relationships with its customers.

Step 4: active communication of the vision

Once a clear story is in place, it should be communicated widely and repeatedly. The 'why', 'what' and 'how' about the transition engage the rational side of employees' minds. This formal communication of information should be supported by relationship-based communications, even at the level of one-to-one discussions which seek to engage the emotions. This must be a hearts and mind campaign. Business leaders must focus on the beliefs and assumptions people have made about the change. Some assumptions such as the possibility of job losses may be negative and need to be addressed. Communication can take the form of developmental coaching, the development of new skills needed for the changed environment, or direct conversations about the employee's own part in the revolution.

External communication and engagement with customers is also vital to avoid those leading the change becoming too inwardly focused. The way a company does business with its customers will change significantly when it introduces this new marketing approach. A company making this change will need its customers to be active partners in creating and adopting the new ways of doing business together. Early adopters and enthusiastic advocates should be targeted and prioritized.

Revolution only works if hundreds of employees are prepared to help and indeed to make sacrifices. Since downsizing is often a characteristic of organizational adjustment, this has a tendency to inhibit proper communication. For communication to be credible it has to be continuous and incorporate within it a confidence in the probability of success. In firms which have won the transformation battle, all communications within the enterprise emphasize the new vision:

- Solutions to business problems must be designed for consistency with the vision.
- Performance appraisals must be adjusted to the new norms.
- Quarterly management meetings must discuss not numbers but progress towards the vision.
- Education and training courses must be recast in terms of the vision.
- Quality reviews have to include judgements about the contribution of executives to vision development.
- Question and answer sessions must be manipulated to stress the radical changes in progress.

Above all, senior management must 'walk the talk'. In communication exchanges, people tend to respond to what is done, not what is said. If customer insights and the management of marketing resources through operational analytics are not the basis of every marketing decision, people will get the (wrong) message quickly.

Error number 4: undercommunicating the vision

If the vision is undercommunicated then no one in the company outside the guiding coalition will understand what is being attempted. If the power coalition delivers a single message then it is likely that the ostrich factor will come into play. Since the change group is not a part of the regular communications network, any isolated message delivered may be ignored, even if anyone turns out to be listening. An article in the quarterly staff magazine or a new link on the website will not be enough. CEO speeches to employee groups alone can fail for the same kind of reason. Only a small portion of the available communication resources have been utilized. The CEO and the marketing director need to use every opportunity to get the message across. If executives fail to 'walk the talk' then cynicism by the troops becomes irresistible and belief in the communication message is eroded.

Step 5: removing the obstacles to vision

Powerful guiding coalitions, an economical expression of the vision and effective communication may all embolden hundreds of employees to embrace new approaches, new ideas and leadership. However, successful managers of corporate change will realize that the first four phases are insufficient in themselves to manifest revolution. Obstacles to change still exist and will inhibit emboldening action. These must be removed.

Common to almost all change conflicts are three elements:

- If job categories are too narrow than these will make it hard to initiate productive change.
- If the old compensation system is in place then employees have to choose between self-interest and the new vision.
- Bosses who refuse to change themselves or make demands inconsistent with the transformation will constrain the new behaviour.

During a revolutionary programme, business leaders often expect employees to change smoothly along with the organization. This does not always happen. There may be a change in the contract between the organization and the employee (reward and job satisfaction for performance and commitment). Employees will expect to be rewarded for creating and delivering the new marketing posture. The emphasis of remuneration and reward might need to change. Employees might even need to be rewarded for developing the skills they will need to perform their new roles.

Changing how employee performance is measured and rewarded signals to employees the importance of the change and encourages the right behaviour from employees such as refocusing efforts to a customer centric approach. Establishing the right set of employee performance measures at the start of the transformation programme is an important step in changing behaviour. Measures should be refined over time, as capabilities and employee performance improve. It can take an organization many years to transform, so rewards should change over time. Rewards can take many different forms. In addition to basic salary, incentives include awards, stock options, recognition via promotion, increased authority and more involvement in leadership activities such as decision making.

Changes to the organization structure may be needed to encourage cross-functional working. Barriers preventing employees from working together need to be identified and removed. The structure is important; behaviour conditioned by the structure should not be overlooked. Irrespective of the organizational structure, individual roles will have to be redefined. Deploying operational analytics will require new skills and responsibilities for most people (in support roles as well as those in the front line). Opportunity spotters and owners, marketing managers, field sales teams, delivery resources and support staff must collaborate. One way to encourage collaboration is to develop and deploy a system of shared targets and rewards for all involved in the creation and delivery process. This helps create an employee 'value chain', in which each member of the wider team depends on the performance of others for their own financial success. Where successful revolution has occurred, these obstacles have been detonated ruthlessly but fairly.

Error number 5: failure to remove managerial blocks

Most studies of organizational change show that the major obstacle to new ways of doing things is often not operations but management. It is managers who fear a loss of power and influence. The reasons for managerial 'blocking' are usually:

- conservative management feel threatened by change;
- managers genuinely believe that the company does not need a revolution;
- they fear that transformation cannot be achieved;
- a worse financial performance is anticipated and they are worried about getting the blame.

Often transformation efforts flounder on this barrier. If the sponsoring team has no experience of confronting the problem, if they are afraid of the change-resisting managers or if they even perceive some value in the blockers, then there will be a temptation to compromise. The result will be that other employees will not be emboldened. Waverers will come down on the side of caution. The message will be that senior management are uncommitted to renewal. Hence individual initiatives consistent with the change vision will be perceived as risky. Investors may get a sense of this and pressure to halt the change will grow from other functions in the company and possibly even from shareholders.

Step 6: planning short-term wins

Almost all revolutionary efforts which have worked actively incorporate short-terms win planning into the change process. The results must be unambiguous and not be subject to interpretative judgement calls, discernible by opponents of change. Specific achievement planning is vital. Short-term wins can be based on metrics such as revenue growth, improvements in the bottom line, increased market share, higher customer satisfaction ratings, higher retention or win-back rates or even the successful introduction of new products and services as a result of deeper customer insights. An additional benefit of short-term win planning is the feedback loop it provides into the initial urgency phase. It also improves the vision analysis. Hence it is consistent with everything that has preceded it in the early stages of the project.

Error number 6: failure to plan short-term wins

Organizational revolution takes time. Failures in the journey often occur because there are no short-term wins to celebrate. Indeed momentum will be lost unless these victories occur. If no bottom line improvement is evident within 12 to 24 months of the transformation effort, then the number of resisters will increase. Managers who have been sitting on the fence will join the ranks of the blockers. Furthermore, the financial markets will get in on the act too. Although the need to create quick wins adds to the pressure on the guiding coalition, without these successes there will be insufficient resources available to reward those in the change party with recognition, promotion and even compensation. This therefore is likely to fragment the transformation effort.

Step 7: postpone victory as long as possible

In companies where radical revolutions have succeeded there is a realization that change has a virtually infinite horizon. Furthermore, even if in some years the rate of change slows down, so long as it continues to be positive, the aggregate of change must increase. This is the objective of the guiding coalition. A good example of such a corporate culture might be Microsoft. Microsoft has rarely hesitated to alter its marketing posture or its central company policies, if it has become apparent that this is somehow out of touch with market trends. The culture is therefore one of 'here is where we are today, we may be heading somewhere else tomorrow'. Such a culture is enervating and stimulating, but it does suit those most comfortable with a dynamic and fluid corporate environment. It will not suit everyone. The short-term wins created in phase 6 provide the credibility to tackle bigger problems and in revolutionary firms are never the excuse for a premature celebration. Instead they create the opportunity for more ambitious adjustments. Typically, systems inconsistent with the new vision are removed. Attention is paid to hirings, firings and promotions. New marketing projects are initiated and these serve to expand the aggregate scale of change continuously.

Error number 7: declaring victory too soon

On the other hand, transformation failures often occur because neither the initial urgency, guiding coalitions nor the vision is sufficiently powerful to sustain the aggregate of change momentum. A sign of this is invariably an early declaration of victory. Change leaders necessarily have to endure a certain amount of hostility. Their job is to make people uncomfortable with the here and now so that they respond to the need for change. That tends to be an unpopular role. Tiredness sets in, it is tempting to declare that the war has been won and the troops may be sent home. Not surprisingly, executives who have witnessed the first six phases with some alarm are quick to congratulate the guiding coalition on their revolutionary achievement. Since no doubt there will have been a considerable degree of corporate tension evident in the early phases of revolution, weak coalitions always give in to the temptation to call a halt at this point. Nothing is more dangerous. The counter-attack goes in with absolute predictability and within two years the corporation is back to business as usual.

Step 8: embedding change

The final phase of the successful revolutionary effort is when the change becomes embedded in the corporate culture. How this is done exhibits wide variations. There are, however, two common features:

- Employees within the company must be made aware how the new behavioural norms have improved performance. The use of company communication channels has once again to be absolute in this value reinforcement process.
- A large quantity of time is spent ensuring the next generation of senior management personifies the new approach. Huge attention is paid to changing the requirements for promotion within the enterprise and this must reflect the new operating criteria.

The idea that a change – even a successful change – is irreversible, is often mistaken. A good example might be British Airways. In the late 1980s British Airways was an unprofitable state corporation. The letters BA were taken as an acronym for 'bloody awful'. On privatization, it was guided by a revolutionary leader who made it one of the most successful and profitable airlines in the world. He was a tough act to follow and his successor embarked on a round of cost-cutting coupled with an appeal to the company's business class and first class passengers. This alienated both staff and passengers and the company suffered a turnaround which the next CEO had to tackle. It took another couple of years before the airline was back on track.

Error number 8: failure to reinforce change values

Unless the new values are rooted in the social norms and shared values of the corporation, then the revolutionary culture is liable to degrade. If the connection between behaviour and performance is ignored, then employees will make their own judgements and inaccurate linkages will develop. Confusions often arise between the individual manager's contributions and that of the team as a whole. Unnecessary departures result.

If little or no time is devoted to succession planning then the work of the guiding coalition, sometimes involving years of effort, can be undermined by a single bad appointment. Indeed the history of corporate revolutions is littered with cases where firms have completed phases 1 to 7 successfully and then, at the end of the day, have fallen from the peak by neglecting reinforcement procedures.

LESSONS FOR MARKETING REVOLUTION

The extent of the change required to revolutionize the marketing approach, to shift the attitudes, beliefs and behaviours of its employees and business partners when undertaking the revolution, should not be underestimated. This change is best managed and turned to advantage by openly recognizing the new demands that the change brings and by managing those demands as part of a change management programme. Companies must accept that the revolution will take time. However urgent and pressing the need, each of the eight phases of the revolution process must be followed, and some of those cannot be rushed.

The development of this process must be supported by the CEO and by the most senior marketing managers. Whilst it is tempting to consider the less radical evolutionary approach to change, the scope of what is needed probably requires a revolutionary approach, a complete rethinking of the relationship between the corporate marketing function and their customers. The approach will be enabled through changes in corporate culture, a new vision, new behaviours and reward systems, performance measurements related to the revolution and a new organizational structure. The short-term measure of success will be observed through various measures such as revenue gains, increased profitability, increased market share and so on. However, the ultimate measure of success will be survival.

12

Case studies

CASE STUDY 1: LOYALTY MANAGEMENT ANALYTICS AND OPTIMIZATION – THE CASE OF THE AIRLINE FREQUENT-FLYER PROGRAMME (FINNAIR)

Finnair wanted to react to increasingly adverse business conditions and grow revenues and profits again. The unfavourable external market conditions resulted from the reduction of air travel following 9/11, the SARS virus, the Iraq war and through intensive competition from low-cost carriers which hampered organic growth. They decided to try to stimulate growth by optimizing Finnair's frequent-flyer loyalty programme, Finnair Plus, to boost sales within the existing customer base. Within this overall objective, they wanted to be able to:

- segment customers based on customer value;
- predict customers' lifetime value and risk over variable time horizons;
- plan and execute targeting campaign sequences to sustain and/or boost customer value;
- optimize marketing budget allocation in order to maximize the value:risk ratio.

What is customer loyalty?

The word 'loyalty' conjures up the image of unquestioning commitment. Loyalty can be defined in two ways:

- A state of mind, a set of attitudes, beliefs and desires. We could call this 'emotional' loyalty. Companies benefit from customers' loyal behaviour consequent upon these attitudes and beliefs. The focus of the resulting loyalty approach will be on maintaining a special place in the mind of the customer. It will try to make the customer feel that their loyalty is being rewarded by a stronger or better relationship, visible perhaps in a higher level of recognition or service. An emotional loyal may buy from a supplier because of the relationship, even when the purchase does not meet all objective criteria.
- A behavioural inclination. It precludes loyalty to some other suppliers but not to all of them. A customer can be loyal to more than one competing supplier. We could call this 'rational' loyalty since it makes sense for some types of situations. Here the focus of the loyalty approach will be on incentives that reinforce behaviour patterns.

Table 12.1 summarizes these two conditions.

Customer situations and loyalty

Loyalty is a composite, as is loyal behaviour. It fits with other attitudes and beliefs that a person may hold, and other cognitions. Loyalty may not always be the primary driver of behaviour. Loyal customers can sometimes appear disloyal. For example, a loyal customer, when coming up to a major purchasing decision, may solicit information from competitive suppliers.

Not all customers are equally loyal, nor will any one customer always demonstrate the same degree of loyalty all the time. Loyalty is

Table 12.1 _The basis of customer loyalty_

Basis of loyalty	Basis of relationship marketing approach
Emotional	Managing loyalty is a constant _theme_ of the company's approach to managing customers
Rational	Loyalty management takes place through _schemes_ to reinforce 'loyal' behaviour

developed by approaches that reinforce and develop a positive state of mind. The aim is not to make all customers loyal but to improve the loyalty of those customers most likely to respond. Different people respond to different things. Some respond to incentives, some to differentiated marketing, some to high general standards of service, some to product excellence and some to strong branding. In addition, some customers will accept switching barriers more easily than others. In other words the relationship between loyalty and purchase behaviour is not linear. It ranges from customers who buy whatever is available at one end, through to customers who will only buy the brand (and will not buy at all if it is not available) at the other. Somewhere in the middle there are customers who like the brand and will buy it if they can, but they will switch from time to time for good reason.

In today's marketing environment, customers expect companies to use the information they have provided at various stages in their relationship positively in managing their account:

- When customers require service, they expect details of their relationship to be available to whoever is delivering the service and to be used if relevant.
- If they are ordering a product or requesting technical service, they expect information they have given about their needs, not just recently but over the years, to be used to identify which product or service is best for them.
- If they are in contact with several different members of an enterprise, they expect the actions of these staff to be coordinated.
- They expect the enterprise to consider their needs for a long-term relationship, not just for individual transactions within the relationship. They want an appearance of care.
- If there are problems on the customer's side, such as meeting payments or service problems which are the customer's fault, they expect their past relationships to be taken into consideration in resolving them.
- Loyal customers expect to have better relationships than if they were not loyal.

So, what can happen in practice? Acquiring a large customer database in even a relatively small business is not difficult. Using it effectively is more of a challenge and that challenge is especially high if your customer database contains perhaps tens of millions of customer records. The promotion in Figure 12.1 was sent to a 31-year-old male, who is single, was never married and has no children. It came as an e-mail from the US-based Safeway grocery chain.

Figure 12.1 _Promotional e-mail to a single male with no children!_

This is almost as bad as receiving a congratulatory message from an ebullient marketer to the effect that your points balance has just reached zero and that with just a few more points and some cash you can enjoy the wonderful benefits of their reward programme! On the other hand, detailed, carefully thought-out schemes can be equally ineffective. Consider, for example, the two airline loyalty schemes in Figure 12.2. Can you tell them apart?

Making the loyalty programme effective

Clearly then, if a loyalty programme is going to be effective it has to appear to be individual in some sense for each customer. Not only will different flyers have different personal demographics and attitudes to flying, but they will also have different patterns of airline usage. One might be the highly mobile executive, on a plane once or twice a week, often flying business class, clocking up miles faster than they can use them, in the gold or platinum level with several airlines and probably disinclined to get on planes in their leisure hours anyway. Another might be the occasional flyer, who makes the odd business trip but when on vacation takes package holidays where the airline is designated by the tour operator. Hardly ever gets enough miles to make

285

	Scheme 1	Scheme 2		Scheme 1	Scheme 2
Number of tiers based upon recent travel	4	4	Purchase miles	Yes	Yes
Tiers based upon lifetime travel	Yes	Yes	Transfer miles	Yes	Yes
Ties bonuses	Yes	Yes	Electronic upgrades	Yes	Yes
Accrued points vary by travel class	Yes	Yes	Family membership	No	No
Miles expire	Not with activity	Not with activity	Website features	—	—
Blackout dates for reward travel	No	Varies	Transaction history	Yes	Yes
Points for domestic travel	25k/40k	25k/40k	Point total	Yes	Yes
Points for Europe/ North America	50k/80k	40k/60k/100k	Updated profile	Limited	Yes
Points for Asia/ North America	60k/100k	50k/65k/125k	Process point redemptions	Yes	Yes
Redeem points with partners	Yes	Yes	Enrol in promotions	Yes	Yes
Number of partners	100+	100+	Request missing credit	Yes	Yes
Credit card	Yes	Yes	Example promotions	—	—
Hotel	Yes	Yes	Booking online bonus	Yes	Yes
Air	Yes	Yes	Fixed point bonus for targeted segment	Yes	Yes
Car rental	Yes	Yes	% bonus for targeted segment	Yes	Yes
Financial services	Yes	Yes	Redemption discounts	Yes	Yes

Figure 12.2 *Can you tell these two airline loyalty schemes apart?*

belonging to a scheme worthwhile. A third might be somewhere in the middle. Makes perhaps half a dozen business trips per year, some long haul, and gains substantial benefits from a frequent-flyer programme if they consistently use the same airline. The airline therefore needs to consider how their scheme is distinctive by asking a few questions:

- How unique is the frequent-flyer scheme, is it distinctive, can the customer recognize the important differences between this scheme and another?

- Does it actually improve loyalty? For example, are there true switching costs if a member wants to leave the programme? If they are a gold member with this programme and they send details of their frequent-flyer points or promotional coupons to your main competitor, will they be made a gold member of that programme instead? If they are, will they see any degradation in service?
- What is the strategy for using your loyalty programme to lock-in customers and create continuous competitive advantage for your airline?

To offer a loyalty programme that creates true competitive advantage for your company it is better to approach the issue by considering the customer experience and the customer journey. The operational analytics can be used to identify moments of truth when the insights from data mining can be deployed to create individual incentives for the customer to remain loyal and to continue to build their relationship with the airline. This requires three main steps:

- Think of loyalty as a cohesive whole. All customers' interactions should be seen as part of the customer journey. A comprehensive loyalty management programme encompasses every way in which an airline deals with its members.
- The programme must continually adapt over time. It cannot remain static since, if it is well designed, it fits into a particular 'time and place'. It must evolve in response to customer needs and competitive changes. In consequence, it must be designed to be flexible and changing must be low-cost. In this way, the airline keeps a continuous incremental advantage over its competitors.
- The programme must leverage customer data to provide unique services and offers. These are based on mined, customer insights. Such offers provide unique advantage, since competitors do not have the data to replicate or match them. They appeal individually to aspects of the customer journey of importance to each customer. As a result, the airline keeps its high-value customers and makes all customers more valuable over time. It also optimizes the use of the marketing budget allocation to maximize customer ROI.

The customer journey

For airline usage, the customer journey extends not only to airline products and services but also to ground handling, transportation and accommodation. Consider the simplified view of the moments of truth in air travel shown in Table 12.2.

The integrated loyalty management life cycle

An integrated, customer journey loyalty management approach would therefore need to address all these possible moments of truth. Figure 12.3 illustrates the tasks that have to be managed.

Customer data are collected at many touch points and the customer experience can be affected, sometimes disproportionately, by the way

Table 12.2 *Moments of truth in the customer experience for an airline*

Stage	Service process	Customer experiences
Before flying	Marketing communications	• Direct mail • E-mail • Corporate publications/promotions
	Sales and reservations	• Availability • Fare options • Upgrade possibilities • Waitlist • Rebooking options • Refund/cancellation options
	Check-in	• Ground transportation (access to airport and terminal) • Check-in routine • Luggage handling • Security routines • Boarding • Possible upgrade at gate
On board the plane	Flight	• Personalized service • In-flight catering • Entertainment • On-board sales • Arrival service • Connections
After arrival	Baggage service	• Baggage damage • Lost baggage/baggage information • Transfer to partner airline or partner ground handling
	Customer feedback	• Claims • Surveys • Depth interviews face to face
	Rewards	• Follow-up marketing • Reservation privileges • Upgrade privileges • Benefits (awards from the airline or its partners)

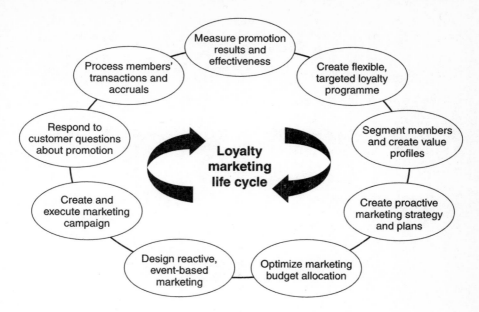

Figure 12.3 *The integrated loyalty management life cycle*

in which each of these is handled. For example, in an otherwise perfect flight, the customer might be heavily preoccupied by a rude check-in clerk, whose poor relationship skills overshadow the rest of the experience. Conversely, a timely intervention by ground staff, possibly even from a corporate partner, to help with a connection or some sort of luggage problem, can put an attractive spin on the rest of the experience.

Between them, IBM and database company Siebel have created a solution that integrates all aspects of customer management, from maintenance of the customer database itself, through data mining and integration with online transaction processing. This is illustrated in Figure 12.4.

To obtain and maintain a competitive edge, advanced analytics and optimization technologies must be combined with deep business insights. The complexity of the task can be highlighted by considering some of the marketing problems that have to be solved:

- How to derive advanced value and loyalty metrics and enhance existing segmentations?
- How to identify customers' different life-cycle phases and dynamics? For example, how can the airline track the value of a family?

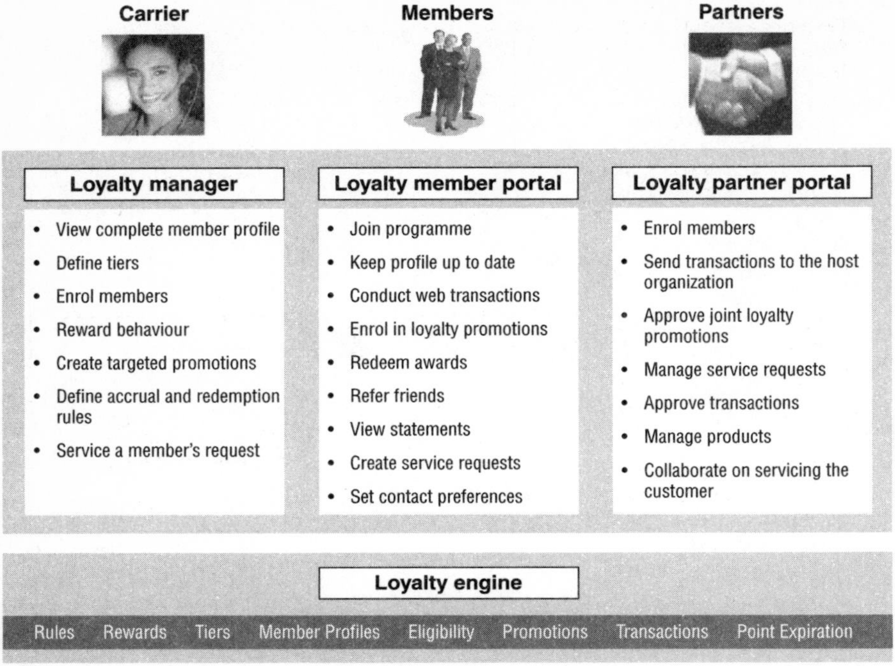

Carrier

Members

Partners

Loyalty manager	Loyalty member portal	Loyalty partner portal
• View complete member profile	• Join programme	• Enrol members
• Define tiers	• Keep profile up to date	• Send transactions to the host organization
• Enrol members	• Conduct web transactions	
• Reward behaviour	• Enrol in loyalty promotions	• Approve joint loyalty promotions
• Create targeted promotions	• Redeem awards	• Manage service requests
• Define accrual and redemption rules	• Refer friends	• Approve transactions
	• View statements	• Manage products
• Service a member's request	• Create service requests	• Collaborate on servicing the customer
	• Set contact preferences	

Loyalty engine

Rules   Rewards   Tiers   Member Profiles   Eligibility   Promotions   Transactions   Point Expiration

Figure 12.4 *Interface of the integrated loyalty management system*

- How to effectively estimate customer lifetime value and risk (their volatility and likelihood of switching) over variable time horizons?
- How to optimize planning of sequences of marketing actions (such as mini campaigns) by segment whilst avoiding customer promotional fatigue?
- How to optimize marketing budget allocation to maximize the value:volatility ratio across the whole customer portfolio?
- How to deliver quality consistently at every customer touch point (call centre, website, sales kiosk, check-in, departure gates, arrival terminals and so on)?

This is where operational analytics and marketing resource management can maximize ROI for the marketing budget. Figure 12.5 gives an example of how this would work for a particular customer, in this case someone who is at the moment very middle-of-the-road.

State: Medium loyalty & Medium value
Sequence of actions: *ExtraP* campaign, *Cash* campaign, *Accrual* campaign
Revenue: $2000
Next state: High loyalty & High value

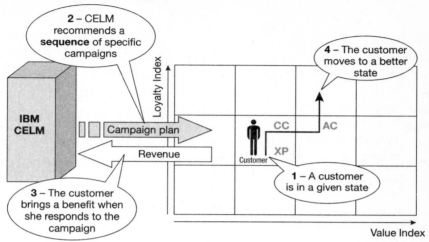

Figure 12.5 *Marketing managers can leverage their customer information for optimal modelling and control of customer dynamics*

Note: ExtraP = extra reward points, CELM is the IBM Customer Experience Lifetime Management Project.

The solution and the benefits

The Siebel Loyalty[1] application is composed of four key products as follows:

1. *The Loyalty Manager*, an employee-facing application that will serve as the foundation for creating loyalty programmes, enrolling members, building loyalty promotions and managing loyalty transactions.
2. *The Loyalty Member Portal* is a customer-facing application that allows members of a loyalty programme to have instant and personalized access to their rewards, profile and transaction history, and it also provides the ability for loyalty programme members to redeem points over the web for products or services.
3. *The Loyalty Partner Portal* is an important application that empowers corporate partners such as reservation services, car hire or hotel companies to have an active role in the loyalty programme ecosystem. By using the partner portal, companies can now allow partners to enrol members, submit transactions, review joint promotions and provide member services with real time information.

4.   *The Loyalty Engine*, a highly scalable transaction engine (a computer program) that processes transactions, credits and debits a member's points, moves a member up and down tiers, deletes expired points, creates statements and handles the day-to-day accounting for the system.

All of this capability is fully integrated into the Siebel CRM framework and sits on top of a powerful transaction and tiers engine that will fundamentally drive member rewards. In addition to integrating across all four loyalty products, a truly successful enterprise loyalty programme must also integrate seamlessly with all other key customer management applications, from operational analytics through the call centre to marketing campaign management. Thus the system allows companies to manage the complete loyalty life cycle with an integrated suite of applications. Operational analytics develop insights which in turn propose loyalty promotions to an identified customer subset. This generates a mini marketing campaign which in turn affects the loyalty disposition of the targeted customer group. This is then the basis for further operational analytics.

No one loyalty programme can be completely effective and generate its promised results unless it manages the entire promotion and member life cycle in an integrated and unified manner. For example, a marketing system that is not integrated with the loyalty and analytic systems will be of significantly decreased value.

This solution brought significant benefits to Finnair in terms of revenue gains and customer satisfaction with significant cost reductions. These are achieved by:

- *Streamlined loyalty promotion management* – coupled with a reduction in the overall time for promotion creation by 20 per cent, and for complex promotion creation time a reduction of 70+ per cent.
- *Maximized marketing ROI* – by optimized marketing strategies that move customers to more valuable segments.
- *Increased sales of distressed inventory* (in this case unsold airline seats) – this is achieved by propensity modelling (picking the right flight for the right customer through the right channel with the right benefits).
- *Reduced system costs* – by releasing up to 30 per cent of the current loyalty IT budget for cost savings or enhancements.
- *Improved customer satisfaction* – by providing consistent service across all channels and creating a 'win–win' relationship.

Source: IBM / Siebel

CASE STUDY 2: THE DRIVER VEHICLE LICENSING AGENCY – MULTICHANNEL MANAGEMENT IN THE PUBLIC SECTOR

Based on a government initiative, the Driver Vehicle Licensing Agency (DVLA) based at Swansea in the UK needed to revolutionize both its business and its operating model. It also needed to identify and deliver new services as part of a long-term vision for change through innovative thinking, high-quality policy proposals and efficient funding streams.

Background

With a 2003/2004 operating budget of £324 million, 40 locations and 5,800 employees, the DVLA is the largest executive agency in the UK Department for Transport (DfT), accounting for 40 per cent of the department's staff. The DVLA's primary responsibilities are the issue, maintenance and enforcement of driver and vehicle records and the collection of vehicle excise duty (VED). These responsibilities are fulfilled almost entirely through the maintenance and application of accurate registers of driver and vehicle information, making the DVLA fundamentally a data management business. The agency maintains 39.5 million driver records and 31.9 million vehicle records, it carries out 200 million transactions per year and collects £4.6 billion of VED revenue, with an additional £609 million revenue from other business. This generates 88 million letters and 10 million telephone calls annually.

In order to modernize its business, the DVLA entered into a 10-year contract with IBM to:

- manage IT and data management;
- provide business strategy development support;
- develop an IT strategy;
- assist with estates and facilities strategic management;
- design and effect a change programme management;
- contribute to the development of people and the organization;
- effect a culture change.

The goals

There were three pressures for change. The first came from the government's transformation agenda. As part of its manifesto, the

Labour government had committed itself strongly to the effective deployment of new technologies throughout the UK, ranging from education through industry and business and even government itself. The aim was to ensure the competitiveness of the country as a whole. Within this there was a recognition that customer expectations had changed. Following a culture shift that took place in the early 1990s, British citizens had come to regard themselves as customers for all sorts of government services. Whereas formerly there might have been some forbearance for poor services from the public sector, after the privatization of some public sector institutions and the publication of numerous customer charters, the general level of service expectations had increased considerably. Whilst the DVLA remained in the public sector (as an agent of tax collection), scandals in other public sector services (notably the passport office where a computerization programme had gone disastrously wrong) had made the reality of effective service improvements, possibly at levels matching those of the private sector, even more distant. Anyone who has experienced vehicle processes such as registration in New York will appreciate the progress needed in this area! In order to meet policy requirement and respond to customer expectations, the DVLA engaged in a transformation agenda that would take the relicensing of motor vehicles on-line. By opening up new channels of citizen access and choice it was at the same time able to increase operational efficiency and effectiveness.

The goals of the project were therefore to:

- open up new channels for better customer access and choice;
- increase operational efficiency and effectiveness;
- compare favourably with other best-in-class service providers.

Solution

At the inception of the project, most vehicle licences were renewed through agencies such as Post Offices on a face-to-face basis. This was both expensive and to some extent error-prone. It also lent itself to fraud in that vehicle insurances (checked at the time of licence renewal) were not always properly validated.

The solution was to design a simplified customer journey which took out the Post Office as an intermediary and delivered the licence directly to the citizen through the mail. The web and IVR (interactive voice response, in which a caller uses a touch-tone telephone to interact with a database) were designated as primary channels, with agents handling more complex enquiries. This approach integrated with the existing DVLA contact centre to maximize cross-service efficiency and allowed electronic checking of insurance and roadworthiness.

Benefits

A quarter of citizens adopted this new simplified approach, which dramatically reduced transaction costs. Figure 12.6 illustrates the cost savings that were achieved. The new electronic systems reduced the cost of licensing renewals up to 40 per cent.

The response

There was a channel shift of 25 per cent which produced massive cost savings in terms of the volumes being processed. Satisfaction levels were high: 91 per cent of customers using Electronic Vehicle Licensing (EVL) said they were either, 'likely to' or 'definitely will' use the service again, which means that the new system had captured the appropriate customer behaviours accurately and encouraged repeat usage. Feedback reports showed that customers considered the new channel management system to be a 'very efficient and time-saving service' and that they would 'recommend the service to other people'.

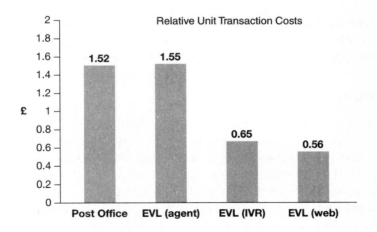

Figure 12.6 _Channel costs for DVLA_

CASE STUDY 3: TESCO – REVOLUTIONIZING THE BUSINESS WITH SEGMENTATION[2]

By April 2005, the giant UK retailer Tesco had achieved reported profits of just over £2 billion and a market share of the grocery retail sector of just over 30 per cent. The figures were a little sensitive for the company as it was concerned about potential customer reactions to the fact that £1 in £3 spent in British supermarkets passed through its tills. However, the figures reflected a period of steady growth for the company, based largely on its very effective use of its customer database and the deployment of data-mining strategies.

Tesco struggled for five years to get its data management, analysis and segmentation right. Indeed, it is the very difficulty of implementation that means those who get it right have a distinct and sustainable competitive advantage. This is one of the most important corporate stories in business history. It remains possibly the outstanding example in the world of how data can be used to change an entire business.

> *The difference between knowing that you could do something and finding out that you can, is five years of work.*
>
> Richard Brasher, Tesco board director

The public face of the Tesco Clubcard[3] is well known in the UK: 10 million customers had signed up for this loyalty scheme, voucher redemption levels were extremely successful and the four customer mailers with these vouchers created 'four Christmases a year' in terms of sales uplift. But the real revolution was taking place backstage. Customer knowledge delivered by Clubcard data triggered a 'quiet revolution' inside Tesco. At the heart of this revolution was a way of segmenting customers that was unique to the industry and proved to possess enormous power.

Clubcard's launch in 1995 had been a success and by 1997 80 per cent of Tesco revenue was spent through Clubcard holders. By this time, however, the team realized that it was time to start some serious work on the data in order to capitalize internally on Clubcard. Apart from the vision of senior managers within Tesco, two of the key people who lay behind the success of Clubcard were Terry Hunt (of direct marketing agency EHS Brann) and Clive Humby (of data analysts dunnhumby). These two key players were important to the marketing strategies that started to be driven by the incredibly powerful data the Clubcard revealed.

Tesco knew that of the 'four Ps', promotion was probably the least important. Much more important to customers was the product–price equation which took shape in the form of the customer proposition. The first issue was price. Fighting on price is as damaging to industry profitability in retail as it is anywhere else. Asda, with its Every Day Low Price brand and set of promises, had assumed the mantle of being perceived as 'the cheapest'. Tesco was keen to fight hard on price but without triggering a price war and without damaging its margins more than it had to. The opportunity for segmentation was to find out that while all customers are interested in low prices, some people will actively shop on that basis alone, while others will not. Was there an opportunity to selectively offer discounts?

Up to 1997 product ranges were largely undifferentiated between stores. Customers were assumed to be a homogeneous mass who, on average, bought the same things no matter which store you picked. Of course Tesco knew all about the geo-demographic products available to the retailer marketplace which allowed them to understand more about the social geography local to each store. Clubcard data told them directly about how their customers differed area by area, without making any assumptions.

However, the segmentation 'Holy Grail' for Tesco was to understand _customer potential_. All firms would love to know not just what their customers are worth to them but their potential worth, what they might be _persuaded_ to spend. People buy different parts of their food supply from more than one place. Also, in the supermarket retail business there has been a consolidation of different product lines under one roof, with giant European operations like Carrefour and Tesco copying the route of Wal-Mart in the United States by diversifying out of packaged goods and into areas like health and beauty, clothing, books, music and even electronic goods such as TVs. The potential for cross-sell is therefore considerable.

The flip-side of potential is customer loyalty and defection. Loyalty is a strange beast in retail, with 'disloyal' customers who buy, say, ready meals and wine being very profitable, while less well-off people buying all their milk and bread at Tesco and who are more loyal, are less profitable.

Data handling was a story in itself. The history of segmentation is littered with ideas that look great on paper but didn't make the transition to action. The core of Tesco's success and the heart of its competitive advantage lie in the success Tesco made of handling the data issues. Credit for this probably starts at the top of the company. Senior managers showed faith in a project for which the end point lay five years away. In 1997 the company faced a massive task of making sense of the mountain of data coming off the online transaction system daily. Data experts warn us not to 'drink from the fireman's hose', a reference to getting swamped by too much data. It was reputed that one of the reasons for Safeway's ABC card problems was just this. Working on the basis that you are what you eat, Tesco analysts began what was to be a five-year journey of hard work in deciding how to handle the deluge (1,600 million data items a month) and how to go about analysing it. Hardest of all, they had to understand how to make this data work around the business.

Credit is also due to the analysts themselves. It takes more than just good technical skills in statistics to nail the problems. Good planners and analysts need to be creative in problem solving, then they must be very determined to overcome obstacles. The detailed knowledge obtained along the way is not easily copied and becomes part of the knowledge DNA of the company. At its best, this capability can become a vital core competence. Tesco's analysts, along with dunnhumby, decided initially to work from samples and then ascribe patterns to the whole, rather than try to work with the entire 10 million record datasets. This saved valuable money and time. Another decision was to look for what might be termed 'rich descriptor' products.

Segmenting 10 million customers and 60,000 products from first principles is well-nigh impossible. It would take years and would be impossible to implement. Tesco needed sensible shortcuts. The insight here was that certain products might be extremely valuable as surrogates to describe important behaviours. For example, 'Value' brand margarine (the economy offering) is a low-cost alternative to well-known branded higher-priced margarines. Tesco's research indicated that those who bought this brand were price-sensitive people. Hence this item could be reasonably used as a shortcut to find those people who were most vulnerable to a price-led attack from competitors. Action could therefore be taken in a highly targeted manner. Tesco was also interested in experimenters who tried new recipes or ready meals; bulk-buy shoppers who shopped once a month; repertoire buyers who bought from many stores; environmentally conscious and ethical shoppers; cash-strapped buyers and so on. Each of these could be identified and targeted based on their basket.

Another inspired idea for Tesco was to use simple, catchy titles for each segment as a way of making each segment translate easily from department to department internally. Tesco could now make its data work within the various company functions. Figure 12.7 illustrates some of the relationships between processes.

Tesco has used its Clubcard-inspired segmentation to target price-sensitive customers. In a business where each player is making over £100 million of price cuts each year, getting this right has had a major impact on margins. Hence it uses rich but simple descriptions like 'High Spending Superstore Families' that create pictures in the executive mindset.

Tesco is one of the first retail companies to use data-driven marketing and segmentation at a corporate strategy level within the business to revolutionize what it does at every level within the company. The sheer complexity and difficulty of its efforts comes out sharply in the story of what it has done. It is this very difficulty that gives it such a strong competitive advantage over its rivals and puts it in a position to dominate the industry in the UK. See Tenby (1999), Johnson (1997), Hunt, Humby and Phillips (2003).

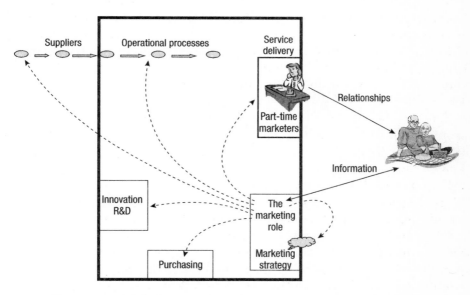

Figure 12.7 *Links between data mining, segmentation and customer relationships at Tesco*

NOTES

1. Siebel Loyalty is a registered brand of Siebel Systems.
2. This case study is based on Hunt, Humby and Phillips (2003).
3. Clubcard is a registered brand of Tesco.

References

Accenture (2001) *How Much are Customer Relationship Management Capabilities Really Worth?*, New York

ANA/Booz Allen Hamilton (2004) *Study of Marketing Organizations*, September, ANA/Booz Allen Hamilton, Boston

Aufreiter, N, Elzinga, D and Gordon, J (2003) Better branding, *McKinsey Quarterly*, 4, pp 29–39

Bates, M, Davis, K and Haynes, D (2003) Reinventing IT services, *McKinsey Quarterly*, 2, pp 143–53

Blasberg, J and Vishwanath, V (2003), Making cool brands hot, *Harvard Business Review*, 81 (6), pp 20–23

Boynton, AC and Zmud, RW (1985) Critical success factor analysis as a methodology for MIS planning, *MIS Quarterly*, 9 (2), pp 121–30

Brady, J and Davis, I (1993), Marketing's mid life crisis, *McKinsey Quarterly*, 2, pp 17–28

Britt, B (2002) Skoda trades on bad rep, *Advertising Age*, 73 (47), p 29

Brown, S (1998) *Post-modern Marketing*, 2nd edn, ITBP, London

Burnes, B (2000) *Managing Change: A Strategic Approach to Organisational Dynamics*, 3rd edn, Prentice Hall, London

Carnall, C (1990) *Managing Change in Organizations*, Prentice Hall, London

Cerasale, M and Stone, M (2004) *Business Solutions on Demand: Transform the Business to Deliver Real Customer Value*, Kogan Page, London

Chartered Institute of Management (2001) The impact of e-business on marketers and marketing, *CIM Canon of Knowledge*, July

Chesbrough, H (2003) *Open Innovation: Using Research from Everywhere for New Product and Service Development*, ibm.com, May

Drucker, P (2001) *The Practice of Management*, Butterworth-Heinemann, New York

Ellwood, I (2002) *The Essential Brand Book*, Kogan Page, London

English, LP (1999) *Improving Data Warehouse and Business Information Quality: Methods for Reducing Costs and Increasing Profits*, Wiley, New York

Forrester Research (2005) *Top Marketing Technologies*, January, Forrester, New York

Foss, B and Stone, M (2002) *CRM in Financial Services*, Kogan Page, London

Gamble, P, Stone, M, Woodcock, N and Foss, B (2003) *Up Close and Personal? Customer Relationship Marketing @ Work*, 2nd edn, Kogan Page, London

Gartner (2004) *The Future of Marketing Automation*, Gartner, New York

Gerstner, L (2003) *Who says Elephants Can't Dance?*, HarperCollins, New York

Glover, M (1999) Skoda has the last laugh, *Automotive Engineer*, **24** (7), p 92

Goold, M, Campbell, A and Alexander, M (1994) *Corporate Level Strategy: Creating Value in the Multibusiness Company*, Wiley, New York

Gronroos, C (1996) Relationship marketing: strategic and tactical implications, *Management Decision*, **34** (3), p 13

Hall, W (1995) *Managing Cultures: Making Strategic Relationships Work*, Wiley, Chichester

Hamel, G and Prahalad, CK (1994) *Competing for the Future*, Harvard Business School Press, Boston

Hammer, M (2002) *The Agenda: What Every Business Must Do to Dominate the Decade*, Random House Business Books, New York

Hammer, M and Champy, J (1993) *Re-Engineering the Corporation*, Brealey, London

Hirschowitz, A (2001) Closing the CRM loop: the 21st century marketer's challenge: transforming customer insight into customer value, *Journal of Targeting, Measurement and Analysis for Marketing*, **10** (2), pp 168–178

Humby, C, Hunt, T and Philips, T (2003) *Scoring Points*, Kogan Page, London

Huyett, WI and Viguerie, SP (2005) Extreme competition, *McKinsey Quarterly*, **1**, pp 46–57

Hyde, P, Landry, E and Tipping, A (2004) Making the perfect marketer, *Harvard Business Review Special Report*, **37**

IBM BCS (2004) *Your Turn: The Global CEO Study*, IBM Business Consulting Services, London

IBM Institute for Business Value (2002) *Global CEO Study*, IBM, Cambridge, MA

IBM Institute for Business Value (2003) *Segmentation Survey*, IBM, Boston

IBM Institute for Business Value (2004) *CRM Done Right: Operationalizing CRM: Global Survey Analysis Wave 1: Global Top Level View*, IBM, New York

Johansson, J, Krishnamurthy, C and Schlissberg, H (2003) Solving the solutions problem, *McKinsey Quarterly*, **3**, pp 116–26

Johnson, M (1997) The application of geodemographics to retailing: meeting the needs of the catchment, *Journal of the Market Research Society*, **39** (1)

Kapferer, JN (2001) *Reinventing the Brand*, Kogan Page, London

Kennedy, R and Ehrenberg, A (2001) There is no brand segmentation, *Marketing Research*, **13** (1), pp 4–8

Kotler, P (2003) *Marketing Management*, 11th edn, Prentice Hall, New Jersey

Kotler, P (2004) Marketing and the CEO: why CEOs are fed up with marketing, *Strategy*, 3 May

Kotter, JP (1995) Leading change: why transformation efforts fail, *Harvard Business Review*, March–April, **73** (2), pp 59–68

LaClair, JA and Rao, RP (2002) Helping employees embrace change, *McKinsey Quarterly*, **4**, pp 17–21

Macrae, C (1996) *The Brand Chartering Handbook*, Addison Wesley, Harlow

Mattern, F, Schonwalder, S and Stein, W (2003) Fighting complexity in IT, *McKinsey Quarterly*, **1**, pp 57–61

McFarlen, F and McKenney, J (1983) *Corporate Information Systems in Management: The Issues Facing Senior Executives*, Dow Jones Irwin, New York

McKiernan, P and Merali, Y (1995) Integrating information systems after a merger, *Long Range Planning*, **28** (4), pp 54–62

Mills, D (2003) Mills on... Skoda, *Campaign (UK)*, **2**, p 19

Mintzberg, H (1994) *The Rise and Fall of Strategic Planning*, Prentice Hall, New York

Oh, TK (1976) Japanese management: a critical review, *Academy of Management Review*, **1**, (Jan), pp 14–25

Pekar, P and Abraham, S (1995) Is strategic management living up to its promise?, *Long Range Planning*, **28** (5), pp 32–44

Peters, TJ (1996) Putting the 'wow' back in strategy, *Strategy*, **1** (Jan), pp 12–14

Peters, TJ and Waterman, RH (1982) *In Search of Excellence: Lessons from America's Best Run Companies*, Harper & Row, New York

Piercy, N (1998) *Market Led Strategic Change*, Butterworth Heinemann, Oxford

Pink, DH (2003) The shape of things to come, _Wired_, May

Porter, ME (1980) _Competitive Strategy_, Free Press, New York

Pringle, H and Gordon, W (2001) _Brand Manners_, Wiley, Chichester

Rackham, N (1998) _Rethinking the Sales Force_, McGraw Hill, New York

Reichheld, F (1996) _The Loyalty Effect_, Bain & Co, Boston

Reinartz, W and Kumar, V (2002) The mismanagement of customer loyalty, _Harvard Business Review_, July, **80** (7), pp 86–95

Rifkin, J (2000) _The Age of Access_, Penguin Books, London

Rock, S, Marsella, A and Stone, M (2004) _CRM Works: CRM Study 2004_, IBM Business Consulting Services, London

Rust, R, Zeithaml, V and Lemon, K (2004) Customer-centric brand management, _Harvard Business Review_, September

Schultz, DE (2003) Marketing gets no respect in the boardroom, _Marketing News_, **37** (24), p 9

Selby, D (2003) Materialisation forecasting: a data mining perspective, in Cirani, T, Fasano, G, Gliozzi, S and Tadei, R (eds), _Operations Research in Space and Air_, Dordrecht, Kluwer

Shaw, C and Ivens, J (2002) _Building Great Customer Experiences_, Palgrave McMillan, London

Stone, M, Bond, A and Foss, B (2004) _Consumer Insight: How to Use Data and Market Research to get Closer to Your Customer_, Kogan Page, London

Stone, M, Woodcock, N and Foss, B (2002) _The Customer Management Scorecard_, Kogan Page, London

Sun Tzu (1971) _The Art of War_, Oxford University Press, Oxford

Tapp, A (2004) _Principles of Direct and Database Marketing_, 3rd edn, FT Prentice Hall, Harlow

Tenby, D (1999) Changing times in retail, _Admap_, May

Woodcock, N, Stone, M and Starkey, M (2003) _State of the Nation iii_, QCi Assessment Ltd, London

Index

Further reading from Kogan Page

Fashion Brands: Branding style from Armani to Zara, Mark Tungate, 2005

The 50-plus Market: Why the future is age neutral when it comes to marketing and brand strategies, Dick Stroud, 2005

How to Write a Marketing Plan, 2nd edn, John Westwood, 2000

Key Marketing Skills: Tools and techniques for building strong relationships with major clients, 2nd edn, Peter Cheverton, 2004

Marketing Communications: An integrated approach, 4th edn, P R Smith and Jonathan Taylor, 2004

The Marketing Plan Workbook, John Westwood, 2005

The New Strategic Brand Management: Creating and sustaining brand equity long term, Jean-Noël Kapferer, 2004

Total Integrated Marketing: Breaking the bounds of the function, James MacHubert, Noel Capon and Nigel F Piercy, 2005